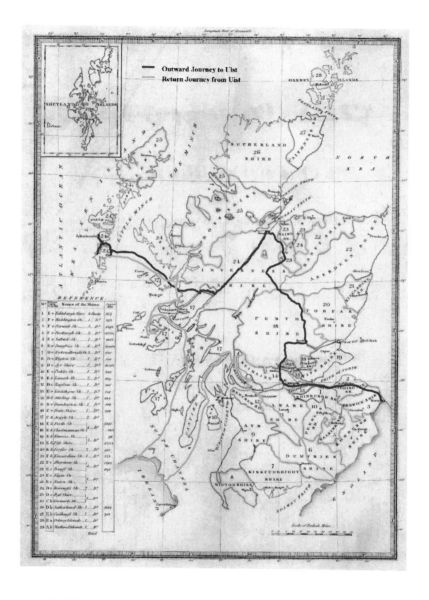

APPROXIMATE ROUTE OF MARSHAL
MACDONALD'S JOURNEY

The French MacDonald

Journey of a Marshal of Napoléon in the Highlands and Islands of Scotland

Marshal MacDonald
Duke of Tarentum

The 1825 Travel Diary of Jacques Etienne Joseph Alexandre MacDonald

With Commentaries by
Jean-Didier Hache and
Domhnall Uilleam Stiùbhart

Published in 2010 by The Islands Book Trust

www.theislandsbooktrust.com

ISBN: 978-1-907443-01-5

British Library Cataloguing in Publication Data. A CIP record for this book can be obtained from the British Library.

Dà Dhòmhnallach by Sorley Maclean is from the book *'Spring tide and neap tide: SelectedPoems 1932-1972'*, Canongate, Edinburgh, 1977

We gratefully acknowledge assistance from the Institut Français d'Ecosse in the publication of this volume

Typeset by Two Ravens Press Ltd, Ullapool, Scotland.
www.tworavenspress.com
Cover design by James Hutcheson
Front cover montage showing portrait of Marshal MacDonald by Casanova (1770-1844), courtesy of OSENAT Sales Rooms

Printed on Forest Stewardship Council-accredited paper by the MPG Books Group, Bodmin and King's Lynn

The Islands Book Trust
Ravenspoint Centre
Kershader
South Lochs
Isle of Lewis
HS2 9QA
Tel: 01851 820946

THE ISLANDS BOOK TRUST
URRAS LEABHRAICHEAN NAN EILEAN

ACKNOWLEDGEMENTS

The publication of the Marshal's Travel Diary has been authorised by the Centre Historique des Archive Nationales, file 279/AP/36. Documents kindly provided by OSENAT Sales Rooms, http://www.osenat.fr, have been selected from the catalogue of the auction sales "L'Empire à Fontainebleau", December 2005. The Islands Book Trust would like to thank the following for their assistance in the publication of this volume: Réunions des Musées Nationaux, Centre Historique des Archives Nationales, Musée National Légion d'Honneur, Mitchell Library, Clan Donald Lands Trust, The National Library of Scotland, Domhnall Uilleam Stiùbhart, Jean-Didier Hache, John Randall, Tommy MacDonald, Donnie Morrison and Margaret Maclennan.

ABOUT THE TRANSLATOR

Jean-Didier Hache is a Frenchman, born and bred in Paris, with a life-long association with Scotland, and with the Outer Hebrides in particular. Though his main line of activity lies with European politics, he has a keen interest in historical research, especially on the ancient relationship between Scotland and France. He has published numerous papers, in French and in English, on European affairs and on island issues.

CONTENTS

LIST OF ILLUSTRATIONS

1. **Foot portrait of Marshal MacDonald in full uniform,** by Casanova (1770-1844). This portrait is supposed to have been offered to MacDonald by Napoléon, after the victory of Wagram and his nomination as Marshal. Catalogue of the auction sales "L'Empire à Fontainebleau" December 2005, Lot 001, (Courtesy of OSENAT Sales Rooms, http://www.osenat.fr).

2. **Coat of Arms of Marshal MacDonald, Duke of Tarentum;** Catalogue of the auction sales "L'Empire à Fontainebleau" December 2005, Lot 369 (Courtesy of OSENAT Sales Rooms, http://www.osenat.fr).

3. **Alexandre MacDonald (son of the Marshal) age 4 in tartan, bearing a Scottish sword,** Portrait by Horace Vernet (1789-1863); catalogue of the auction sales "L'Empire à Fontainebleau" December 2005, Lot 397, (Courtesy of OSENAT Sales Rooms, http://www.osenat.fr).

4. **Portrait of Flora MacDonald,** This portrait was sold amongst different items having belonged to Marshal MacDonald. Catalogue of the auction sales "L'Empire à Fontainebleau" December 2005, Lot 412 (Courtesy of OSENAT Sales Rooms, http://www.osenat.fr).

5. **Marshal MacDonald wearing the sash of the Order of Saint Esprit** (Courtesy of the Musée de la Légion d'Honneur et des orders de chevalerie, www.legiondhonneur.fr). The Museum is located 2, rue de la Légion d'honneur, 75007 Paris, and opens Wednesday to Sunday, 13.00 to 18.00. Entry is free. Photography by Fabrice Gousset.

6. **Marshal MacDonald's Seal** (reproduced courtesy of Clan Donald Museum, http://www.clandonald.com).

7. **French 'birth certificate' of Neil MacEachen (MacDonald) by Paris Scots College** (reproduced by kind permission of the Centre Historique des Archives Nationales, Paris. File 279 AP 36. The photography comes from the Atelier photographique du Centre Historique des Archives Nationales).

8. **Map of Prince Charles Edward Stuart's travels In Scotland 1745-46** (from Walter Biggar Blaikie 'Itinerary of Prince Charles Edward Stuart', Edinburgh, 1897).

9. **Sir Reginald MacDonald Steuart Seton, Bart. of Staffa,** Touch & C & C; Catalogue of the auction sales "L'Empire à Fontainebleau" December 2005, Lot 400 (Courtesy of OSENAT Sales Rooms, http://www.osenat.fr).

10. **Ruins of Neil MacEachen's birthplace at Howbeg.** The person in the picture is Duncan MacEachen, first cousin five times removed from Neil MacEachen. (Courtesy of Tommy MacDonald).

11. **Glen Corrodale from Rubha Hellisdale** (John Randall).

12. **Looking down on cave and buildings at Corrodale** (Jean-Didier Hache).

13. **Cave (souterrain) at Cas fo Deas, Corrodale** (Jean-Didier Hache).

14. **Site of bothy at Rossinish** where the Prince spent his last night before going "Over the sea to Skye". (Jean-Didier Hache)..

15. **Loch Skipport** (Jean-Didier Hache).

16. **Sketch by John Schekty of ship off Armadale,** from 'Sketches and Notes of a Cruise in Scotch waters...' by John Christian Schetky and Lord John Manners. London: Thomas McLean, 1850 (Reproduced courtesy of the Mitchell Library, Glasgow).

17. **View of Edinburgh from Calton Hill,** from 'Modern Athens, displayed in a series of views, or Edinburgh in the Nineteenth Century ... from original drawings', Mr Thomas H. Shepherd, London: Jones & Co., 1829 (reproduced by permission of the Trustees of the National Library of Scotland).

18. **Jacobite exiles in France** often enlisted in one of the Irish or Scottish Regiments in the service of France. Here, the Régiment Royal-Ecossais, a sister unit to Neil's Ogilvy's Regiment.

19. **Chapel of Scots College, Paris** (Jean-Didier Hache).

20. **The castle of Courcelles-le-Roy,** near Beaulieu-sur-Loire, residence of Marshal MacDonald, where he died in 1840 (Jean-Didier Hache).

FOREWORD

We are delighted to publish this updated edition, based on new research into this truly extraordinary story:

It is based on the previously unpublished travel diary in 1825 of Marshal MacDonald to Uist and other parts of Scotland to see the birth-place of his father Neil MacEachen and meet some of his MacDonald/MacEachen relatives.

In doing so, the Marshal was remembering, in a very different era, the exploits of Neil MacEachen and Prince Charles Edward Stuart in 1746, when Neil played the major role in hiding and protecting the Prince after Culloden.

Born in France, where his father lived after the failure of the '45, his son Jacques Etienne Joseph Alexandre MacDonald, achieved a meteoric rise to power in military and political circles, a Marshal of Napoleon during the latter's supremacy but also eventually negotiating Napoleon's abdication.

As a retired elder statesman, the Marshal (who spoke little English and no Gaelic) visited Scotland with the assistance of the British Government, meeting people like Sir Walter Scott, and eventually setting foot in the land of the MacDonalds, including Howbeg where his father was born, and the cave at Corrodale where his father and the Prince had hidden all those years before.

Only a few years ago, the Marshal's travel diary, not written with a view to publication and containing many frank comments about the Scotland of his time and the people he met, was discovered in the French National Archives in Paris by Jean-Didier Hache, a Frenchman who has been associated with Benbecula for over thirty years.

Jean-Didier Hache has translated the Scottish part of the Marshal's travel diary into English for this publication. Alongside it appear commentaries on the French and Scottish backgrounds to the Marshal and his visit by Jean-Didier Hache and Domhnall Uilleam Stiùbhart of Edinburgh University, with some beautiful colour illustrations. Jean-Didier visited many of the locations while working on Caledonia TV's film 'Dòmhnallaich na Frainge' for BBC Scotland and the Gaelic Media Service.

This new publication is important on many different levels – as a valuable record of Scotland, and particularly the Highlands and Islands at a time of rapid economic and social change, and as a fascinating footnote to the momentous events of Jacobite and Napoleonic history. The story also, to my mind, demonstrates the genuinely dramatic quality of life in the Hebrides, which goes way beyond the cosy romantic myths – a society which to this day is remarkably outward looking with many links to the wider world, living in an environment which can be harsh as well as inspiring.

John Randall
Chairman
The Islands Book Trust
March 2010

INTRODUCTION
by Jean-Didier Hache

My first acquaintance with Marshal MacDonald happened in Paris, in the 1970s. The catalogue of an auction sale at Drouot's sales rooms had advertised a "MacDonald" print, which, as a collector of Scottish memorabilia, I assumed to be directly related to Highland history. I had not bothered to go to the preview exhibition, so when the print was produced on the day of the auction, I was surprised to see, not a kilted MacDonald clansman despatching some Hanoverian troops, but a Marshal of Napoléon proudly leading his troops over the Alps in winter.[1]

The decision whether to bid or not was a split second affair. On one hand, the item appeared to be irrelevant to my field of interests. On the other, if that man's name was MacDonald, there was bound to be a connection of some sort with Scotland, so perhaps it was worth collecting after all. The bidding being slack, the price remained affordable, and so I was able to leave with Marshal MacDonald under my arm, and thought no more of it for some years.

Fate struck a second time, indirectly, in the summer of 1975, when I met John MacDonald in Mallaig. A lobster fisherman, and a keen accordionist from Island Flodda, Benbecula, he was overseeing the building of his new boat at the Mallaig shipyard. This fortuitous meeting got me acquainted with Island Flodda, where I eventually purchased the old home of the MacLellan family, which I have now enjoyed for over thirty years. Without this chance encounter with John, who died tragically at sea on his way back from the Monach Isles in the winter of 2003, the story would not have gone much further.

In those days, the Island and Kyles Flodda area of Benbecula had very limited infrastructure: no piped water, no electricity, no refuse collection, barely a couple of phones, and a road in

---

1   *The illustration is slightly inaccurate in historical terms, for he was only a general of the Republic when he took his troops into Switzerland.*

pretty dismal condition. The reading of a book on the "Origins of the '45",[2] which included the reprint of an old manuscript describing the flight of Prince Charles Edward Stuart through Benbecula in 1746 gave me the idea of an innocent joke. Quoting a passage which said that *"[The Prince] fell almost at every step in some ditch or mire, where, very often, he lost his shoes, which gave Neil a vast amount of trouble before he could fish them up"*, I wrote a letter to the Stornoway Gazette[3] pointing out that since the situation had hardly changed since 1746, the road might as well be listed as an historical monument.

The published letter did not markedly improve the state of roads in the Flodda area at the time, but it attracted the attention of Dr Alasdair MacLean, GP for South Uist and local historian. Dr MacLean had recognised the quote, and contacted me to point out that the aforementioned "Neil" was Neil MacEachen of Howbeg, who was no less than the father of Marshal MacDonald. The print acquired in Paris some years before duly rose to prominence above the chimney in my sitting-room.

Dr MacLean, with whom I was to become friendly, was then working on a history of Neil MacEachen. Since Neil had been an officer in the French service, and had ended his life in France, he asked me to perform some research for him in the French archives. Having previously published some work on that period,[4] I was glad to oblige and to contribute in a small way to his authoritative book *"A MacDonald for the Prince. The story of Neil MacEachen"*.[5] This book, which was successful enough to be reprinted, was to be followed by a second one, written together with John S. Gibson, on the

2   *"**Origins of the '45**", Edited by Walter Biggar Baikie, Scottish Academic Press, 1975, p 255.*

3   *"Prince Charlie in the Hebrides", This week's letters to the Editor, **Stornoway Gazette**, 24th of November 1979.*

4   *Jean-Didier HACHE, « Déstabilisations et stratégies indirectes dans la périphérie européenne. L'affrontement franco-anglais en Ecosse, en Irlande et en Corse, au XVIIIème siècle », in **Stratégique**, Fondation pour les Etudes de Défense Nationale, 2/88, Paris, 1988.*

5   *Dr. A. MACLEAN, "**A MacDonald for the Prince. The story of Neil MacEachen**", Acair, Stornoway, 1982.*

"*Summer Hunting*" of Charles Edward Stuart.[6]

Dr. MacLean retired to Skye and, regrettably, is no longer with us today. My own involvement in that field of research became more remote, but for the occasional collection of relevant books or documents. However, in 2004, BBC Radio Scotland contacted me about a short radio programme with Mark Stephen and Louise Yeoman on the story of Neil MacEachen. Could I be of assistance? I was reluctant at first to step into the shoes of a Gaelic-speaking scholar and historian such as Dr MacLean, having none of his local contacts and in-depth knowledge of Uist history. However, having stressed that my degree of expertise, if any, was limited to the French side of the story, and being reassured by the presence of another Gaelic-speaking scholar and historian of the younger generation, Donald William Stewart, I accepted.

Dusting my files, freshening my memory, and checking information for this programme set the wheels of research grinding once again. One thing led to another, and I subsequently found further information on Neil MacEachen which was unavailable in Dr MacLean's days. I also realised that a lot remained to be said about the relationship his son, Marshal MacDonald, had with Scotland. Last but not least, I was fortunate enough to find a remarkable document in the French National Archives; viz. a copy of the travel diary of his visit to the land of his forefathers in Scotland in the year 1825.

This "discovery", so to speak, amazed me, for these files, which had been given to the public archives in the 1960s, had certainly been perused by many researchers before me. I can only assume that this diary, post-dating the fall of the Empire by 10 years, and relating to events of a private nature, was found too marginal to be of interest by specialised Napoléonic historians, and thus remained in obscurity. However, it is undoubtedly of great potential value to two categories of readers: those interested in the history of the Highlands and Islands of Scotland in the early XIXth century; and those interested in the life and family history of Marshal MacDonald.

---

6   Dr. A. MACLEAN and John S. GIBSON, "**Summer hunting a Prince. The escape of Charles Edward Stewart**", Acair, Stornoway, 1992.

This research also made me realize that there was a considerable dearth of publications on the topic of Marshal MacDonald and his amazing career. But for the Marshal's own "*Recollections*"[7] there is, to this day, and to the best of my knowledge, no book written specifically about him, be it in English or in French. Whilst his life and his military career have been referred to in many publications, no complete biography of him seems ever to have been published, nor is there any major work on his achievements. This seems extraordinary for a man who was once asked to lead the Coup d'Etat which ended the French Revolution, and who eventually negotiated Napoléon's abdication.

I can only hope that, in the very near future, an editor will make this comment obsolete by publishing a proper biography of Marshal MacDonald, and that the present book, which merely highlights the Marshal's Scottish dimension, will make a useful contribution to such an undertaking.

Last but not least, in my (unending) quest on Marshal MacDonald and on his father, Neil MacEachen, many people in France, in Scotland and even in America have given me very useful assistance by providing me with information, or by sharing their comments or analysis with me. Others would certainly have done so if I had been fortunate enough to be acquainted with them earlier. To the former, far too numerous to be quoted individually, I wish to address my sincere thanks; and to the latter my hope that this work will act as a catalyst in fostering future exchanges.

❀ ❀ ❀ ❀ ❀

Notes on the publication of the Second Edition

The fact that this book sold out within two years of its first publication, and is now being reprinted is excellent news for a number of reasons:

Firstly, as anyone who has ever written will know, the very minute a book is out of print, new facts or documents emerge, proving or disproving the author's pet theories. This publication

---

7   Marshal MACDONALD, *Recollections of Marshal MacDonald, Duke of Tarentum. Introduction by Camille Rousset, London, Richard Bentley and Son, 1893, 501pp*

has not escaped such a fate, with the finding of fresh evidence which sheds new light on the relationship between Marshal MacDonald's father and mother, and even raises interesting questions, if not serious doubts, about his legitimacy.

Secondly, no matter how hard one tries, or how carefully one has proof-read, the first edition of a text is seldom immune from errors or omissions of various sizes, scales, or gravity – the more obvious ones inevitably being also the most invisible to the author's eyes. In this second edition, it has been possible to weed out some of these mistakes. A word of gratitude must be addressed to all those unpaid correctors – specialised historians or ordinary readers – who have made such improvements possible through their comments. Special mention will be made of Susan Howard, not only for her sharp but fair criticism in reviewing this book,* but also for giving me the hope that, thanks to her own impressive research on Marshal MacDonald, a comprehensive publication covering the man's life and deeds will eventually see the light of day.

A final reason to celebrate this second edition is that its very existence proves that, no matter what the pundits say, highly specialized works or documents of a local historical nature can still attract a fair degree of attention from the general public. It also demonstrates that small publishers located in 'remote' areas, such as the Islands Book Trust, can successfully target a 'niche market', thanks to the combined use of local retail outlets and of the internet, not forgetting a strong commitment by the Editor and the Trustees. In that respect, special mention must be made of Alasdair MacEachen (himself a distant relative of Neil MacEachen, and perhaps accordingly motivated!) who deployed considerable efforts to promote not only this book, but, more importantly, this story, in his own homeland of Uist and beyond.

*See http://www.napoleon-series.org/reviews/memoirs/ c_MacDonald.html

Jean-Didier Hache

DÀ DHÒMHNALLACH

'Na do ghaisgeach mòr làidir;
'Nad churaidh miosg nan curaidhean,
Dhùin thu geata Hougomont.
Dhùin thu 'n geata 's air a chùlaibh
Rinn do bhràthair an spùilleadh.
Thog e tuath an Gleann Garadh –
Am beagan a bh'air fhàgail dhiubh –
Is thog e tuath mu Cheann Loch Nibheis
Is thog e tuath an Cnòideart.
Cha b'fheàrr e na Fear Dhùn-Bheagain:
Rinn e milleadh air Cloinn Dòmhnaill.

Dè rinn thusa 'n uair sin,
A churaidh mhòir làidir?
Fiach na dhùin thu aon gheata
An aodann do ghalla bràthair?

Bha ann ri d'linn-sa fear eile,
Curaidh eile de Chloinn Dòmhnaill,
Curaidh Bhàgram, Leipsich, Hanau.
Cha chuala mi gun do thog esan
Aon teaghlach mun Mheuse
No mu abhainn eile.
Cha d'rinn esan milleadh
Air Frangaich no air Dòmhnallaich.

Nach bochd nach tàinig esan
Le Bonaparte a nall.
Cha thogadh esan tuath
Air sgàth nan caorach òraidh,
'S cha mhò chuireadh esan gaiseadh
Ann an gaisge mhòir Chloinn Dòmhnaill.
Nach bochd nach robh esan
'Na dhiùc air Tìr an Eòrna
Is 'na phrionns' air Albainn.

Nach bochd nach tàinig esan
Le Bonaparte a nall
Fichead bliadhna mun tàinig,
Cha b'ann a dh'èisteachd sodail
O'n t-sliomaire sin Bhàtar
No a chruinneachadh na h-ùrach
As an t-seann làraich,
Ach a chur an spionnaidh ùrair
Ann am fuidheall a chàirdean.

Nach bochd nach tàinig esan
Gu cobhair air a chàirdean.

TWO MACDONALDS

You big strong warrior,
you hero among heroes,
you shut the gate of Hougomont.
You shut the gate and behind it
your brother did the spoiling.
He cleared tenants in Glengarry –
the few of them left –
and he cleared tenants about Kinloch Nevis,
and he cleared tenants in Knoydart.
He was no better than the laird of Dunvegan.
He spoiled Clan Donald.

What did you do then,
you big strong hero?
I bet you shut no gate
in the face of your bitch of a brother.

There was in your time
another hero of Clan Donald,
the hero of Wagram, Leipsig, Hanau.
I have not heard that he cleared
one family by the Meuse
or by any other river,
that he did any spoiling
of French or of Mac Donalds.

What a pity that he did not come
over with Bonaparte!
He would not clear tenants
for the sake of the gilded sheep,
nor would he put a disease
in the great valour of Clan Donald.
What a pity that he was not
Duke of the Land of the Barley
And Prince of Caledonia!

What a pity that he did not come
over with Bonaparte
twenty years before he did,
not to listen to flannel
from that creeper Walter
nor to gather dust
from the old ruin
but to put the new vigour
in the remnant of his kinsmen!

What a pity that he did not come
to succour his kinsmen!

Source: Sorley MacLean, "Spring tide and neap tide. Selected poems 1932-1972"
Edinburgh, Canongate, 1977

COMMENTARY
by Jean-Didier Hache

Section I

On the 1ˢᵗ of July 1825, the people who lived in remote Corrodale, an isolated glen on the eastern side of the island of South Uist, in the Outer Hebrides, must have felt a sense of relief and curiosity.

Relief, because they knew that the Customs & Excise Revenue Cutter HMS Swift which had just dropped anchor in the bay was not following its normal course of duty, which would have implied a search of the area for illicit stills and contraband whisky, an illegal but prosperous activity in all the West coast of Scotland at the time. Curiosity, because the Cutter was there to bring a very special visitor from France. The day before, this visitor had been in Howbeg, on the West side of the island, where a very large crowd of six hundred people had greeted him, and had drunk a toast to his health. Messages had been sent over the hills with news that he wanted to see the caves of Corrodale, and that he would soon be on his way by sea.

He was an important man, they had been told. A Duke, a Minister of the King of France, and also an ex-Marshal of Napoléon – the same Napoléon which some of them had been sent to fight in Portugal, in Spain or at Waterloo, a decade before–. But more importantly, he was by descent one of their own, for his father, Neil MacEachen, had been born on this island of South Uist. The old ones remembered that he had held lands in this very glen, and there were a few in the area who were related by blood to the visitor.

The story had been told time and time again, and transmitted down the generations by oral tradition. Nearly eighty years before, in 1746, after the Rebellion had been crushed on the Battlefield of Culloden, it was Neil who had been asked by MacDonald of Clanranald to take direct care of Prince Charles Edward Stuart who had taken refuge in the Hebrides. The Prince had spent two months in the islands, in its most remote

11

caves and peninsulas, including a few weeks in this very Glen Corrodale. There were tales of some tense moments, when the Royal fugitive had been hiding in some of the area's numerous caves to escape the government's troops, and also some more relaxed ones, when Charles Edward had gone hunting or fishing, or partaken in drunken carousing with the local gentry, but always under the watchful supervision of Neil.

The Prince had eventually left over the sea to Skye, disguised as a servant of Flora MacDonald of Milton, then gone to the mainland, and later on to France after being rescued by some French Privateers. Neil had left for France with him, and his brother, Ronald, who did not escape arrest, also managed to join him after a spell in the Tower of London. It was rumoured that, like many other Jacobite exiles, Neil had become an officer in the French army, that he had married a French woman, and that he had children with her. The slim old man in black in the rowing boat, who had the greatest difficulty to climb onto the slippery rocks with the oncoming swell from the Minch, was his son. They rushed to help him ashore.

❈ ❈ ❈ ❈ ❈

The visit of a Napoléonic Marshal to the Outer Hebrides must have been an extraordinary event for the inhabitants of Glen Corrodale; indeed anyone in Scotland at the time, and it still seems so to us nowadays. What could have brought one of the highest dignitaries of France, an old man of sixty years with mediocre health, to travel, not without risks nor discomfort, to one of the remotest corners of Western Europe?

If we take the literary archives as a yardstick, the number of French travellers who had visited Scotland before 1825 out of curiosity (and not out of professional obligation, like sailors, soldiers or merchants) was fairly limited. Those who had toured the Highlands were even more of a rarity, and it was practically unheard of to reach the Western Isles.

According to Martin Rackwitz,[8] only about one hundred

---

8   Martin RACKWITZ; *Travels to terra incognita: The Scottish Highlands and Hebrides in early modern travellers' accounts c. 1600 to*

of such travellers had visited the Highlands between 1600 and 1800. Less than a third had gone as far as any of the northern or western islands, of which barely more than a dozen to Skye or the Outer-Hebrides. Of those hundred or so travellers, about fifteen percent had come from outside the British Isles – the bulk of them French or German –. We have evidence of only two Frenchmen who came to the Hebrides: Faujas de Saint Fond, who went as far as Mull in 1784,[9] and Pierre Nicolas Chantreau, who circumnavigated Scotland in 1788-89, stopping en route in Orkney, then in Lewis, Harris, Skye, Canna, Rum, Mull, and Jura.[10]

The first quarter of the XIXth century saw the number of Frenchmen touring Scotland increase, but only very progressively. According to Margaret Bain,[11] the French who visited up until 1789 were mostly motivated by a philosophical approach, and especially by the quest of first hand information about the "primitive races" of Europe. It will be recalled that the Ossianic lays were extremely popular in the whole of Europe at the time. MacPherson's work was said to be one of Bonaparte's favourite books, and Ossian was to become an inspiration for many famous French painters of the early XIXth century such as Ingres, Gerard, or Girodet.

This enthusiasm for Ossian and the Celtic heroes did not prevent the numbers of French travellers to Scotland from declining during the period between 1789 and 1815 due to the French Revolution, and the ensuing Napoléonic wars. Those who came were generally "forcible" visitors, either because they were in exile (like the court of the King's brother, the Comte d'Artois, who stayed at Holyrood), or because

1800, *Dissertation zur Erlangung des Doktorgrades der Philosophischen Fakultät der Christian-Albrechts-Universität zu Kiel vorgelegt von Kiel*, 2004.

9   Barthelemy FAUJAS DE SAINT FOND, *Travels In England, Scotland, And The Hebrides* (London, 1799)

10   Pierre Nicolas CHANTREAU, *Voyage Dans Les Trois Royaumes D'Angleterre, D'Ecosse Et D'Irlande, Fait En 1788 Et 1789*, (Paris, 1792)

11   Margaret I. BAIN, *Les voyageurs français en Ecosse 1770-1830 et leurs curiosités intellectuelles*, Librairie Ancienne Honoré Champion, Paris, 1931, 227p.

they were prisoners of war. It was only after 1815 that the flow of French travellers resumed, but only very gradually. Less than twenty are recorded between 1815 and 1825, and most of those from 1821 onwards. Their motivation had also changed. Philosophers were replaced by romantics who came to see the land celebrated by Sir Walter Scott, whose poetry and historical novels were now translated into French, and becoming increasingly popular.[12] Of those French visitors, very few explored Scotland's periphery, and even less its islands. In 1817, J.B. Biot went to Shetland for some scientific research. In 1816 and 1820, Charles Dupin went as far as Inverness, and so did the Marquis de Custine in 1822. In 1821, Edouard de Montulé visited Oban and Staffa. None went to the Outer Hebrides.

However, in 1822, just three years before the Marshal's visit, a Swiss citizen, Necker de Saussure, reached the Western Isles, and moreover the very island of South Uist, where he stayed at Kilbride, in the house of MacDonald of Boisdale. Necker de Saussure, who had been introduced to MacDonald of Boisdale by his relative MacDonald of Staffa (who was later to chaperon the Marshal during his tour) got a very warm reception there. He expressed amazement at finding that a most elegant society was living in the midst of this wilderness, and noted the islands' extreme isolation, as *"for want of regular packet-boats, a person may be several months in succession without the arrival of either letters or friends."*[13]

But for that single exception, it will be appreciated that Marshal MacDonald's visit to Uist was a novelty. Of course, neither he nor Necker de Saussure were the first persons from the European mainland to set foot in the Uists. Well before him, there were all those who had journeyed from France, Spain or Holland to the West coast of Scotland and the Hebrides because of their trade. Dutch fishermen had fished around these waters. Merchants, and especially wine traders had supplied

---

12   *"Guy Mannering"* was translated into French in 1816.
13   NECKER DE SAUSSURE, A Voyage to the Hebrides, 1822. Quoted in Derek COOPER, The Road to the Isles. Travellers in the Hebrides 1770-1914, Routledge &Keagan Paul Ltd, London, 1979, p 56.

the well-stocked cellars of the clan chiefs.[14] There were even craftsmen, like those French masons who supposedly built Clanranald's castle at Ormaclate at the express request of the Chief's demanding French wife.[15] There were, of course, those who came on military business, like the officers from the French or Spanish Navy, not to mention the privateers from places such as Dunkirk or Saint-Malo, who navigated these waters on some mission to support the Jacobite cause in the XVIIIth century.[16] There were also the priests, for instance the Franciscan missionaries trained in Louvain, in Flanders, who rekindled the Catholic faith in these islands in the XVIIth century.

However, all of them came to fulfil a specific commercial, military or spiritual mission, and none were motivated by his own curiosity, be it literary, scientific or historical. This dearth of visitors is hardly surprising when one bears in mind the lack of public transport which characterised the area right till the first part of the XIXth century. Guides were equally scant. Of the *Traveller's guide through Scotland and its islands*, published in 1780, and regularly re-edited till 1811, "*only 12 of 570 pages devoted to the islands of the west.*"[17] It was not till 1820 that "*Lumsden & Son's Steamboat Companion or Stanger's guide to the Western Isles and Highlands*" appeared with the development of steam navigation. Two more modern guides, the *Scottish Tourist*, and the *Account of the Pleasure tours of Scotland* were printed around 1825, but both were still very imprecise.

So Marshal MacDonald's visit to South Uist in 1825 was extraordinary first of all simply because, in itself, it was an event which was rare in the extreme. It was also unique because

---

14   Billy KAY and Cailean MACLEAN, **Knee deep in Claret. A celebration of wine and Scotland**, Mainstream Pulishing, Edinburgh, 1983. Chapter 11, "Fion Dearg Na Frainge"

15   "How Clanranald built Ormaclate House", in Angus MACLELLAN, Stories from South Uist, Birlinn, Edinburgh, 1997, p 89.

16   For an example of such sources, see the "Notes and Sources" section of Alasdair MACLEAN & John GIBSON, **Summer Hunting a Prince. The escape of Charles Edward Stewart**, Acair, Stornoway, 1992, p75.

17   Derek COOPER, **The Road to the Isles**, Op.cit, p 58.

of the exceptional social and political status of the visitor, as was clearly demonstrated by the loan of a British warship for his personal use. But this visit was also markedly different for one reason: because of its motivations.

For it was not a quest for Ossian, Oscar, or any other other Fingalian heroes which had made the Marshal leave his palatial Hotel de Salm, in Paris, where he presided over the affairs of the elite order of the Légion d'Honneur. Nor was it a step-by-step, book-in-hand, search for the characters and locations mentioned in Walter Scott's celebrated epic novels which had made him abandon his beautiful castle of Courcelles-le-Roi, near the Loire river. Instead it was interest in his own family history, and especially in the life of his father, Neil MacEachen of Howbeg, born in that remote island of South Uist. It was a search for Clan Donald, and especially the MacDonalds of Clanranald, with whom he had identified all his life. It was also an exploration into the historical past and present realities of Scotland,the country of his ancestors, as well as an appraisal of this Great-Britain to which it now pertained.

To appreciate Marshal MacDonald's travel diary and to understand why this journey took place and how it was organised, it is necessary to go back into this past.

Section II
The MacDonalds of France

The story of the relationship between Marshal MacDonald and Scotland begins in the Outer-Hebrides, in the Island of South Uist, in the parish of Howbeg (or *Tobha Beag* in Gaelic). There, on the 26th of December 1719, his father, Neil MacEachen,[18] was born. The story of Neil MacEachen of Howbeg has been told in detail by Dr Alasdair MacLean in his Book *"A MacDonald for the Prince"*.[19] It will be only summarized here, with the addition of some information from other sources, and hitherto unpublished elements.

Equally, this paper does not pretend to give a comprehensive description of Marshal MacDonald's complex and eventful life story, nor does it dream to provide a full account of his extensive military and political career. In that respect, we shall direct the reader to the Marshal's own *"Recollections"*[20] which, to this day, remains the main source available to us regarding his life. Though only the main events of his career will be mentioned hereby, some more in details than others, our ambition is merely to explain how he rose to prominence in France, while highlighting the role played by his Scottish and Jacobite roots in the process.

Neil MacEachan (MacDonald)

Neil MacEachen was apparently the son of Alexander of Glenuig (though Dr MacLean mentions a possibility that he was only fostered in that family, and that his true father was a MacDonald). Records indicate that he had no less than four brothers, John, Alexander, Angus and Ronald, which explains that whilst Neil himself does not have any remaining

---

18   *The spelling of the name is often distorted in documents as MacEchin, MacEchan, MacEchain etc. In Gaelic, his name is Niall MacEach-ainn.*

19   *Dr A. MACLEAN, « A MacDonald for the Prince. », Op.cit.*

20   *Marshal MACDONALD, **Recollections**, Op.cit.*

descendant in the male line, there are still today a number of people in the Uist area who bear the name of MacEchen and descend from that sept.

The MacEachen, or "Sons of Hector" were historically based in the MacDonald of Clan Ranald's lands, be it in the Glenuig area on the mainland, or, in the Outer-Hebrides, in the Uist area. Whether they were themselves a cadet branch of Clan Donald is open to doubt, and Dr MacLean thinks that they were in fact descended from the MacLeans of Kingerloch. Whatever the truth, there is no doubt that they had close ties with Clanranald, and that they were under the political influence of that clan; namely, they were staunchly Catholics and pro-Jacobites. These points are not without influence upon the rest of the story, for they explain why Neil was sent to France to study for the priesthood at the Scots College.

A view of the ruins of Neil's family home near the Howmore river indicates a substantial settlement, and would suggest that the MacEachens of Howbeg belonged to what would be called in modern terms the "upper-middle class", at least by local standards. Neil was reportedly a *"Daoin'-uasail"*, or small gentry of ClanRanald, and his brother Alexander was the tacksman of Howbeg. Who financed his journey to France is not known. Apparently funding came from the Catholic Church, perhaps with the help of Clanranald himself or, as Donald Nicholas suggests, the financial assistance of the Jacobite Paris banker, Aeneas MacDonald.[21]

Whatever the source of the finance, Neil went to France when he was about seventeen years old, after a brief stay at the seminar in Scalan, in Glenlivet.[22] His son, in his *"Recollections"*, mentions that he was sent to the Scots College in Douai, in the North of France, but his name does not appear on the College Records. On the other hand, Canon Halloran quotes evidence of his journey from Leith to the Paris Scots College in 1736.

Neil stayed at the Scots College for about a year, during

---

21   Donald NICHOLAS, « Trusty Neil MacEachan », in **Scottish Historical Review** XXIX, 1950, p 167.

22   See Brian M. HALLORAN, « Neil MacEachan at Scots College in Paris », in The Innes Review, Vol. XLIII, N°2, August 1992, pp 17-181.

which time his name changed from MacEachen to MacDonald. Various explanations have been given for this change, a practice which apparently was not unknown at the time.[23] For some, the change was an expression of loyalty to the MacDonalds of Clanranald, who were the superiors in Uist. Another explanation may lie with the difficulty to pronounce "MacEachen" in the French language, whereas "MacDonald" raises no difficulty. However, we would suggest a third possible reason, namely the desire to keep a degree of anonymity at a time when the anti-Catholic Penal laws, which were in force in Scotland, could have had disastrous consequences for him and his relatives. For a Scottish Catholic family, sending a child to study in a Scots College abroad could legally mean the forfeiture of all its belongings.[24] The more fortunate Catholic and Jacobite families were powerful enough to ward off these repressive measures, for, should the worst come to the worst, they had acquired sophisticated techniques to avoid putting their wealth at risk by laundering money across Europe, by scattering their assets, or leaving them in the hands of those of their names who were nominally Protestant. However, this option was clearly not open to Neil, who may have wished to improve his safety, and that of his next of kin, by sheltering behind a fairly widespread patronymic such as that of MacDonald.

It is said that when Neil left the Paris Scots College in September 1737, he could speak not only his native Gaelic, but also English, French, Latin and that he had a fair knowledge of Greek. Considered a bright pupil, a "spark", perhaps he could have gone further in his studies, but he was apparently having health problems, with severe leg pains. Such physical ailments

---

23   Canon Halloran thus mentions Evan MacEachan (1769-1849), a student at the Scots College in Valladolid, who became Evanus MacDonald. (See Supra, p 178).

24   In 1762, when the Paris Parliament undertakes an enquiry in view of unifying the various foreign Colleges, the Scots College makes representation in view of preserving the anonymity of its pupils, which could have been compromised in the process. See: Pièces Justificatives Données à l'Appui du Mémoire de Gordon & Riddoch du 31 Octobre 1762. Extrait des Lois Pénales Contre les Catholiques d'Ecosse. Archives Nationales, H3 2561 A. Quoted in **Souvenirs du Collège des Ecossais**, Paris, 1962.

were to recur during his life; since he broke a knee-cap in the army, and suffered a dislocated hip in his later years, which left him crippled.[25] Neil, who was considered as a possible tutor for the Catholic College in Arisaig, eventually decided not to become a priest, or, as an illustrative Gaelic expression puts it: "*He came home without going under the hands of a bishop at all. Some of the vows of the priesthood were too hard for him...*"[26]

According to Canon Halloran, the Catholic authorities, whether in Scotland or at the Paris Scots College, also discovered that his behaviour was not flawless. On various occasions, he managed to swindle some money from the viatick of his fellow students, which did not endear him to his superiors. Robert Gordon, Procurator of the Mission in Edinburgh wrote that he was "*both cunning and interested.*" Yet, that behaviour was perhaps not without its reasons, since Neil, unlike the more fortunate *alumni* of the Scots College, did not have the financial backing of an aristocratic family to cater for his personal needs.

What happened after his return to Scotland at the end of 1747 is unclear. Various sources mention that he was a local teacher in Uist, or perhaps the tutor to the children of the Laird of Clanranald. Since Ranald MacDonald, son of the 15th chief of Clanranald himself became a pupil of the Scots College between 1739 and 1742, it is not impossible that Neil accompanied him to France on that occasion.

Neil surfaces again in historical documents in 1746, in the aftermath of the battle of Culloden. In a letter to the Stuart court in Rome dated 1764, he mentioned, "*There is no one who knows it better than my Royal master how I had the happiness to accompany in his most eminent dangers and hardship from the battle of Culloden until his arrival back in France*", but this is a general statement, and it does not mention precisely when and how his involvement began. Neil does not

---

25   For all these facts on Neil at the Paris Scots College see HAL-LORAN, Op. cit ; and HALLORAN, "*The Scots College Paris. 1603-1792*", John Donald Publisher, Edinburgh, 1997,226p.

26   Carmichael WATSON, MS 363, Fo 20; Edinburgh University.

appear in the list of officers who fought in the Prince's army at Culloden, and when the Prince lands in Benbecula on the 27th of April, less than two weeks after the battle, he was having dinner at Clanranald's house in Nunton. In the absence of other evidence, it is therefore reasonable to assume that he was not at Culloden himself, and that his association with the Prince started in Benbecula.

What happened in the Western Isles during the months of May and June 1746 is an epic adventure. An initial attempt to find a suitable ship in the island of Lewis having failed, with the protestant inhabitants showing clear signs of hostility, the Prince and his few followers had no other option but to remain in the largely catholic Southern Isles. There, Neil was put in direct charge of the Prince's safety, and undertook to guide him from islands to isolated peninsulas, through hills and fords, in a complex pattern of wanderings throughout a 30 mile area, stretching from Benbecula in the north to Loch Boisdale in the south. Together with the Prince, he sheltered in various remote places: a shepherd's hut on the Rossinish peninsula, some discreet caves in his own lands of Glen Corrodale, or even at times, for want of better or safer options, under mere rocky ledges.

What we know of these adventures has been recalled in various papers written by eyewitnesses, and, more prominently, by an exceptional manuscript found – so we are told – in France around the 1820s, and published some twenty years later by the *New Monthly Magazine*. This document, though it provides us with a very detailed account of Charles Edward Stuart's movements through the islands, is both incomplete (for it stops abruptly when the Prince is in the Isle of Skye), and anonymous. However, the wealth of details and precise local knowledge it contains indicate, with near certainty, that Neil himself was the author.[27]

---

27   Neil MACEACHAIN (attributed to), "The wanderings of Prince Charles in the Hebrides", in **Origins of the '45 and other papers related to that Rising**, Reed. By Walter Biggar BLAIKIE, Scottish Academic Press, Edinburgh, 1975, pp LXX and following, and pp. 226-266. See also Walter Biggar BLAIKIE, **Itinerary of Prince Charles Edward Stewart**, University

Spoken of in the third person, Neil appears through this account as instrumental in the Prince's safekeeping and eventual escape. His task was not easy, for the Prince often behaved in a rather heedless way, partaking in long drunken carousing with the local gentry on the braes of Corrodale, or foolishly rowing out to sea to seek French vessels. During that time, it was up to Neil to ensure the safety of the Royal fugitive, to keep him supplied with commodities, to gather information on enemy movements, and to keep a lookout for possible rescue ships. Eventually, on the 28th of June, Neil, Flora MacDonald, and the Prince, in his famous female disguise as Betty Burke – Flora's servant – managed to sail "Over the sea to Skye" in a celebrated episode. There, they headed for Raasay, where the Prince and Neil were to part for a time.

Because of its romantic dimension, history has mostly remembered the role of Flora MacDonald, herself a cousin of Neil, in the affair. However, there is little doubt that Neil, by far better-educated than Flora, was the key player. Not only was his knowledge of French, acquired at the Paris Scots College, essential in establishing contact with any French rescue mission, but also it proved especially useful when communicating discreetly with the Prince, the two of them reverting to that language when wishing to have private discussions.

After meeting up with the Prince again in Loch nan Uamh, Neil and a number of Jacobite followers set out for France on board the ships *l'Heureux* and *Le Prince de Conti*, landing safely in Roscoff some time later. The Prince then returned to Paris, to live a rather lavish existence, fêted by the Court of Louis the XVth and basking in popularity with French public opinion. What happened to Neil? According to Dr. MacLean, he seemed to have remained fairly close to the Prince's household, and was perhaps sent to Scotland in 1747, meeting Flora MacDonald in Edinburgh on the occasion.[28] Flora's extreme discretion about him when interviewed at the time (she refers to him as a mere "servant") seems to bear evidence that his presence in Scotland

Press, Edinburgh, 1897

28   Dr. A. MACLEAN, *A MacDonald for the Prince* , Op. cit., Chapter 10.

was related to some secret mission.[29]

By the end of 1747, Neil officially appeared in the French army records as a Lieutenant in the Albany Regiment, which was be incorporated in 1749 in Lord Ogilvy's Regiment. His army files referred to him as being initially *"a Captain in the Prince of Wales Army"*, and a footnote commented *"Excellent individual who has always served Prince Edward and who greatly helped his rescue."*[30] The mention of his rank as a Captain in the Jacobite army might well have been a mean for the Prince to reward his services, the Jacobite officers being then offered commissions – albeit usually on a lower rank – in the Scottish Regiments in the French service.[31]

Neil's involvement with the Prince seemed to end in 1748. Following the Peace Treaty of Aix-la-Chapelle with Britain, France agreed to end its support to the Stuart cause. Prince Charles Edward was asked to leave the Kingdom but, confident in the support he enjoyed from the powerful Jacobite lobby at the Court, and with Parisian public opinion on his side, he chose to ignore Louis XVth's injunction. Matters came to a head on December 10th 1748, when Prince Charles Edward Stuart was arrested on his way to the opera, in a spectacular police operation which involved no less than a whole Regiment of Guards, because of the risk of riots. The Prince was immediately sent to the state fortress of Vincennes, on the outskirts of Paris, while his household was raided and some thirty-nine of his followers incarcerated in the Bastille. After four days, the Prince relented and agreed to leave France, heading for Avignon.

Various authors (Dumont Wilden, Francisque Michel, etc.[32]),

---

29   According to the *"Journal taken from the mouth of Miss Flora MacDonald"* by Dr. Burton of York, and published by Bishop Robert Forbes in *"The Lyon in Mourning"*.

30   Archives historiques de l'Armée, Vincennes.

31   Officers in the Jacobite army were supposed to keep the same rank in the French army, but this was not necessarily applied in practice. For a similar experience to Neil's, see the Chevalier de JOHNSTONE, **Memoirs of the Rebellion of 1745-1746** , Longman, London, 1822, p 426.

32   Francisque MICHEL, **Les Ecossais en France. Les Français en Ecosse**. London, Trübner & Co, 1857, 2 Vol. 548 p et 551p. ; and

obviously quoting one another, have mentioned that when in Vincennes jail, Charles Edward Stuart was allowed as his sole companion, his "faithful Neil MacEachen", or that Neil went with him to Avignon afterwards. This is highly unlikely, for none of the existing archives[33] make any reference to Neil's presence at Vincennes, nor at the Bastille. It is doubtful that anyone would have had access to the illustrious prisoner without clearance at the highest level, and without the visit being reported in some way in the Governor's papers. Moreover, a letter to Flora MacDonald attributed to Neil mentions that he was having dinner with Clanranald and *"somebody"* (the Prince?) *"the day that they were took;"* and comments *"My God, what fright we got."* If authentic, this document would suggest that he escaped arrest himself.[34]

Barring the discovery of new evidence, our personal view is that the story of Neil's supposed presence with the Prince at Vincennes might have been part of a Jacobite propaganda ploy, since pamphlets were later circulated condemning French callousness, and extolling the Prince's fortitude during his brief incarceration. These papers claimed that the French officers were appalled by the orders they had received, that the Prince was lamenting the presence of his "brave Highlanders", etc. But such propaganda work, probably dictated by Charles Edward himself, required someone to bear witness to these events, and the story of Neil's supposed presence at Vincennes may have arisen from there.[35]

Neil's service as a Lieutenant in the French army lasted for sixteen years. Had France (again at war with Britain, and supporting the Stuart cause) succeeded in its attempt to land its Scottish and Irish troops across the Channel, his fortunes

---

L.DUMONT-WILDEN - *Le prince errant. Charles-Edouard le dernier des Stewarts*, Paris, Librairie Armand Colin, 1934, 362p.

33   *See the Fonds Bastille at the Bibliothèque de l'Arsenal, Paris.*

34   *See Dr A. MACLEAN, **A MacDonald for thePrince** , Op.cit, Chapter 10.*

35   *Arrest of Prince Charles (Authentic account of the Young Chevalier, London, 1749). For a detailed account of the Prince's arrest, see LL. BONGIE, **For the love of a Prince. Bonnie Prince Charlie in France**, University of British Columbia Press, 1986, Chapter XII.*

might have been different, and he may have returned to his native land in a position of power and influence. Such hopes ended in 1759 when, at the naval Battle of Quiberon, the French fleet was soundly defeated by the British Navy, and the last determined effort in that direction aborted. Neil's regiment only saw action on mainland Europe, during the war against Prussia. In 1763, following the Treaty of Paris, these troops were surplus to requirement and the Ogilvy's Regiment was disbanded.

Neil was then living in Saint-Omer, the garrison town of Ogilvy's Regiment, a short distance away from the Channel. He had married – or so we are told - Alexandrine Gonant, who was twenty years younger than him, and came, says the Marshal in his "Recollections", from a 'good family', her father being a soldier by profession who was a stranger in the town. His spouse had no fortune, and the meagre pension of 400 Livres a year he was receiving was insufficient to keep the household in comfort,[36] especially when their first child, a daughter, Eulalie, was born in 1764. Neil, mindful of the pledges of eternal gratitude he had received from the prince during the Uist escape, started the first of a series of letters he was to send over the years to the Stuart Court in Rome to beg for financial assistance. These calls for support met with some success at first, but then less so, until eventually he received no response at all.

The couple first moved towards Lorraine, where the cost of living was supposed to be cheaper than in Flanders, but had to stop in Sedan for lack of funds. There, their second surviving child, Jacques Etienne Josef Alexandre MacDonald, future Marshal of France, was born, on the 17th of November 1765.

---

36   *By comparison, Lord Nairn, who was heading the small Jacobite community in Sancerre, was receiving a gratification from France of 2400 livres per year. The same list of gratifications indicates that three exiles, who are also Cadet officers in the Scottish Regiments, will receive a payment of 200 livres per year as a supplement "because of the mediocrity of the pay." Neil was obviously not fortunate enough to receive this extra assistance. (See J. BROWNE, "Appendix N°CXXIV, Etat des gratifications proposes pour les Ecossais", in* **History of the Highlands and of the Highland Clans**, *Glasgow, 1838.)*

It is then that the MacDonald family went to Sancerre, in the Berry area, though, as we shall see, in circumstances which are less than clear. If we believe the Marshal's *"Recollections"*, his father moved to that town because of *"the cheapness of living and, probably, of the wine which is good."* He also moved to Sancerre because a small group of Jacobites had settled there under the Patronage of Lord Nairn where *"they formed a kind of colony and invited their Old Brother Officier Neil MacDonald to form part of their Society"*[37]. In this small community, between twenty and thirty strong, we see names such as Nairn, MacNab, Dalmahoy, Murray, Urquhart, Maxwell, Stuart as well as Neil's brother, Ronald.[38]

Neil was to remain in Sancerre until his death, on the 9th June 1788, never returning to Scotland. Apparently his latter years were not happy ones, since he lived with his wife and two children in extreme poverty, in a small house with *"a single room with a single window and a door"*,[39] as well as in poor health due to a dislocated hip. Despite this, according to his son, *"In his retreat, with his friends and his books, he consoled himself for the cruelty of fortune. He was very studious, well versed in the Greek and Latin tongues, which he spoke easily, as well as French, English and Gaelic, his native language (...) his memory was well stored, full of anecdotes, and he was a good musician, playing the violin; he was much esteemed after by the society of that time."*[40]

Thus goes the official story of Neil MacEachen, from the moment he left his native Howbeg, in the Outer-Hebrides, to his death at Sancerre, in the heart of France. However there are, in the story of Neil's life, a number of question

---

37   *"Pedigree of MarshalMacDonald Duke of Tarentum by Sir E. MacNab, 1814"*, in **Dunstaffnage Papers**, GD202/85.

38   *Ronald MacEachen was also involved in sheltering the Prince in Corrodale, and was later arrested. It is noteworthy that he appears in the list of Scottish refugees in Sancerre as Ranald MacDonald and not as a MacEachen.* (Maurice SUPPLISSON, **Les réfugiés écossais à Sancerre au XVIIIème siècle**, Bourges, 1918, p 9.

39   *See Léopold Bonnin's Manuscript*, **Description de la Ville de Sancerre**, *1877. Accessible at the Mairie de Sancerre.*

40   *Marshal MACDONALD*, **Recollections**, Op.cit, pp 5-7.

marks which cannot be ignored, at least because of their consequences upon the life and career of his son, the future Marshal MacDonald.

The first relates to the nature of Neil's relationship with his wife, Alexandrine Gonant. MacDonald liked to claim that François-Laurent Gonant, Alexandrine's father, was a professional soldier like himself, from an impecunious but 'well-respected' family; simple local townsfolks, or as Guillaume Lévêque (author of an interesting paper on MacDonald's French origins) puts it, *'le petit peuple urbain de l'Artois'*.[41] Gonant however, was not a military man but a violin player – a profession which Neil must have found attractive, since he himself was known to be a fair practitioner of the instrument. Earlier on in his life, François-Laurent had been a servant of the local Bishop. Alexandrine's mother, Jacqueline Lecat's parents were local butchers. According to registers, both François-Laurent and Jacqueline were illiterate.

Interestingly, the baptism certificate of Eulalie Sophie, the Marshal's eldest sister, reveals that she was born illegitimate, her mother Alexandrine being at the time *'fille libre'* – that is an unmarried mother. The father was officially unknown. Did Neil and Alexandrine legalize the situation after her birth? Guillaume Lévêque assumes so, but only by relying upon the evidence of Alexandre's own baptism certificate, written in Sedan about a year later, for Saint-Omer's archives of that period show no record of such a marriage.

However, by the 17th of November 1765, when the future Marshal is baptized in the Royal Parish of Saint-Charles de Sedan, Alexandrine and Neil are at last declared *'married together'* as well as living in that parish. The original baptism certificate no longer exists, but we know of its exact contents through transcripts, such as the one made in 1791 for the Parish of Saint-German-en-Laye for the purpose MacDonald's first marriage. A couple of points in this document draw the attention:

Firstly, Neil is described as *'Niell* Etienne *MacDonald'*

---

41 Guillaume LEVEQUE, *'L'ascendance obscure du Maréchal Mac-Donald'*, Op.cit.

27

(spellings were quite flexible at the time). This is, to our knowledge, the first and only occurrence of the first name *'Etienne'* being used by him. Where does this *'Etienne'* come from? There is little doubt that this typically French first name was not acquired in the Gaelic-speaking Hebrides, but later on, during his stay in France. Two possible explanations exist. One is that Neil was confirmed in the Catholic faith upon his arrival at the Scots College in 1736, and that being asked to chose a confirmation name as is customary on such occasions, he chose one related to the College's local parish of Saint-Etienne-du-Mont. He seldom used this name except for important occasions such as the baptism of his son. Another possibility is that the local priest in Sedan who performed his son's baptism was unsure about Neil's adhesion to the Catholic faith, him being a foreigner, and applied a cautionary procedure of 'conditional baptism' – hence the addition of a new first name.[42]

A second point worthy of note is the choice of the future Marshal's first names: Jacques Etienne Joseph Alexandre. His everyday first name, *'Alexandre'*, was probably chosen in reference to Neil's own father, Alexander Glenuig, and *'Etienne'* might be an echo to Neil's other declared first name. As for the *'Jacques'* and the *'Joseph'*; the register shows that the new baby's godfather was called *'Jacques Joseph Burtin'*. Did Neil choose these names to ingratiate himself with this witness, who, incidentally, was also confirming his marital status?

But if these events in Saint-Omer and Sedan raise some queries, they are like the calm before the storm in comparison with those which happened afterwards in Sancerre; events which have been brought to our knowledge mostly thanks to research undertaken by the town clerk of Sancerre, Leopold Bonnin, more than a century later. In a comprehensive work dated 1877 and entitled *'Description of the Town of Sancerre'*, Bonnin endeavours to describe every street and every house

---

42   We are thankful to both Canon Halloran, of Saint Andrew's University, and to Father Ross Crichton, Paris Priest of Benbecula, for these suggestions.

of the town, and to relate its history.[43] Coming to the modest house occupied by Neil and his family, he mentions, with profuse apologies to the Marshal's memory, the following story,

Neil had arrived from Sedan to Sancerre not with his wife and children, but after having abandoned them in Sedan because he could not afford to keep them going with his miserable pension. He had settled in Sancerre, '...*when on a winter evening, a wretched woman in rags, holding a child under each arm, came to knock on the door of his house. It was Alexandrine Gonant who had undertaken the whole trip from Sedan to Sancerre* [200 miles as the crow flies] *to join him, begging her way along the road.*'

At first, Neil refused to accept her in his home, but under pressure from the Jacobite community, he eventually relented. Yet, matters did not stop there, for says Bonnin,

'*The thought of leaving his mistress and his two children once again crossed his mind, but he repelled this and chose another option. On a fair morning, the mother being away, he took the two children to Bourges* [25 miles away] *and deposited them at the foundlings hospice. The poor mother was outraged by this behaviour and, gathering in her maternal love the necessary strength, set out on her own for Bourges. Alone, without any money, surviving from alms, she withdrew her children from the orphanage, and undertook once again the journey between Bourges and Sancerre, laden with two children. But her strength did not match her courage, so she used a heroic means, which only a mother could conceive. She took one of the children, carried it for a certain distance, then after leaving him in a safe place came back to get the other one which she took where the first one was. Taking that one again, she carried it further and came back to get the second. The same operation was repeated till she reached Sancerre, exhausted.*'

---

43   This manuscript was printed privately in 1998 by Mr Jacques Faugeras, former Deputy-Mayor of Sancerre, and is now out of print. The original is owned by the Mairie de Sancerre.

Neil then accepted her, and made no further attempts to get rid of the children, but, on,

'The 11th of March 1769, that is a few months after the events I have just mentioned, Alexandrine Gonant gave birth in Sancerre of another daughter which was baptised on the same day by Mr Girault, Vicar of the Parish and registered as the daughter of an unknown father and of Alexandrine Gonant. The death certificate of that child, issued on the 26th of the same month, bears the same indications.'

Bonnin (who clearly writes without any notion of what had happened previously in Saint-Omer) then notices the obvious contradiction between Alexandre's baptism certificate (a copy of which he acquires from his colleague in Sedan), in which Neil and Alexandrine are declared as married, and the above documents, which state that four years later, Alexandrine gives birth to a child *'of an unknown father'*. Having no evidence of Neil's marriage, either in Sancerre or Sedan, he concludes that Neil and Alexandrine were not in fact husband and wife, but instead were living in sin. In Sedan, where the couple were not well known, they managed to convince the priest of their marital status, but in Sancerre, where the small community of exiles (including Neil's own brother!) was intimate with Neil's real situation, that was not possible – hence the *'unknown father'*.

Thus an extraordinary situation is revealed, in which Alexandre, born 'officially' legitimate in Sedan in 1765, finds himself sandwiched between two illegitimate sisters (Eulalie Sophie, born in Saint-Omer in 1764, and Alexandrine, born in Sancerre in 1769).[44]

It will be recalled that divorce did not exist in eighteenth century Catholic France, which rules out a temporary marriage. Moreover, any child born in wedlock was, by law, assumed to be the husband's, whether this was the case or not. This means that had Neil been married to Alexandrine Gonant in 1769,

---

44 According to the Marshal, Neil and Alexandrine had another boy, who also died in infancy. We have no information about where this birth took place, or whether he was also declared illegitimate.

he could not have denied being young Alexandrine's father. Since it was stated that child's father was *'unknown'*, then the conclusion is that Neil and Alexandrine were still unmarried.

Bonnin's theory about Sancerre and Sedan (i.e. that the couple's real situation was known in the former town, when it was probably not in the latter) also applies to Saint-Omer. Not only was Saint-Omer Neil's last garrison town, but it was also Alexandrine's home town, so their unmarried status would have been common knowledge. Only in Sedan, where the couple lived temporarily, could witnesses be persuaded (or bribed) to certify that the parents had been lawfully wedded.

The logical conclusion of all this is that Marshall MacDonald's parents were unmarried and that his birth certificate was most likely based upon fraudulent declarations. Legally speaking he was illegitimate.[45]

Can Bonnin's information be considered as reliable however? According to local sources, he was a rather fanciful historian, prone to serious errors or mistakes, and his manuscript provides ample evidence of that.[46] However, there are two grounds over which he cannot be so easily dismissed. One is that, for all his failings as an historian, as a town clerk he had a professional approach to official registers. Indeed, Sancerre's civil registers confirm the birth and death in 1769 of a child borne by Alexandrine Gonant and whose father was *'unknown'*. The other one, of crucial importance, is that Bonnin had access to first hand information about Neil's life because of his own family connections (his mother was the niece and goddaughter of Mme Denizot, a widow who was the governess at Lord Henry Nairn's house).[47]

45　Not that this would be so exceptional. Dorothy Carrington, in her remarkable book on Napoleon's parents, says that Napoleon's father and mother were probably never religiously married, and that the registers were 'doctored' at a later date. See Dorothy CARRINGTON, **Napoléon et ses parents au seuil de l'histoire**, Ed. Alain Piazzola & La Marge, Ajaccio., p23.

46　To give but one example, in the aforesaid description of Neil's life, he happily confuses the Treaty of Westphalia and the Treaty of Aix-la-Chapelle, separated by no less than a hundred years!

47　For all the information about Sancerre and Léopold Bonnin, I am

Bonnin's claims are also validated, to a certain extent, by snippets of information provided by both Neil and his son. For example, Neil tells us, in a letter to Rome written in his own hand, that he was considering leaving France and returning to Scotland in 1768.[48] This suggests that he was indeed prepared to part with Alexandrine, who would have been unlikely to follow him as far as the Outer Hebrides. As for the nature of Neil and Alexandrine's relationship, MacDonald himself does not hesitate to acknowledge that it was not good. In his *"Recollections"* (which were initially written for his son, and not intended for publication) he makes this rather frank admission,

'...*while I was moving from garrison to garrison, your grandfather and grandmother had, two or three years before the death of the former, differences of so serious a nature that they voluntarily separated. I fancy that your grandmother, perhaps embittered by trouble, had some slight affection of the mind, but it was scarcely noticeable, and certainly not so apparent to others as to me. She retired to Fontainebleau, where she ended her days twenty-five or twenty-six years ago. Your grand-father was very gentle, she was quick-tempered; she was a great talker, he was naturally silent.*'[49]

It is clear that the couple were unmarried in 1769, but did they remain so till Neil's death in Sancerre in 1788? Bonnin mentions some hearsay that Neil did try to regularise his marital status before he died, but he could not find any evidence to support it. Furthermore, MacDonald's story that his parents had separated a few years before his father's death does not give much support to this theory, though it does not necessarily rule it out.

On his burial certificate, Neil is mentioned as being married to Alexandrine Gonant. This however did not convince Bonnin

thankful to Mr Jacques Faugeras, ex-Deputy-Mayor of Sancerre, and Mr Ribault, retired archivist at Archives Départementales du Cher and specialist in the history of the Scots in the Berry area.

48   Alasdair MACLEAN, A MacDonald for the Prince, Op. cit., p 74.
49   Marshall MACDONALD, **Recollections** , Op.cit., p 6.

who, for want of any corroborating evidence, suspected that the document was drafted purely and simply on the basis of the information in his son Alexandre's baptismal certificate.[50] It is noteworthy that the aforesaid certificate records the name of Neil's old friend, Alexander MacNab, as a witness. There is a possibility that MacNab, who was Neil's executor and the depositary of his papers, applied some pressure to keep unsavoury details at bay, either by having Alexandre's dubious birth certificate accepted as sufficient evidence, or by spreading the tale of a last minute wedding. MacDonald was then a young officer in the French army, and any indication of illegitimate descent would not have helped his career at a time when aristocratic favour was still key to reaching the higher echelons (but not for much longer – the Bastille was taken a few months later!). MacNab, who was an ex-bodyguard to the King of France, and a person of some substance in Sancerre, was certainly not without the necessary influence to ensure that the sanitized version prevailed.[51]

Indeed, the possibility of the story 'coming out' must have become an increasing worry as MacDonald rose in rank and renown: that one of Napoleon's famous Marshals, the Duke of Tarentum, the High-Chancellor of the Légion d'Honneur and Second Major-General of the King's Bodyguards, etc. was after all no more than the illegitimate child of a broken family, who had narrowly escaped being dumped by his father

---

50 On the rumour of Neil having married eventually, Bonnin thus states: *"Mr Alexandre MacNab having told me that he thought he could remember his forefather having mentioned in front of him that this marriage effectively took place in Saint Satur [next to Sancerre] shortly before Neil MacDonald's death, I went to the Courts to verify this assertion, and after having read and re-read all the acts registered in the parish of Saint Satur for the aforementioned period, I have acquired the certitude that the assertion made by Mr MacNab is inaccurate. It is likely that the burial certificate has been drafted purely and simply on the basis of the indications mentioned in the act of baptism transcribed elsewhere."*

51 And he seems to have kept to this sanitized version in his later years, if we believe the "Pedigree of Marshal MacDonald" passed on by his son, Duncan MacNab, to Major General Campbell in 1814 (see GD202/85 Dunstaffnage Papers).

in a foundling's home...[52]. MacDonald, whose steady nerves had been proved on many occasions, would probably have confronted such revelations with calm if they had been made public, however undoubtedly he would not have relished the prospect.

But who knew the story? Seemingly, more than one would expect. Leopold Bonnin, reporting it in 1877, and making use of family sources, clearly shows that Neil's mischief had not been forgotten in Sancerre, and that local people within the Jacobite community were passing the tale along from one generation to the other. However, the circle of those 'in the know' went well beyond Sancerre, as demonstrated in 1845 with the publication of the 'Mémoires secrets' of Armand François d'Allonville.[53]

In his book, d'Allonville, an aristocrat who went into exile to fight in the Prince's Army at the time of the Revolution, expresses his respect for MacDonald, with whom he became acquainted during the campaign of Naples. However, he deems it necessary to provide some details about his birth, not to cast any slight upon him, so he says, but *'to prevent biographers making errors'*. D'Allonville also emphasizes that he has taken care to await the Marshal's death to publish these facts, *'not because they were a blemish upon his memory, but because there are some self-esteem susceptibilities which can easily be bruised'*. What d'Allonville says is in fact a garbled version of the much better account which Bonnin, who had access to superior sources, provided some thirty years later.

---

52   I have not found any evidence in the Archives du Cher of two children with the right names having been abandoned around that period at the *Hôpital Général* of Bourges, but the records may be incomplete, names may have been changed, or the children might have been left elsewhere. Callous in our day and age, the practice of abandoning children to a foundling home was not uncommon at the time. For example, in Paris, between 1772 and 1776, 32,222 children were admitted to the *Hôpital des Enfants Trouvés*. See Camille BLOCH, **L'assistance de l'Etat en France entre 1764 et 1790**, Paris, 1908, p 105. See also Arlette FARGE, **Vivre dans la rue à Paris au XVIIIème siècle**, Folio Histoire, 2005, pp 62 – 68.

53   Armand François Allonville, 'Mémoires secrets', Passard, Paris, 1845. See Chapter XIX.

The tale is riddled with confusion and inaccuracies which are too convoluted to detail here, but the gist of it is similar: first that MacDonald's parents were unmarried; secondly that Neil supposedly married Alexandrine when in the throes of death, and thirdly that the mother of his children had to hunt Neil throughout France, carrying one child after the other along the road for miles (a dramatic story, as well as a considerable feat, which seems to have made great impression). D'Allonville adds that when, towards the end of his life, Alexandrine separated from Neil and went to live in Fontainebleau, she was financially supported by her son, on his officer's pay. This assertion is plausible, since Neil hardly had the means to pay any sort of alimony.

The main thing that d'Allonville's book tells us is that the skeleton in the MacDonald family cupboard was not a very well kept secret, which suggests that the story must have circulated around during the Marshal's lifetime, at least in some Royalist circles.[54] And did the Marshal himself know about his shady familial past? In his *"Recollections"* he makes abundantly clear that he had fairly little information about his parents, not least because Neil's papers disappeared when in MacNab's custody, following the latter's arrest during the Revolution. However, there is some evidence that he could have known much more than he pretended.

For a start, MacDonald's *"Recollections"* indicate that he was fully aware of his parents' strife, though he tends to attribute it not so much to Neil's callousness, as to his mother's *'light affection of the mind'*. He does not elaborate on whether Alexandrine's supposed condition was caused by his father's behaviour, or if on the contrary, Neil's sins were exaggerated by his mother because of her illness. It is noteworthy that he always speaks very affectionately of his father, which hardly portrays Neil as a reckless man. Alexandre may not have been

---

54 My inclination would be to attribute d'Allonville's information source to Hyde de Neuville, a hardline Royalist conspirator whose Jacobite grandfather had been a companion of Neil in Sancerre. Hyde would have been close enough to the source to know the general story, but too distant to provide an accurate report.

at home often, either because he was educated at boarding-school (even in Sancerre!), or because of his military career, but he was not altogether ignorant of what went on in the house.

Moreover, MacDonald was apparently aware that his parents had not two, but four children, two of which – a boy and a girl – seemingly died in infancy. Did he make inquiries about them? If he did, the details of his younger sister's birth and untimely death, available in the parish of Sancerre, would have quickly informed him of his parents' real marital situation. In much the same way, his sister Eulalie Sophie, who was married in Paris in 1790 to Frederic Weltner, must have asked for a transcript of her own baptismal certificate in advance of the ceremony.[55] Had she been unaware of her illegitimate birth, a reading of the certificate would have been sufficient to inform her of it. In 1821, the widowed Eulalie Sophie died at her brother's castle of Courcelles-le-Roy, where she had retired. Alexandre, who had her buried in the graveyard of nearby Beaulieu, must have dealt with her papers and her estate. There again, the truth would have become apparent in the process.

All in all, it is hard to believe that MacDonald was never informed of his parents dubious marital situation when other people, who were in no way family relations knew, and when he and his sister were confronted with administrative formalities which would, in all likelihood, have let the cat out of the bag.

In conclusion, and unless new documents to the contrary are produced (not least of all Neil's hypothetical marriage certificate), the weight of evidence available to us points to Marshal MacDonald being born illegitimate, and suggests that he probably remained so thereafter. There is also a fair degree of likelihood that he was not ignorant of his situation, but chose to keep quiet about it for understandable reasons. Such facts do not demean in any way the valour of the man or the quality of his deeds, nor do they dismiss the fact that his upbringing and career were certainly influenced by his Scottish origins and his Jacobite environment. But, and this is what is of interest to us, they throw a special light on his visit

---

55   MacDonald's first marriage took place in Saint-Germain-en-Laye in 1791, thus a transcript of his baptism certificate in Sedan was necessary.

to Scotland in 1825, which might have been motivated not only by curiosity about his ancestral homeland, but also by the desire to consolidate a questionable legitimacy.

There is an extra twist to the story. When the manuscript relating the flight of Prince Charles Edward Stuart in the Hebrides, attributed to Neil, surfaced in France in the 1820's, the editor of the *New Monthly Magazine* tells us it was bought by one of his friends from a hairdresser who claimed to be the author's son, and who said that his father had accompanied the Prince at some stage. With the narrative came, '*... two miniatures, beautifully executed on copper; one that of himself, one that of the Duke, afterwards Cardinal of York. This document and its accompanying relics were bought by our friend for a moderate amount of argent comptant, and they are now before us.'*[56]

Is this story authentic? Should it be accepted unreservedly? It is somewhat hard to understand how the owner of this diary and of these miniatures, a modest hairdresser who was unlikely to have much English, far less a detailed knowledge of the '45 Rising, could know anything about the historical value of such artefacts, never mind find the right people who would be interested in their purchase. But if we assume that it is true, then one may wonder if these items formed part of the papers which were given into MacNab's custody following Neil's death, and which were supposedly scattered during the Terror; or if they came from totally different sources.

There is nothing extraordinary in papers lost during the turmoil of the Revolution resurfacing years later in the most unexpected hands, and perhaps the mysterious hairdresser's claim to be the son of the manuscript's author was nothing more than a ploy to justify a dubious ownership. However, in view of the clear evidence that we have of Neil's troubled

---

56   New Monthly Magazine, 1840, 3rd part, p 323. *"Neil Mac Eachain's narrative of the wanderings of Prince Charles in the Hebrides"* was reprinted by W.S BLAIKIE in, **Origins of the '45 and other papers related to that rising,** Scottish History Society, 1916; and again by the Scottish Academic Press, in 1975. I would welcome any information on the whereabouts of this manuscript, which could be compared with letters written and signed by Neil.

marital relationship, there could be another option.

What we know with reasonable certainty, due to its style and its contents, is that the manuscript could hardly have been written by anyone but Neil. If its owner in 1820 (when the Marshal was still alive) was really his son, then this would mean that Neil MacEachen had fathered children with a woman other than Alexandrine Gonant. Could this woman have been his lawful wife? Hypothetical and farfetched as it may sound, this theory at least has the merit of explaining why Neil, who lived more than 20 years with Alexandrine and had four children with her, always refused to marry her in spite of pressure to do so. Perhaps the reason he did not wed her was simply because he was already married! It must be remembered that even at that time, when abandoning your wife was frequent, and leaving your children to an institution commonplace, bigamy remained a criminal offence. Then again, until further hard evidence becomes available, we cannot dismiss this hypothesis altogether.

Another question mark lies over Neil's life story: was he a mere failed priest, a brave schoolmaster from Uist, who happened to be in the right place at the right time, and was brought by extraordinary circumstances to play a small role in Scottish history? Or was he a clever, cunning adventurer, and a first rate Jacobite agent, if not a spy in the service of France? There is a substantial amount of circumstantial evidence, but very limited hard facts, which point towards the second option.

For a start, Neil was educated at the Paris Scots College, which was not a mere Catholic school, but renowned to be a centre for Jacobite intrigue. Apparently, the political role of the College prevailed over its religious function when it became suspected by the Church of Jansenist sympathies. Thus, the Paris Scots College did not ordain any priest between 1737 and 1764, but many of its *alumni* figured prominently in the numerous Jacobite attempts of the first part of the XVIIIth century. During the '45, many of its former pupils, such as the Duke of Perth and his brother Lord John Drummond, Bishop MacDonald (who blessed the Prince's standard at Glenfinnan), the Earl of Traquair, the Jacobite banker Aeneas

MacDonald, son of Kinlochmoidart, Alan MacDonald (the Prince's Chaplain), and others played a key role in the Rising. Significantly, when the Prince arrived in Scotland, he was said to have been dressed in the garb of an *alumni*. A centre for Jacobite intelligence, the College was itself under surveillance from the opposite side, Young Glengarry – alias "Pickle the Spy" – being also one of its pupils. Neil's presence in such an environment cannot have been neutral in its consequences.[57]

Then there is the fact that Neil was a Uist man, belonging to a Catholic clan renowned for its Jacobite loyalties. This Uist background is of extreme importance, for this remote part of Scotland, loyal to the Stuarts' cause, remained then largely out of government control, and a prime area for communications with France or Spain. It is not without significance that the Prince landed in Eriskay in 1745, or that he headed for the Uists after Culloden to be exfiltrated to France. With no army barracks or Royal Navy port, the place was ideal for bringing agents, gold or arms into Britain. In August 1745, on hearing of the possible arrival of the Prince in Scotland in Mull, the Marquess of Tweedale, then Secretary of State for Scotland, wrote to the Lord Advocate:

"I think, if he is in Scotland, the Isle of Uist would be a likelier place than the Isle of Mull; and, if he is in any other part of Scotland, I think it impossible that he should remain long there, without some of his Majesty's servants receiving intelligence of him, either from the officers employed in the recruiting, or from those belonging to the revenue in those parts."[58]

However, the waters surrounding the Outer-Hebrides are notoriously dangerous, and the information provided by the maritime charts available at the time were very limited, if not erroneous. Having a contact person in Uist who had a native's knowledge of the place, impeccable political loyalties, and who

---

57   See Canon Brian HALLORAN, *The Scots College Paris, Op . cit.,* Chapter 6.

58   John Heneage JESS, **Memoirs of the Pretenders and their adherents,** London, Richer Bentley, 1845, Vol II, p281.

could master French, English and Gaelic would have been a key asset for the French Navy. Neil certainly met all these criteria to perfection, and his supposed absence from the Culloden battlefield may have been related to that role.

In terms of hard evidence, we know that Neil was on some secret mission in Edinburgh after the '45, so he was undoubtedly used as an agent at some stage.[59] But was it so before the Rising? An interesting document may answer that question. In June 1764, Neil wrote from Saint-Omer to the Stuart Court in Rome to ask for some financial support. In his letter, he related his existence in these terms *"I will only say that I was made a Lieutenant in Lord Ogilvy's Regiment where I had the misfortune to continue in the same station till the dissolution of that corps, and after 28 years service, am now reduced to the miserable station of a Lieutenant reform with 400 Livres a year."*[60]

The figure "28" is poorly written and there is a fair amount of uncertainty whether the "2" is not a "1" somewhat squashed. Hence two options: if it is eighteen years, a simple subtraction brings us to the year 1746, shortly before he is officially listed as an officer in the French army records. If it is twenty-eight, then it brings us back to 1736, when he was also in France, but as a pupil at the Paris Scots College. This would mean that he had been enlisted by France as an agent well before the Rising.[61]

Did Neil have the qualities one would expect of a secret agent? The evidence we have is contradictory, much in the same way as that which we possess about his family's behaviour. Described as clever, but "cunning and interested" at the Scots College, he is mentioned as "an excellent

---

59   *Neil's letter to Flora MacDonald, dated February 1749. Quoted by Alasdair MACLEAN, A MacDonald for the Prince, Op. cit., Chapter 10.*

60   *Royal Archives, Vol 421/210.*

61   *I am, again, indebted to Mrs Genet-Rouffiac, not only for her own comments and analysis on this affair, but also for showing this document to a colleague palaeographer. The latter's opinion was that whilst "28" was apparently written, a distorted "18" could not be ruled out, the more so since it matched official military records. The advice given to me was to remain cautious, and to avoid building a theory on the basis of this sole document.*

individual" in his French army records. Similar ambiguity appears in a comment from MacDonald of Kingsburgh, about Neil's behaviour during the Prince's escape:

"[Kingsburgh and his Lady] *told likewise that they had never been so much afraid of any person's conduct as that of MacKechan, because he was a good-natured man and very timorous in his temper. But they frankly owned they had done him great injustice by entertaining any suspicion about him; for that he had behaved to admiration, and had got abroad with the Prince, the great wish of his soul; for he could never think of parting with him at any time but upon condition of meeting again, which MacKechan was so lucky as frequently to accomplish even when at parting they could scarce condescend upon a place or time when and where to meet.*"[62]

This description reminds us more of the behaviour of a professional "minder" than that of someone brought in by fortuitous circumstances to accompany the Prince; the vicinity of the latter being probably the last place where a "timorous" person would want to be in the aftermath Culloden.

In the end, Neil was probably a "spy"; not in the sense of being a full-time paid operator (those were comparatively few in number, and we have no evidence so far that he was one of those), but simply because his political, religious and educational background all contrived to make a Jacobite agent out of him. An avowed supporter of the Stuart cause, brought up in the Catholic faith and educated at the Paris Scots College, later on serving in one of the Scottish regiments in the service of France, his career is eminently representative of that of those thousands of Scots or Irish who, in the late XVIIth and in the XVIIIth century, fled repression at home to constitute the impressive Jacobite network in Europe, and in France in particular.

---

62   *Quoted in Rev* FORBES, **The Lyon in mourning**, *Ed. Edinburgh University Press for the Scottish History Society, 1895, Vol. I , p 80.*

Marshal MacDonald

If the life of Neil MacEachen–Mac Donald provides us with a rich array of travels, plots and adventures, that of his son Jacques Etienne Joseph Alexandre MacDonald gives us more of the same, but on a far grander scale altogether. In some ways, the son's life echoes that of his father: a military career taking him well beyond his native land, involvement in political intrigue, and a staunch loyalty to an espoused cause. It is also markedly different for, unlike the father, the son was not to be a pawn on the chessboard of French, British or European politics, but a player: General of the Revolution, Governor of Rome, Plenipotentiary Minister and Extraordinary Envoy to Denmark, Marshal of France, Governor of Catalonia, *Ministre d'Etat* (Secretary of State), Member of the King's Privy Council, Arch-Chancellor of the Legion d'Honneur, etc...[63] His shadows loom at some crucial times in French early XIXth century history, such as the very moments of the rise and fall of Napoléon. The contrasting fates of father and son are also illustrated by their opposite economic fortunes; Neil dying in great poverty in a single room, and his son in his castle, in the midst of a vast estate.

However, there was little hint of such future wealth when the young MacDonald spent his childhood in Sancerre. In fact, if we believe Bonnin, the family was close to misery:

"...Neil MacDonald working little or not at all, the mother working as a cleaner or a washerwoman, and the children being sent out of the town to collect dead wood for the fire, or manure along the roads to sell it to the wine yard owners."

It is hard to tell if Bonnin was prone to exaggeration in this description, but a tell-tale sign lies with the fact that, according to local sources, Neil's son was a boarder at Sancerre's school, even though his parent's home was barely a few streets away. We can assume that the school fees were paid by the more

---

63   Not to forget, eventually Deputy Grand Master of the Free Masons in France.

42

fortunate members of the small Jacobite community, such as the Nairns or the MacNabs, perhaps as a way to give the family more space, or simply to ensure that the child was being fed properly.[64] Another sign may be found in MacDonald's constant generosity in his later life; a generosity which one of his aides-de-camp, Philippe de Ségur, was to depict as "to the point of prodigality."[65] This trait of character may be read as the reaction of someone who knew poverty all too well.

Following a "somewhat neglected" education in Sancerre, the young MacDonald, gave up the initial thought of a religious vocation (another common point with his father!) and was sent to Paris, to the School of the Chevalier Pawlet,[66] with the view of becoming an engineer. He did not succeed in that line, but the fact that this establishment was a kind of military school provided him with the necessary background to fulfil his real ambition, which was to join the army.

Here, one must pause to underline the importance of the Jacobite network in the education and early career of the future Marshal. Amongst his patrons, we find not only the Sancerre community, and especially Edward MacNab (then in the King of France's Bodyguards), but also Lady Mary and Lady Lucy Stuart,[67] the Prince Ferdinand de Rohan (then Archbishop of Cambrai[68]), as well as the Countess of Albestrop. These people

64   His sister Sophie Eulalie was sent to a convent in Rouen, to be educated. She later married a Swiss doctor, Frédéric Weltner,who himself joined the French army to become a Colonel, and who died in Russia during the crossing of the Berezina. Sophie-Eulalie retired to her brother's house, and is buried at Beaulieu-sur-Loire.

65   See Philippe DE SEGUR, « Mémoires ».

66   The Chevalier Pawlet ran a school for military orphans, located in Popincourt

67   This appears to be a reference to the name of Stewart of Traquair, a well-known Scottish Catholic family, with close links with the Paris Scots College. See Sir E. MACNAB "Pedigree of Marshal MacDonald, Duke of Tarentum", 1814; Document transmitted by Duncan MacNab to Major General Campbell, **Dunstaffnage Papers**, GD202/85. Edward MacNab was a close friend of Neil.

68   According to information received from Ian Grant-Suttie, a lifelong Marshal MacDonald researcher, the Bishop of Cambrai had for a mistress Charlotte, illegitimate daughter of Prince Charles Edward Stewart and of Clementina Walkinshaw. (Ian GRANT-SUTTIE, "Le sabre de Mourad Brey",

either financed his studies, or helped him to get his very first commission as an officer.

His first posting was not, however, in the French army, but in the Maillebois' Regiment which was recruited as foreign troops by the Dutch, on the verge of a confrontation with Austria. War was eventually averted by negotiations, and the young lieutenant quickly found himself in search of fresh opportunities. Courageously, he began his military career all over again by joining the French army in 1787, even though this meant relinquishing his rank of Lieutenant and beginning again at the bottom of the ladder. Once more, thanks to his patrons, he was able to find a position in the Regiment of Dillon, a corps seeped in Jacobite traditions, which was part of France's Irish Brigade. Incidentally, Dillon's Regiment had played a decisive role in the victory of Fontenoy, in 1745, when the French army resoundingly defeated the Duke of Cumberland's troops during the Flanders' war.

We now enter the long, rich and complex military career of Alexandre MacDonald, of which we shall only give brief glimpses, since our purpose here is to focus upon the Marshal's Scottish dimension. As he began his career, MacDonald still had links with Scotland, obviously inherited from his father's. We know from his 1825 travel diary that he was visited in Paris in 1787 by MacDonald of Clanranald, uncle of Sir Archibal MacDonald, and also that he met Lady Lucy Stuart at the time. But these links were about to be interrupted as France entered the turmoil of the Revolution, and as she began a long succession of wars with Europe, and with Britain in particular. Except for some brief interruptions, the conflict was to last from 1792 till 1814; the communications between both countries being at their weakest during the period of the "Terror" (between 1793 and 1794) when any relationship with foreign powers was viewed as rank treason, and carried a risk of death, and again during the "Napoléonic Blockade" when, from 1806 onwards, any trade or exchanges with Britain were totally banned.

Conférence to the Association Franco-Ecossaise, Paris, 2005. Paper in my possession).

For MacDonald's career, the wars of the Republic provided a formidable opportunity which he was able to exploit when, unlike many officers belonging to the nobility, he decided to remain in the French army rather than to emigrate. His decision to stay in France was not really motivated by politics, but rather by personal considerations, as he later confessed in his *"Recollections"*. More prosaically, "he was in love", namely with his first wife, Marie-Constance Jacob, whom he married in 1791, and whose family were Republicans.[69]

In the early 1790s, France not only became embroiled in numerous external conflicts against various successive coalitions of European powers, but was also torn apart by internal civil wars as opposing partisans of the Republic fought those of the Monarchy, or Republican factions battled between themselves. At war on all fronts, the army was desperately short of officers, the more so since many of the Royal army officers had emigrated or been arrested and executed.[70] Those who were skilful enough to contribute to victories, and astute or lucky enough to avoid the various political purges, found themselves in a position to benefit from promotions at lightning speed. With the abolition of privileges, soldiers from very modest backgrounds could now reach ranks which would, beforehand, have been the sole preserve of the higher echelons of the French aristocracy, or would have required a life-time career.

Whilst MacDonald considered himself of noble blood, he only originated from the small local gentry of a foreign country, and more importantly, he had no personal fortune whatsoever. His prospects of reaching the higher echelons in the King of France's army would have been very limited indeed,

---

69   *MacDonald was to marry three times during his life, but was unfortunate to see each of his wives dying after a few years. Marie Constance Jacob died in 1797, leaving him with two daughters. His second wife, Félicité Françoise de Montholon, whom he married in 1802, died in 1804, leaving him one daughter. His third wife, Ernestine Thérèse Gasparine de Bourgoing, whom he married in 1821, as he was 55 years old; died in 1825, aged 32, leaving him with a boy.*

70   *Such as Arthur Dillon, Colonel of Dillon's Regiment, guillotined in 1794.*

and the Revolution undoubtedly provided him with unique opportunities. This, in his later life, he quite frankly confessed to the King of France's brother in the course of a dinner, saying that he *"... adored the Revolution."* The future Charles X recoiled in horror, but MacDonald hastened to say, to the latter's relief, that whilst he *"hated its men and its crimes"*, he also could not deny that it had made him, for: *"Without it, would I have had the honour of being at the King's table, beside your Majesty today?"*[71]

In 1792, five years after enlisting, MacDonald was still a Lieutenant, but his fortunes were to change with considerable speed. France was at war on its northern borders, when he was made aide-de-camp to General Beurnonville, who was to become his mentor, and later a lifelong friend. In June 1792, he was promoted to Captain, in August of the same year he became Lieutenant-Colonel and in March 1793 he was made Colonel. In April 1793 he refused a further promotion to Deputy-General, but later that year he accepted the rank of General Commanding a Brigade. By December 1794, barely more than two years after being a mere Lieutenant, his rank was that of General commanding a Division.

The list of actions and battles in which he participated in order to reach that rank is long and impressive. They are too numerous to list here, except to mention as examples the battles of Valmy and Jemmapes, decisive as they were in securing the future of the young French Republic, and the winter campaign in Holland. To the best of our knowledge, that campaign was the sole occasion in MacDonald's career when he confronted British land forces, repelling an army led by the Duke of York, the son of George III.

Like all soldiers, MacDonald met with danger during military action in the field, but he also had to face it, and potentially more treacherously, in the changing political scene. The Army of the North, in which he began his career, was the cutting edge of the Republic, but it was also rife with plots and treason. No less than two of his commanders (Dumouriez and Pichegru)

---

71   Marshal MACDONALD, *Recollection*, *Op.cit.*, p 459.

under which MacDonald served, were eventually to cross over to the Royalist side. The former added insult to injury when, in the process, he delivered to the enemy General Beurnonville (by then French Minister for War) and four Commissars who had come to arrest him for treason.[72]

In such dicey circumstances, MacDonald, with his foreign name and noble origins, could not avoid falling under suspicion. He had a number of potentially lethal brushes with some of the Representatives sent by the Convention to supervise the army's high command. At one point he was even advised by his friends and superiors to flee, but, to his credit, he refused to do so, despite the consequences.[73]

It is indicative of the atmosphere at the time to recall that, if MacDonald's skills and loyalty brought him rapid promotion, he did not always welcome it. This was partly because he considered himself insufficiently experienced to become a commanding officer at such an early stage in his career, and partly because of the political risks involved. In 1793, following one of his feats of arms, Levasseur de la Sarthe, Representative for the Convention, wanted to make him a general, but, according to Levasseur, he reacted thus:

"–Representative [he told me], I am a foreigner.
– What does it matter? The Republic will need another man of talents to serve and defend it.
– You will make me enemies.
– You will answer them by your merits."[74]

This conversation is extremely interesting, for it shows MacDonald claiming to be a "foreigner" to ward off a promotion of which he was wary. It raises this simple, but obvious question: was he French or not?

---

72   *Beurnonville was incarcerated in Austria for thirty months before being exchanged. This was perhaps just as well, for at the time he was himself under accusation from Robespierre, and would probably have lost his head had not he been already in enemy hands. See Mortimer TERNAUX,* **Histoire de la Terreur** *(1792-94), Levy Frères, Paris, 1867, p 568.*

73   *Ibid, p 574.*

74   *René LEVASSEUR DE LA SARTHE,* **Mémoires** *, Tome II, p 35.*

The mere fact that he emphasised his foreign origin is a clear indication that he was not French by birth, for the question would not have arisen otherwise. In France, from 1715 onwards, all English, Scottish or Irish foreigners who had served for ten years in the army were entitled to claim French nationality if they wished to, a mere declaration to the courts being required.[75] Neil MacDonald obviously did not bother to do so, for his son, born in France, with a French father and mother, would have automatically acquired French citizenship the day he was born. However, Alexandre MacDonald was truly French for more than one reason.

By 1793, the various legislations and Constitutions enacted by the Republic since its inception had made a number of changes to the methods of acquiring French nationality. The law of 1790 specified that any foreigner established in France for five years was to become French automatically if he had property in France, traded in France, or had married a French wife. MacDonald, as we have seen, had married Marie Constance Jacob in 1791. The Constitution of 1791 also required the taking of a "civic oath", but we know that this is precisely what MacDonald did on the 27th of July 1791, when a Lieutenant in Dillon's Regiment.[76] When rejecting Levasseur's offer of a deputy-generalship, he must have known that he had already acquired French nationality through the aforementioned legislation. So why did he claim to be a "foreigner?"[77]

The explanation undoubtedly lies with the dangerous political climate in the year 1793, when France, increasingly

75   Claude NORDMANN, « Les Jacobites écossais en France au XVIIIème siècle », in *Regards sur l'Ecosse du XVIIIème siècle*, Publications de l'Université de Lille III, 1977, p 85.

76   This oath is mentioned in the *Journal des Chercheurs et des Curieux*, 10th of February 1894, p 134.

77   On this issue of French nationality, see Patrick WEIL, *Qu'est-ce qu'un Français?* Edition Grasset, Paris. Accessible on www.edition-grasset. fr/chapitres/ch weil.thm . It is worthy of note that the rules regarding the acquisition of French citizenship were changed again, in a restrictive way, by Napoléon's Civil Code which required "being born of a French father." Born after 1803, MacDonald would have remained a foreigner, or would have had to undergo a long an expensive naturalisation process.

threatened both externally and from within, was run by the hardline regime known as the "Terror". Foreigners then became increasingly associated with traitors or spies in the public mind, to the point when a hard-line legislation specified that those "...*born subject of governments with which the Republic is at war will be incarcerated till the peace.*"[78] Moreover, the situation of the Army of the North was an especially exposed one, for in the year 1793, out of his five successive commanders, one (Dumouriez) was to desert to the enemy, one was to be dismissed (Charles Edward Jennings of Kilmaine, of Irish Jacobite origin), and two were to be arrested under suspicion of treason and executed (Houchard and Custine). MacDonald's immediately lukewarm response to the prospect of promotion, and his opportunistic reference to his "foreign" origins must be appreciated in that context.[79] Whilst he was to relent, and accept a generalship only a few months later, there is no doubt that his life was under serious threat when the Terror held sway over France.[80] He undoubtedly inherited from that period a deep dislike of hard-line Republicanism, which was to shape his political attitude in the years to come.

In 1798, MacDonald was sent to Italy, where he was to command the French troops, becoming General-in-Chief of the Army of Naples, winning a series of victories over the army of the King of Naples. Only when confronted by veteran general Suvarov at the Battle of Trebbia, with 50 000 men against his own 30 000, was he forced to give up. This he did after three days fighting, but organized a masterly retreat to Genoa,

---

78   *Décret de la Convention of the 16th of October 1793.*

79   *In his "Recollection" MacDonald recalls a similar incident involving his noble origins. As he was being asked to command the front line, he argued that recent legislation prohibited, under pain of death, aristocrats to come within 30 km from the borders. Being ordered to go just the same, he asked for a written discharge, lest he should be accused of treason if his troops were to be defeated...but he was refused that too. So, he had no other option but to succeed. For more evidence on the same matter, read Guillaume LEVEQUE, 'L'Ascendance obscure du Maréchal MacDonald', in* **Revue du Souvenir Napoléonien***, N°463, pp63-66.*

80   *The "Terror" ended when Robespierre and his allies themselves fell to the Guillotine in July 1794.*

bringing the Russian general's comment: "*Another success like this one and we shall have lost the Peninsula.*"[81]

Meanwhile, France was once again in turmoil. The ongoing government of the Directoire, itself of dubious democratic credentials (it was issued from the Fructidor Coup d'Etat of September 1797), was notoriously corrupt and inefficient. Another Coup d'Etat, led by some of its members, was in the offing, to replace it with a less discredited and more efficient government structure. However, such a move could not succeed without serious army backing, and the plotters, looking for a military leader, approached various generals whom they knew to be political moderates. General Joubert was initially considered, but he was killed in Italy at the battle of Novi. General Moreau was then approached, but refused to lead the Coup. The conspirators then turned to MacDonald, then in France recovering from illness, but he also refused to lead, though he agreed to give his support. Eventually, General Bonaparte, miraculously back from Egypt in spite of the French fleet's destruction by Admiral Nelson, offered his services, and agreed to command what was to be known as the "18th of Brumaire Coup d'Etat" (9th of November 1799).

The importance of MacDonald in the advent of Bonaparte was openly acknowledged by the former in his "Recollections", and indeed was quite obvious to his contemporaries, since Bonaparte paraded surrounded by his key supporters in the army.

"On the 18th of Brumaire a great number of military, amounting to about 10 000 men, were assembled in the gardens of the Tuileries, and were reviewed by Bonaparte, accompanied by General Beurnonville, Moreau and MacDonald. Bonaparte read to them the decree just issued by the commission of inspectors of the Council of the Ancients, by which the legislative body was removed to St. Cloud; and by which he himself was entrusted with the execution of that decree, and appointed to the command of all the military forces in Paris,

---

81   *Quoted in Louis de LA ROGNE,* **Catalogue des Généraux Français de 1724 à 1813***, p 184 .*

50

and afterwards delivered an address to the troops."[82]

MacDonald's role during these events was to ensure the safety of the Versailles military area, on the road to Paris, and near Saint Cloud where the deed actually took place. This he did, immediately closing the Republican Club of the latter town in the process, thus preventing its use as a rallying point.[83] It is of course tantalizing to imagine what would have happened if MacDonald had decided to lead the Coup himself, rather than following Bonaparte. Perhaps he would have failed (as nearly happened with Bonaparte, when things turned awry at Saint Cloud), and perhaps he would have lost his head in the venture. But he would possibly have succeeded, and his presence in government would have given a totally different twist to early XIXth century French and European history, not to mention the nature of the relationship between France and Britain at the time.

Following the Coup, and the advent of the Consulate, MacDonald was put in charge of the Reserve Army, which became the Armée des Grisons. There, he executed one of his most daring successes, by taking a whole army across the Splügen Pass, in the Alps, in mid-Winter, a feat which was considered impossible, and which flushed the Austrians out of the Tyrol. However, this military prowess did not necessarily endear him to Bonaparte. On his way to absolute power, the First Consul had no wish to see any other army leaders outshining him; especially when they had proved to be potential "Coup d'Etat" material like MacDonald or Moreau.[84] Moreover, the risk of internal rivalries within the army – the clan of those who had fought mostly in the North confronting those who had made their careers with him in the South – had to be avoided at all costs.

---

82   BOURIENNE, *Memoirs of Napoléon Bonaparte.*

83   *He probably did so with some satisfaction, because that club – the Breton Club – was the historical birthplace of the dreaded hardline Jacobin faction, whose policies had put his career and his life at risk when he was an officer on the Northern front.*

84   *From Ist Consul, he became Life Consul in 1801, and Emperor Napoléon in 1804.*

"It was with that aim in mind, with Moreau especially, that all the possible conciliatory and generous means– honours granted, praise given, family ties even, it has be said - were employed; but we have already seen the resistance of that general. With others, such as Bernadotte, Augereau and MacDonald, Napoléon used more efficient means. They were scattered by various errands, some military, some diplomatic and military at the same time. Bernadotte was sent to command the Army in the West, and Saint-Cyr to Spain, to lead the French division sent against Portugal. Lannes and Brune left, one for the Embassy of Lisbonne, the other for that of Constantinople. As for MacDonald, with his free and mocking speech, with his proud and independent character, and because of his relationship with Moreau which made him a cause of concern, he was earmarked for Denmark well before his return to France in the first months of 1801."[85]

MacDonald was then sent as Plenipotentiary Minister and Extraordinary Envoy to Denmark, but his mission served little purpose other than that of expediency in France's internal politics, for the Danish fleet had just been destroyed by the British. Frustrated at being stranded in a political and military backwater, he campaigned vigorously and ceaselessly to be recalled. This very process may have triggered a long-lasting conflict in the relationship between himself and Foreign Affairs Minister Talleyrand, whom he suspected of employing his considerable skills in prejudicing Napoléon against him.

In 1802, he was back in France, but matters did not improve – far from it. An assassination attempt against Bonaparte had nearly succeeded, and a ruthless clandestine war set his police against Royalist plotters who were allied to dissatisfied Republican officers. In 1804, the main conspirators, Cadoudal and Pichegru had been arrested, and along with them, General Moreau. All were brought to trial, but there was a strong suspicion that Bonaparte had had Moreau linked to the case to discredit the popular general who was a strong potential

---

85   Philippe DE SEGUR, *Mémoires*. General Beurnonville was also *sent as Ambassador to Berlin.*

opponent in the army. Cadoudal was to be executed, Pichegru died mysteriously in prison, and Moreau was sentenced to two years in jail, which was commuted to exile in America. The official story has it that MacDonald, who had fought with Moreau, was highly critical of his colleague's condemnation and expressed it in no uncertain terms; hence his ensuing disgrace.

Evidence found in the police archives[86] seems to indicate that matters were somewhat more complex, and that MacDonald was not an unknown quantity at the court of Louis XVIII. The correspondence between a mysterious Royalist Committee in Paris and the court highlights that the exiled King of France thought he could benefit from some support from within the French army, and that officers such as MacDonald, Lecourbe, Mallet, Berthier, and especially Moreau, ranked high on the list of his possible partisans. As a certain Bourlac reported, following a mission to London in 1808:

"[In case of a takeover] *Moreau was all designated to become the provisional generalissimo, till the King's agreement, and, in the absence of Moreau, the commandment would have alternated between MacDonald and Lecourbe*" [87]

Further:

"[in London] *Louis the XVIIIth, Moreau, MacDonald, Lecourbe, Malet are the topics of all conversations.*"[88]

These documents are known to us because the supposed Royalist Committee of Paris was in fact a decoy run by Bonaparte's formidable Minister for Police, Joseph Fouché, and Bourlac – alias Perlet – one of his agents. Though it would not have been beyond Fouché to plant evidence against such or such personality in one of his agent's reports, there is a ring of

---

86   See *Affaire Fauche-Borel et Charles Perlet (1806-1809) in Archives Historiques de la Préfecture de Police, Paris,Série Aa 311.*
87   *Ibid, folio 396*
88   *Ibid, folio 388.*

truth in these assertions. Moreau eventually came back from exile to fight in the armies of the enemies of France, and met death by French fire. Malet was involved in a famous plot which nearly toppled the regime in 1812, when Napoléon was still in the snows of Russia. MacDonald himself, though totally loyal to Napoléon till the Emperor's first abdication, was to become an equally loyal supporter of King Louis XVIII.

The police archives provide us with references which suggest that the King had *"reasons to rely upon MacDonald."* What were these reasons? How could he have been so sure of MacDonald's feelings and sympathies? Information may have come from some of his colleagues like Mathieu Dumas, who once belonged to the Royalist "Club de Clichy", or from General Pichegru, who had him under his command before crossing to the other side; but another possibility may lie with Hyde de Neuville. A top Royalist agent (he tried to negotiate the King's return with Bonaparte, and was also suspected in the Cadoudal/Moreau conspiracy), Hyde was no less than the grandson of James Hide, an English refugee from the '45 Rising, who had belonged to the Jacobite community of Sancerre at the same time as the Marshal's father.[89] It is therefore not unthinkable to see in Hyde an ideal contact person between MacDonald and the Royalist side, the two of them sharing the same Jacobite roots, and the families having known each other for fifty years.[90]

Whatever the extent of MacDonald's involvement with the Royalist side (if any at all), the suspicion which surrounded him put a brutal stop to his career. He was awarded no command for five years and his name was bypassed when Napoléon drafted the first list of his Marshals. This led him to withdraw from Paris and the Napoléonic court to his estate of Courcelles-le-Roy, near the Loire. There, in a beautiful 16th century castle[91] surrounded by 600 hectares of land he had acquired, he took a keen interest in agriculture, and led the life of a gentleman-

---

89   Maurice SUPPLISSON, Op.cit..
90   At least till he himself went into exile in America.
91   Located in the commune of Beaulieu-sur-Loire, this delightful castle is now regrettably in a ruinous state, and is threatened with collapse.

farmer, though always under the watchful eye of Fouché's secret police.[92]

How did he come to be part of the landed gentry? It is worth remembering that, on his marriage in 1791, he was a junior officer with no personal fortune whatsoever, to the extent that he had to get his superior officer's support in convincing his first wife's father to give him his daughter's hand. At her death in 1797, when he was a young general, the notary had valued his fortune at only 3,306 Livres, mostly tied up in horses and equipment and of which 1,029 Livres had to be deducted in expenses and wages owed to domestics. By 1802, when he was remarried to Félicité Françoise de Montholon,[93] his assets were valued at 284,000 francs, and his bride's at 350,000 francs. The estate he was to purchase in Courcelles in 1805 cost him 200,000 francs, and he was also involved in property dealing with an even larger estate at Bois-Sir-Amé.[94]

It is understood that the MacDonald family's long tradition of gruelling poverty had by then become a thing of the past, and this was to be increasingly so.[95] Where did this wealth come from? Whilst his pay as a general, or his pension as a Grand Officer of the Légion d'Honneur did certainly provide him with a substantial income, we must probably turn to the campaign in Italy for an explanation, when the seizure of Italian cultural treasures, considered as spoils of war, enabled France to richly reward its generals. By Napoléonic standards, when plunder was the norm, MacDonald was an honest man, pointedly refusing to accept certain gifts or bribes which many

---

92   His gardener was apparently an agent of Fouché (Information from Ian GRANT-SUTTIE, Op.cit.)

93   She was the widow of General Joubert, who was supposed to lead the Coup d'Etat which eventually befell to Bonaparte. There is a remarkable consistency, in this whole story, in the way potential or effective plotters such as Generals Joubert, Moreau, MacDonald or Beurnonville associate with each other in their professional as well as their private lives.

94   We are thankful to Michel Mazué, who has researched MacDonald's notarial documents, for this information.

95   Besides his property at Courcelles, he also had a hotel in Paris, in which was a library with an extensive collection of books, maps and paintings.

others would gladly have taken or even expected. There is however no doubt that his military career, as well as his marriages, helped him to acquire substantial wealth, despite the fact that Napoléon himself considered MacDonald to be "without fortune" – everything being relative.[96]

MacDonald's disgrace ended in 1807, when he was offered the possiblility of seeking service in the army of Naples, then run by King Joseph, Napoléon's brother, an offer he did not accept. In 1809, Eugène-de Beauharnais, Napoléon's stepson and Vice-Roy of Italy, was confronted by an Austrian military offensive and was in severe difficulties. Sent to his rescue, MacDonald quickly turned the tables around, flushing the enemy out of Italy in a series of victories. He pursued them back to Austria, joining with Napoléon's forces on the battlefield of Wagram, where a considerable confrontation was looming; probably one of the largest in the world's history to date, involving 360,000 soldiers from both sides.

In Wagram, MacDonald was to perform one of his most celebrated military feats by breaking through the enemy centre and organising his troops in a square formation backed up by artillery. No subtle strategy there, but a brutal and massive confrontation of forces, resulting in horrendous losses: out of the 8000 soldiers who advanced with MacDonald in their midst, only 1500 were to remain standing when the action was finished. Thanks to "MacDonald's column" the enemy centre had been broken, and the two day battle, whose outcome had been uncertain, was won.

Napoléon, who had witnessed the deed, came to him after the battle, hugged him with force and said:

"Let us be friends henceforward.'
'Yes,' I answered, 'till death.' And I have kept my word, not

---

96   *In 1809, he was given an annual pension of 60000 francs upon Naples, in 1810, one of 20000 francs over Galicia. His many ranks and positions under the Empire, and later under the restored monarchy also attracted various incomes. As for MacDonald's disinterestedness, and for Napoléon's comments on his lack of "fortune", see Infra, their last conversation when the Emperor abdicated.*

only up to the time of his abdication, but even beyond it.

He added, *'You have behaved valiantly, and have rendered me the greatest services, as, indeed, throughout the entire campaign. On the battle field of your glory, where I owe you so large a part of yesterday's success, I make you a Marshal of France* (he used this expression instead of 'of the Empire'). *You have long deserved it.'*[97]

MacDonald was made Duke of Tarentum. Though two other generals were also nominated along with him (Marmont and Oudinot), he was said to be the only one whose nomination was the direct consequence of his deeds on the very field of battle. In the army, a ditty describing the reason behind each of these nominations ran:

"France chose MacDonald
   The Army chose Oudinot
  Friendship chose Marmont"

In a letter dated July 1809 to Edward MacNab, his father's old friend in Sancerre, MacDonald sent a description of the battle, telling how, all around him, his soldiers and their horses had been killed or wounded, how his own horse had been wounded and his sword broken by a bullet, and how he himself had miraculously escaped with ... a bad horse kick. The letter, embellished with appropriately sycophantic praise of the Emperor's leadership, was dutifully recorded and published by the Municipality of Sancerre – a wise diplomatic move which advertised his renewed loyalty, and perhaps also his appreciation at having been released from the military doldrums.[98]

To avoid straying any further into French military history, we shall only give a fleeting description of Marshal MacDonald's campaigns between 1809 and 1814, and of his life thereafter. In 1810, he was in Spain as Governor of Cataluña, and successfully regained the key fortress of Figueras, which had been captured

---

97   *See **Recollections**, Op .cit.*
98   *Archives of the Mairie of Sancerre.*

by the Spaniards. He let the Spanish commanding officers keep their swords, a rare gesture of chivalry in a conflict otherwise characterised by atrocities. In 1812, he was in the Baltic, commanding the left wing of the Great Army during the invasion of Russia. There, his troops, suitably equipped with sheepskins, were able to face the ferocious winter better than any others, consequently returning home in better condition. In 1813, he took part in the German campaign, in which he won some victories, but also suffered a crushing defeat at the Battle of Katzbach – an event for which he took responsibility fully and personally, gaining the respect of his fellow officers.[99] The same year, at the battle of Leipzig, when Napoléon's military might was brought to a halt, he narrowly escaped drowning when swimming across a river whose bridge had been blown prematurely.

In 1814, as the Imperial army rolled back within France's national borders, he took an active part and distinguished himself in many of the battles of this defensive campaign. However, temporary successes were not enough to stem the progress of the coalesced forces from all Europe. France was exhausted by years of war, and the army, too depleted to withstand the pressure, could not stop Paris being occupied. Napoléon, in nearby Fontainebleau, considered unleashing the remnants of his forces in an ultimate battle to regain his capital or perish. Painfully aware that this battle would be lost and only result in the city's destruction, the army refused to go any further. A delegation of high-ranking officers, including MacDonald, went to meet the Emperor to convince him to abdicate.

Napoléon having finally bowed to the pressure, a delegation comprising Marshal MacDonald, Marshal Ney and the Minister for External Relations. Caulaincourt was sent to negotiate his terms of abdication with the Allies, in the person of the Czar of Russia. The situation was difficult in the extreme, and worsening by the minute, for whole army corps were now deserting to the enemy or concluding separate truces, while a

99   See *Général Baron de MARBOT*, **Mémoires**, *Plon, Paris, 1891, Volume III, Chapter XXVII*.

provisional government proclaimed the Emperor's dethroning. Unbowed and totally loyal to his master when so many were deserting him, MacDonald endeavoured to the best of his means to defend the latter's interests. Though his arguments for a Regency (Napoléon abdicating in favour of his infant son) were not to convince the Allies, he secured a reasonable deal. Napoléon was to abdicate and leave for exile, being given a symbolic Kingdom in the small island of Elba, between Corsica and Italy.

The climax of these crucial negotiations took place in the palace of Fontainebleau, when Napoléon handed his act of abdication to MacDonald, in a scene which the Marshal himself thus recalled :

"Sire, the Duke of Tarentum is waiting. The deed which he is to take with him ought to be delivered to him, seeing that the delay will expire I twenty-four hours, and that the exchange is to be made in Paris.

The Emperor, rousing himself for a second time from his meditations, got up more briskly, but his colour had not changed, and his face was melancholy.

'I feel rather better', he said to us, and then added: "Duke of Tarentum, I cannot tell you how touched by, and how grateful for, your conduct and devotion I am. I did not know you well; I was prejudiced against you. I have done so much for, and loaded with favours, so many others, who have abandoned and neglected me; and you, who owed me nothing, have remained faithful to me! I appreciate your loyalty all too late, and I sincerely regret that I am no longer in a position to express my gratitude to you except by my words. I know that your delicacy and disinterestedness have left you without fortune; and I am not unaware of the generous manner in which you refused to accept a present of considerable value at Gratz in 1809, which the States of the Province offered you in token of their gratitude for the strict discipline and order you maintained among my troops, and where your impartial rule did justice to all. Formerly I was rich and powerful, and now I am poor'.

'I flatter myself', I answered, ' that your Majesty thinks too

well of me to believe that I would accept any reward in your present position; my conduct, upon which you place too high a value, has been entirely disinterested'.

'I know it', he said, pressing my hand; 'but , without hurting your delicacy, you can accept a present of another kind, the sword of Mourad-Bey, which I wore at the battle of Mont-Thabor; keep it in remembrance of me and of my friendship for you'.

He had it brought to him, and offered it to me. I thought I might accept this present. I thanked him very warmly; we threw into each other's arms, and embraced one another effusively. He begged me to come and see him in Elba if any chance took me to Italy; I promised. I made my preparations for departure, and since then I have never seen Napoléon again."[100]

Napoléon having abdicated, MacDonald considered himself freed from any obligation to him, and took the decision to offer his services to the restored King of France, Louis XVIII. This offer was gladly accepted, and MacDonald was nominated Peer of the Realm. After sitting for a while in the War Council, he was given a new military command.

However, Napoléon's story was not finished yet. In 1815, well-informed of the dwindling popularity of his successor, Bonaparte escaped from the Island of Elba and, having landed on the Riviera coastline, undertook to march to Paris to regain power. Everyone thought that this small troop was going to be easily dispersed, but the opposite happened, for by the sole persuasion of its leader, it swayed all the forces sent against it to its side, one after the other. Remaining loyal to the King as he had been to the Emperor, MacDonald did not change sides, unlike many of his colleagues, but his soldiers did so. In Lyon, as he was preparing to oppose Napoléon's advance, his army joined the general trend and walked to the other side, leaving him with no option but to withdraw, narrowly escaping arrest. In a few weeks, Napoléon was back in power.

MacDonald, after escorting the King Louis XVIII to the

---

100   *Marshal MACDONALD, **Recollections**, Op.cit. p 328-9.*

border, refused to go into exile and returned to his Paris home. There, he steadfastly refused Napoléon's repeated attempts to bring him back to his side, and waited for an end which he knew to be the unavoidable.[101] It came a few months later, on the Battlefield of Waterloo, ending the Empire forever as MacDonald had thought.

The return of Louis XVIII to power brought the Marshal's career to its pinnacle. Having clearly demonstrated his unflinching loyalty in the most trying of circumstances, he was first given the delicate task of disbanding the remnant of Napoléon's army. This he performed with regret, but also with great tact, sheltering his erstwhile colleagues threatened with arrest for treason, and defending some who were court-martialled.

Nominated a *Ministre d'Etat* (or Secretary of State) in the new government, MacDonald was considered as a possible incumbent for the War Ministry, but he eventually took the post of Arch-Chancellor of the Légion d'Honneur.[102] There, he performed with great skill to safeguard this elite order created by Napoléon, which was threatened with disbanding. He also redressed the order's finances – which were bankrupt – and undertook a long lasting reform of its rules and institutions.[103]

MacDonald was also made a member of the King's Privy Council, a Second Major General of the King's bodyguard, and a Grand-Croix of the order of Saint-Louis as well as a Commanding Knight of the Order of Saint Esprit. A Peer of the Realm, he stood as a moderate liberal, and endeavoured to

---

101   It has been said that, at the time, he also enlisted in the National Guard as a mere foot soldier to underline the fact that he was not deserting.

102   An interesting parallel may be drawn between Marshal MacDonald's career and that of Henri Jacques Guillaume Clarke, who got the post of Minister for War in that same government. Of Irish Jacobite descent, Clarke started his career during the French Revolution, became Minister for War under Napoléon, and eventually paid allegiance to Louis XVIII after the latter's downfall.

103   Marshal MacDonald's portraits may be seen in Paris at the Musée de la Légion d'Honneur, 2 rue de la Légion d'Honneur, 75007 Paris.

find acceptable compromises to the intricate issue of properties confiscated by the Revolution. He was still to serve for fifteen years, first under Louis XVIII till the King's death, and then under his successor Charles X. He retired from most of his official posts in 1830-31, some ten years before his death at Courcelles-le-Roy on the 25th of September 1840. [104]

MacDonald was certainly a physical survivor; for thirty years he had escaped the slaughter of countless battlefields, from Russia to Spain, from Holland to Italy. He was also, undoubtedly, a political survivor, for he had pursued his career through many coups d'Etat, intrigues and revolutions, and under regimes of every hue and shade, from the monarchy of Louis XVI to that of Charles X, from the radical republicanism of the Terror to the Imperial absolutism of Napoléon. More important, he had done so without compromising his name, honour and reputation.[105]

In 1765, Alexandre MacDonald had been born the son of a poor Scottish exile, who had neither career nor prospects. His only inheritance from his father was "the example of his virtues" – but perhaps also some good contacts with the Jacobite network. Fifty-five years later, his situation was markedly different. In 1820, as he married his daughter Alexandrine Aimée Sidonie to the Marques of Rochedragon, the marriage deeds registered as witnesses, amongst others, the King of France himself and eight members of the Royal family. The deeds also detailed the marriage's financial arrangements, revealing the young couple's joint assets to be well over 1,000,000 francs – and Alexandrine was only one of his three daughters.[106]

Such was the man who was going to visit Scotland and the Outer-Hebrides five years later, in search of his Scottish roots.

---

104   MacDonald was also a Free Mason (as were many officers of Napoléon), being the Deputy Grand Master of the order in France.

105   The link between physical survival and political survival may be illustrated by the fact that, out of 26 Marshals of Napoléon, 3 died on the battlefield, but 5 died by assassination or execution.

106   Archives Nationales, Etude Bertinot, cote CXVI/681. Mariage du 26 Août 1820 entre le Marquis de Rochedragon et Sidonie MacDonald.

Section III
A Very Special Visit

In the spring of 1825, MacDonald might have been at the top of his career, but he was experiencing severe personal grief. His third wife, Thérèse Gasparine de Bourgoin had just died, aged only thirty-two, leaving him with a son barely one year old. This untimely death (she was twenty-two years younger than him) was part of a recurrent pattern of tragedies in his life, his first wife having died prematurely, after less than six years of married life, and his second wife too, just two years after their marriage.[107]

Being nearly fifty-five years old, MacDonald had little prospect of re-engaging into matrimony, and was to die a widower. His chagrin was great,[108] and he looked for comfort and solace in two directions. One was by writing his "Recollections", which he did not do for the purpose of publication,[109] but to serve the future education of his infant son, Louis Marie Alexandre. The other one was to research his own family roots by travelling through the British Isles, and especially to Scotland, to his father's birthplace in the Hebrides.

The close relationship between the writing of his memories and the trip to Britain is underlined in a letter dated May 1825, which opens the first Chapter of the "Recollections":

---

107   *However, his love life was not limited to these three marriages. MacDonald is supposed to have had an affair with the beautiful, but rather light-headed, Pauline Bonaparte, Napoléon's younger sister. There was also talk, at some stage, of him marrying Hortense de Beauharnais, daughter by a first marriage of Bonaparte's first wife, Joséphine de Beauharnais. Napoléon apparently opposed this union which would have made MacDonald his relative.*

108   *Local history has it that he never occupied again the conjugal room on the first floor of his castle at Courcelles-le-Roi, and moved to the room below, where he was to die in 1840.*

109   *His « Recollections » were to be published fifty years after his death by his grand-daughter, the Baronne de Pommereuil.*

"The idea has occurred to me, my son, of beginning this sketch of my life for you, without caring to know when it will be finished; nevertheless, I set to work, having for guide assistance nothing but my memory. I let my pen travel on and I write these lines, as you will observe, in the simplest and most familiar style possible. Truth needs no adornment, and, moreover, I am not writing for the public; these lines are not intended for the light of day. I write in haste from an old habit of never letting anything till tomorrow; besides, my return to Paris cannot be long postponed, and once there, I shall have no time to continue this work, as I am contemplating a journey of six weeks to two months, in order to see the three kingdoms of the British Empire, with which I am acquainted, and to visit my father's birthplace in the Hebrides" [110]

MacDonald was well aware that he had only imperfect knowledge of his father's life, and of his family's history. Neil had obviously fed him with stories and anecdotes about his Scottish ancestry in his youth, but these memories were remote. A youth, at most in his late teens, Alexandre had left Sancerre for Paris to be educated at the School of the Chevalier Pawlet. Then, in 1785, he had enlisted in the army, and at the time of his father's death in 1788, he was quartered in Calais, in the north of France. As a consequence, he was unable to attend his father's funeral, and to take possession of the latter's archives. These were collected by Edward MacNab, to be given to him in due course, but it never happened, since MacNab was arrested as a suspect during the Revolution and all his papers seized and scattered. So, whilst the purpose of this journey was certainly *"to occupy the isolation caused by his sorrows"*, as his commentator Camille Rousset pointed out, it was also to bridge the gap between the past – a father whose life he knew little about – and the future – a son which, in all likelihood, would probably be still young at his own death. [111] The Marshal

110   *Letter dated 16th of May 1825, quoted in Chapter 1 of the "Recollections."*

111   *Which is indeed what happened, since his son was only sixteen years old when he died in 1840.*

was obviously anxious that his only male heir, the most tangible memory of his third wife, would not find himself in his later life as bereft of information about his family past as he had found himself to be.

The interest that MacDonald had in the land of his ancestors went well beyond mere genealogical curiosity. Obviously, the information passed on by his father in his early years must have left him with a keen interest in Scotland, but another factor was that, forty years after Neil's departure for exile, the links between his family and Scotland were far from extinct. In his travel diary, the Marshal mentions being reacquainted with people he had seen in France before the Revolution, such as Lieutenant-Colonel MacDonald of Clanranald, uncle of Sir Archibald, who saw him in Paris in 1787, or such as Midlady Lucy Stuart, whom he had last seen in France, some thirty four years before (i.e: in 1791). Last but not least, it will be remembered that it was the old Jacobite network which had provided the young MacDonald with patrons to support his studies, and which had helped him to get a first posting in the army.

The successive wars between France and Britain between 1793 and 1815 had the potential to weaken, or destroy totally these contacts, but the seeds had been well sown. Given the opportunity, MacDonald showed himself extremely eager to underline his Scottish origins. This was demonstrated in a rather striking way in 1809, when he was made a Duke of Tarentum by Napoléon, in the aftermath of the battle of Wagram. The coat-of-arms he chose was *"...in quarterly, 1st arg, a lion rampant gules, armed or; 2nd a dexter hand coupée fesswise, holding a cross crosslet fitchee, gu; 3rd a lymphad or galley, oars in saltire, sable, and in base a salmon niant proper in sea vert; 4th arg., an oak tree, vert, surmounted by an eagle displayed, or."*[112] In plain terms, it was an exact replica of the one used by the MacDonalds of ClanRanald's, to which he added a small Tarantula, obvious allusion to his Dukedom of Tarentum. He also borrowed the Clanranald's motto of "My

112   R.R MCIAN, *The Clans of the Scottish Highlands, first published in 1845, Reprinted by Webb & Bower, Exeter, 1980, pp 91-93.*

hope is constant in thee" (in English), as well as Clanranald's war cry (in Gaelic) of "Dhan Deon Co-Theiragha" [113] ("In spite of all opposition"); such features being certainly unique in the heraldry of a Marshal of France.[114]

The downfall of Napoléon in 1814-1815 immediately reopened the lines of communication across the Channel, and MacDonald was not slow in re-establishing contact with whatever relations he had in Scotland. He lost no time in writing to MacDonald-Buchanan, grandson of MacDonald of Boisdale who had been in Glen Corrodale with his father, and asked him for an abstract of the family's genealogy, which the latter duly supplied. Such contacts paved the way for his visit, ten years later, when MacDonald-Buchanan was to welcome him in the land of his forefathers, and when his brother, MacDonald of Staffa, acted as his guide during his tour of the Highlands and Hebrides.

Also revealing of his interest in Scotland were his contacts with various historical or cultural societies.[115] The Inverness Journal of the 13th of October 1815 thus reported:

"The Society of True Highlanders" met at Inverlochy on the 5th inst. Glengarry was re-elected President, and Mr Ewen Maclachlan, librarian at Aberdeen, was appointed Gaelic secretary. Marshal MacDonald, Duke of Tarentum, was elected an honorary member."

The fact that, barely four months after Waterloo, a Highland Society would adopt one of Napoléon's Marshals

---

113   Also spelt "Dhaidheoin cotheir-aid e".

114   Amusingly enough, a beautiful painting of Marshal MacDonald's great armorial, once in his possession, contains a spelling error with the "h" being omitted in "hope", and "My" and "ope" being joined, which makes the motto more suited for an optician than for a Marshal.

115   This extended well beyond Britain. When Captain John MacDonald of Glenaladale, who had emigrated to Canada, returned to Europe "... he visited Marshal MacDonald, Duke of Tarentum, one of Napoléon's most famous generals, who was much interested to hear of the Caledonian Society of Prince Edward Island, sent a donation, and was enrolled as Honorary Member. Tarentum, on the Island, is named after him."

as an honorary member clearly indicates that MacDonald was also viewed with some interest and sympathy in Scotland, at least within such quarters. After more than two decades of Franco-British conflict, it was now time to turn a leaf, and rediscover each other.

In search of Clan Donald.

On the 1st of June 1825, Marshal MacDonald began his two month tour of the British Isles. He was nearly sixty years old, and in mediocre health. In 1795, during the Campaign of Holland, he had contacted Walcheren fever,[116] which nearly cost him his life, and was to plague him for years. On various occasions during his military career (in Holland, Italy, Spain...), illness or wounds had compelled him to withdraw on sick leave. In his old age, he was also affected by gout, of which he had severe bouts which seriously impaired his ability to walk. In such a physical condition, one may appreciate that his decision to travel to some of the most remote areas of Europe was a clear indication of his determination to see the land of his forefathers. At times, these efforts proved too much, and the brevity of the entries in his diary, especially on his return from Scotland, suggests that the journey had fairly exhausted him.

This poor physical condition did not go unnoticed by the local press; for instance, the Inverness Courier dated 29th of June, which published this rather unsympathetic portrait of the famous visitor:

"Marshal MacDonald is described as thin in person and rather above the middle size; his hair quite grey, his eyes dark, his countenance rather round and sedate, and not indicative of the mental qualities he was reported to possess. He was plainly dressed in black, and like Napoléon took snuff in large quantities. He spoke little English, and that little imperfectly. The fatigues of a soldier's life and the anxieties of political

---

116   *Walcheren fever, described as "a lethal combination of malaria, typhus, typhoid, and dysentery" was to cause havoc on the British side too, killing 4,000 soldiers during the 1809 expedition to Holland.*

struggles appear to have brought on premature age, for he walked rather feebly, and with a manner that indicated an infirm state of health."

Walter Scott, after meeting him in Edinburgh, put it in nicer terms:

"Sir Walter gave us a very pleasing account of Marshal MacDonald, not at all like a soldier in looks, slight and delicate in appearance, but his conduct seems to have been much more steady than any of the other generals."[117]

MacDonald did not leave for Britain alone, but travelled with two companions. One was the Count of Jean de Coüessin, who belonged to an old aristocratic family from Brittany, and the other Auguste, his manservant. Coüessin was not only his aide-de-camp, but also a family relative. His wife, Adélaïde Weltner, was a grand-daughter of Neil MacEachean by his daughter Eulalie MacDonald, and thus the Marshal's niece. It was therefore Neil's son and grandson-in-law who headed together towards the Hebrides.

As they reached Scotland, they were joined by Sir Reginald MacDonald Steuart Seton, Baronet of Staffa, who accompanied them to the Hebrides, and through most of the journey along the west coast. As grandsons of MacDonald of Boisdale, MacDonald of Staffa and his brother MacDonald of Buchanan, were the obvious links with his own father's past; Clanranald himself then living in London. Being the Sheriff of Stirlingshire, and a ruling elder for the General Assembly of the Church of Scotland, MacDonald Staffa was a member of the Scottish establishment with good connections, both in the literary circles of Edinburgh (he was a friend of Sir Walter Scott), and with the Highland gentry. An Honorary Secretary to the Highland and Agricultural Society of Scotland, he had land on the west coast, and owned the island of Staffa itself, with

---

117   *Letter from Edgeworthstown dated Saturday, July 30, 1825, in* Hon. Emily LAWLESS, *Maria Edgeworth, The MacMillan Company, New York, 1904. pp. 162-179.*

its famous Fingal's cave, which the Marshal was to visit in his company. Also of great importance for the Marshal, Staffa was a Gaelic speaker, and acted as a guide and interpreter during the tour. He sent various reports of the journey to the press, and published a short account of it.[118]

The role of MacDonald of Staffa must be underlined. The Laird of Staffa was a perfect illustration of the patriarchal, and often dictatorial, kind of landowner who held sway at the time over large estates of the West coast of Scotland and its islands. Staffa's attachment for the old traditions did not prevent him adhering at the same time to rather more mercantile preoccupations. Walter Scott, who visited his estates in 1810, gave this rather sharp description of him:

"By dint of minute attention to his property, and particularly to the management of his kelp, he has at once trebled his income and doubled his population, while emigration is going all round him; But he is very attentive to his people, who are distractedly fond of him, and he has them under such regulations as conduce both to his own benefit and their profit; and keeps a certain sort of rude state and hospitality in which they can take much pride. I am quite satisfied that nothing under the personal attention of the landlord himself will satisfy a Highland tenantry, and that the substitution of factors, which is now becoming general, is one of the great cause of emigration. This mode of life has, however, its evils, and I can see them in this excellent man. The habit of solitary power is dangerous even to the best regulated minds, and this ardent and enthusiastic young man has not escaped the prejudices incident to his situation."[119]

---

118   This document entitled "*Tour of His Exellency Field-Marshal MacDonald, Duke of Tarentum, Marshal of France, High-Chancellor of the Légion d'Honneur, etc.*" in June 1825, is available at the National Library of Scotland, with the reference Abbot 103 (46). It is anonymous, and wrongly attributed to the Marshal himself in the Library's catalogue. Its contents, and the details it provides on certain parts of the journey in the Highlands, clearly indicate MacDonald Staffa to be the source, if not the author, since he was the only one to accompany the Marshal's party on these occasions.

119   Quoted by Derek COOPER in *The Road to the Isles.Op.cit, p 48*

With a foot in the old society, and another in the new one, MacDonald of Staffa was to be the Marshal's guide as well as his translator.

Various authors have stated that the Marshal himself could speak some Gaelic. Alexander Carmichael thus reports that when in the Uists *"He addressed his relations in French and in broken Gaelic, they answering him in Gaelic, for none of them could speak English."*[120] Some go even further, and say that the Marshal could speak *"fine accurate Gaelic, but with a French accent."*[121] This is probably totally untrue, for there is no hard evidence of the Marshal having any Gaelic, and even his English was very limited – which did not help him to get all the information he would have wanted from his relatives -.

There is a long, and still ongoing, tradition in the Hebrides of flatteringly describing as a "fluent speaker" anyone who can barely utter a couple of words in the Gaelic language. It is not impossible that this treatment was applied to the Marshal, who may have remembered the odd Gaelic word taught by his father nearly half-a-century before. However, his travel diary makes no reference whatsoever to any capacity, however modest, to converse in that tongue, whereas it mentions explicitly the necessity to use the linguistic skills of MacDonald Staffa to communicate with the islanders.

The Marshal's visit of the British Isles lasted 57 days, from the 1st of June to the 27th of July. The itinerary began at Portsmouth, and followed a course along the South-West of England (Salisbury, Bath, Bristol, Clifton, Oxford, Windsor...), before reaching London on the 11th of June. After a few days in the capital, the Marshal headed for Scotland via the Eastern route (Cambridge, York, Durham, Newcastle), reaching Berwick and the Scottish Border on the 18th of June. Going straight to Edinburgh via Dunbar, he remained for three days in the Scottish

---

120   Footnote by Alexander Carmichael in the first Chapter of the Marshal's "Recollections", in the edition by Richard Bentley and Sons, London, 1893, p4.

121   Moray McLAREN, **Bonnie Prince Charlie**, Granada, London, 1974, p 193.

capital before heading northwards. At first the journey to the Highlands followed a classic itinerary: Linlithgow, Stirling, Perth and Inverness. From there he sailed down the recently opened Caledonian canal on a steamer, but branched off at Fort William to take the road to Arisaig, where a British Navy Ship, HMS *Swift*, awaited him. He sailed for the Hebrides on the 29th of June, and was to spend a couple of days in the Uists, before following a southward course along the West Coast.

Stopping en route in Skye, Moidart, Staffa and Oban, he headed to Antrim before returning to the Kintyre peninsula. There was a brief visit to Inverary, then onwards to Loch Lomond, sailing from there to Glasgow, which he reached on the 11th of July. Leaving Scotland via Gretna two days later, he made his way South to Carlisle, Manchester and Liverpool. After a brief two day visit to Dublin, he returned to England via Wales (Holyhead, Bangor, Shrewsbury, Birmingham and Banbury) and was back in London on the 22nd of July. He then took the route via Brighton, and sailed back to France on the 27th of July, nearly two months after his departure.

Whilst the Marshal claimed his intention to visit the "Three Kingdoms" of the British Isles, the emphasis of his journey was clearly on Scotland and the Highlands. It is significant that, out of fifty-seven days, twenty-six days (nearly half of the journey's duration) were spent north of the Border, and sixteen days (close to a third) in the Highlands and Islands.

Looking at the selection of places he visited during his tour of the North, a clear pattern emerges. The visit to his father's birthplace in the Uists might have been brief – barely a couple of days – but he also spent much time visiting areas associated with either Clan Donald history or with Highland history. During his relatively short journey, he managed to see Armadale Castle in Skye, Castle Tioram in Moidart and the castles of Mingary, Aros and Ardtornish in the Mull area. He also visited the battlefield of Culloden, and even went to the Clan Donald lands in Antrim, and saw Glenluce and Glenarm castles. Whilst he also visited many other places in the Highlands (such as Inverary castle), his main interest was undoubtedly focused on anything related, one way or another, to Clan Donald and its past. The list of people he met echoes this preoccupation.

As a Minister of State in the French government, MacDonald was a high-ranking dignitary as well as a man of wealth, and it is not surprising that most of the people he saw during his tour belonged to the gentry. Those he met during his stay in London not only belonged to the more prosperous classes, but were also part of the first circle of power and wealth in the British Isles. Though the Marshal's tour, decided upon at very short notice following his wife's death, was certainly of a private nature, it had in many respects, the trappings of a State visit.

Being a French Peer of the Realm, and henceforth a fellow parliamentarian, he was welcomed in Westminster by the Speakers of both Houses, and Lords Montrose, Athol, Beresford and Melville came to speak to him. This welcome was not merely formal, extending well beyond the boundaries of ordinary courtesy. Being informed of his plans, Lord Melville, First Lord of the Admiralty thus offered him the use of a British Navy vessel to take him wherever he wished to go in the Hebrides, and arrangements to that effect were made right away. By the time he arrived in Edinburgh, they just had to be finalised, and when he reached Arisaig, barely two weeks after London, Revenue Cutter HMS *Swift* was already awaiting, to convey him according to his desires. One will appreciate that this courteous treatment was certainly in stark contrast to that which his father would have met from the same British Navy, had they had the opportunity to catch him, some eighty years before...

The semi-official nature of his visit was also made apparent on a number of other occasions. At Loch Lomond, another Customs vessel awaited, to ferry him to the south side of the Loch. In Edinburgh, as he visited Holyrood Palace, where the guard, discreetly informed, made a show of arms in his honour. In Edinburgh, Stirling and Fort Augustus, officers in charge of Royal castles and forts made a point of showing him around, and on numerous occasions, gun salutes were fired in his honour from land or sea.

Many amongst the high and mighty of the land, such as the

Duke of Montrose, the Duke of Argyle, the Duke of Hamilton, Lord Belhaven, Lord MacDonald, Lord Gray, General Sir David Baird, Sir. Jas Steuart and Sir Cumming Gordon, etc. also invited him to their house as their private guest. However, the Marshal's priority was the visit to the Highlands and to the land of his ancestors, which meant he had to keep time-consuming social obligations to a minimum. But for a few exceptions, he generally refused such hospitality, preferring the use of local inns or hotels. This desire for privacy also included the Masons for, when returning to his hotel in Perthshire, he realised that a Masonic function was taking place in the premises, he immediately fled to his bedroom... lest anyone would realise that he was Deputy Grand-Master of the Order in France.

But even if he had to decline many of their invitations, the list of the Marshal's social contacts with the "better classes of society", as they were known at the time, clearly shows an emphasis on Highland gentry, and on people of the name of MacDonald in particular. In London, he was thus feted at a dinner featuring no less than Sir Archibald MacDonald, Lord Clanranald, General MacDonald (Adjutant to the Duke of York),as well as Lt-General Murray (Commanding the British Forces in Ireland), General Major Doyle, Sir John Sinclair, the Duke of Sussex (as Count of Inverness).

Similar emphasis can be observed during his stay Scotland, where a substantial number of the representatives of the gentry he meets are namesakes: the two grandsons of MacDonald of Boisdale, MacDonald of Staffa and MacDonald Buchanan, of course, but also MacDonald of Glenaladale, MacDonald of Scotos, MacDonald "Saint Martin" near Perth, Bishop MacDonald in Oban, as well as MacDonalds of Rhue, Arisaig and Morar, etc. This Clan Donald interest even spread to Antrim, where, though he failed to meet the Countess of Antrim (*née* MacDonald of Glenaladale), he was much gratified to hear from a local old woman that *"... the MacDonalds of Scotland and Ireland are always welcome in her house."*

The Marshal's social contacts in Scotland were of course not

73

strictly limited to people bearing his name, but, even in the cities of Edinburgh, Perth or Glasgow, he was mostly gravitating in what could be termed as "Highland circles"; the apotheosis being a dinner organised in the presence of Sir Walter Scott, grand master of the "Highland revival."[122] Pleasant anecdotes seem to have been exchanged on that occasion, and Walter Scott wrote to a friend:

"We have had Marshal MacDonald here. We had a capital account of Glengarry visiting the interior of a convent in the ancient Highland garb, and the effect of such an apparition on the nuns, who fled in all directions."[123]

But if Marshal MacDonald's warm reception by the gentry in general, and that of his namesakes in particular, was rather predictable, more formidable perhaps was the one he got from the people themselves, especially in the Highlands.

In the Hebrides *"... the inhabitants of South Uist, being appraised of the arrival of their distinguished visitor, upward of six hundred of them had assembled near Houghbeg to greet him on his arrival in the isle which gave birth to his father and a long line of ancestry."*[124] Even if exaggerated, the figure was impressive enough, since the population of South Uist at the time was around 6,000 people. *"We are welcomed by a quantity of MacDonalds, large and small,"* noted the Marshal in his diary, adding *"The whole west side of the island was in movement."* The gathering was, of course, not entirely spontaneous, the people having been forewarned of his arrival not only by the papers, but also by letters from Clanranald and from MacDonald Buchanan to Mr Shaw, Clanranald's factor in the Uists. Moreover, the timely purchase of a barrel of whisky by the Marshal in Arisaig, before sailing to the islands, indicated a degree of preparation, and its subsequent gift to

---

122   On the role of Sir Walter Scott in the Highland Revival, see Arthur HERMAN, *The Scottish Enlightenment. The Scots invention of the modern world*, Fourth Estate, London, 2003., Chapter seven.

123   Letter from Scott to Skene, 24*th* of June 1825.

124   *"Tour of His Exellency Field-Marshal MacDonald, etc"*, Op.cit.

the crowd in order to raise a toast may certainly have made "the distinguished visitor's" presence all the more attractive.

The large crowd gathering in Uist, his family land, was nevertheless not a one-off, and in the Isle of Skye, the scene repeated itself. According to the Edinburgh Annual Register:[125]

"This day Marshal MacDonald landed from the swift revenue cruiser at Armadale Castle, Isle of Skye, about seven in the evening and was met on the shore by many gentlemen. At this time a salute was fired from the cutter, which was returned from the Castle. The party then proceeded headed by Lord MacDonald's piper. On coming near the Castle two hundred men of Lord MacDonald's tenantry, who were drawn up on an eminence, gave the Marshal three cheers, waving their bonnets in the air. The Marshal, much pleased with their appearance, went amongst them and requested MacDonald of Staffa to address them in Gaelic, stating his delight to be amongst them. He told them he had the warmest feelings of attachment to the Highlands, for, independently of its being the birthplace of his father, it was the nurse of heroes and the grave of tyrannising foes. The Marshal called for a glass and drank in mountain spirits the health of their noble landlord, with all the honours, which was warmly pledged by the whole group."

If accurate, the quote regarding "tyrannising foes" is interesting, and deserving of further investigation, there being a number of potential candidates for such an appellation, not all of them belonging to a distant historical past... In Moidart, as the Marshal visited Castle Tioram, the old seat of the MacDonalds of Clanranald and again the scene repeated itself:

"At castle Tyrrim, about four hundred of the Moidart and Arisaig tenantry were assembled to receive their distinguished clansman and visitor, whom they cheered as he ascended the

---

125   *Report on Marshal MacDonald, Duke of Tarentum, at Armadale 8th July 1825.* **Edinburgh Annual Register 1825**

rock and approached the revered walls of the ancient edifice, in
a style which few could sufficiently appreciate, who were not
accustomed to the ancient usage of these, attached, honourable
and faithful people."[126]

It would be easy to dismiss the importance of these popular gatherings by attributing them purely to the pressure exerted by local MacDonald landlords. It is true that in Skye, the rousing welcome which the Marshal received came from Lord MacDonald's tenants who were busy landscaping the castle grounds, and who may have had little other choice but to raise their hat and cheer. However, this would not explain why similar scenes took place in other parts of Scotland where the landlord-tenants relationship was not an explanation. Thus was the case each time the Marshal used public transport on the waterways. On the Caledonian Canal, the passengers raised their glasses to toast him. On Loch Lomond, his fellow steamer travellers saluted his transfer to another boat with hoorays and by hoisting the dinner table-cloth as an improvised French flag (then white, the colours of the monarchy). When he reached the urbanised part of Scotland, the interest did not abate. As his vessel approached the end of Loch Lomond, it was greeted by a small fleet of boats loaded with onlookers from Glasgow, to the extent that the Marshal jokingly gave the title of "Commodore" to the captain of his ship. In Glasgow itself, where he stayed at the Star Inn, witnesses mentioned that "a great multitude" was waiting to have a sight of him.[127]

Bearing in mind that two decades of nearly continuous wars with France had ended barely ten years before this visit; and that 240,000 British soldiers had lost their lives in the process,[128]

---

126   *"Tour of His Exellency Field-Marshal MacDonald, etc", Op.cit. The Marshal, in his diary, noted a crowd of some forty people, and not four hundred. So, we must wonder whether a missing zero or an excessive imagination can be held responsible for such a flagrant discrepancy.*

127   *KN MACDONALD, M.D, "A noble trait in the character of Marshal MacDonald, Duke of Tarentum", in* **The Celtic Review***, Vol 5, 1909, p 115.*

128   *The majority of them from illness... See Martin R HOWARD, "Doctors in conflict. Walcheren 1809: a medical catastrophe",* **British**

amongst them many Scots, and especially Highlanders,[129] this was, by all accounts, an extraordinary welcome. Only a few years before, people in South Uist sang songs such as this one:

> "'S ged a dh'fhiach e fhéin 's na Frangaich
> Ri tighinn do Bhreatainn le aimhreit,
> Tillidh sinn a null gun taing thu,
> 'S fheàrr dhut fuireach thall dhad'dheoin"

("Although he [Bonaparte] and the French should try to come to Britain with violence, we will drive you back willy-nilly; you had better stay over there of your own accord.")[130]

Now, 600 people from that island congregated to drink to the health of a man who had played no small role in bringing the same Bonaparte to power. Whilst there is no doubt that such crowds were probably drawn to see him by mere curiosity, curiosity alone would not account for the warmth of that reception. The Marshal was not just a foreign personality, and we can assume that the public's awareness of his Scottish ancestry undoubtedly played a role in this sympathetic welcome. He was after all, deep in his roots, a Scotsman (and in the Highlands, even more so, a scion of Clan Donald) who had been given the opportunity to succeed "on the other side", and had done so remarkably well. If the French had kept Europe at bay for so long, was not it because they had officers like him with them? MacDonald might have been an enemy commander in the past, but more importantly, he was another perfect demonstration of the universal qualities of the Scottish people.[131]

Medical Journal, 18 December 1999;319; pp1642-1645

129   For example, four thousand soldiers were enlisted in the British army between 1793 and 1805 from Isle of Skye alone. See: John PREBBLE, **The Highland Clearances**, Penguin Books, 1963, p297.

130   "O! Gum B'Aotrom Linn an t-asar." Quoted in Margaret FAY SHAW, **Folksongs and Folklore of South Uist**, Oxford University Press, 1977, p 92.

131   Things went apparently further than that. The archives of folklorist Alexander Carmichael, hold a note, apparently written by a Capt Alexander

However, the chief aim of the Marshal's visit was not just to meet the MacDonald gentry, or bask in popularity amongst crowds, but to find his own, direct relatives. This he did on two occasions, in the Uists and in Glasgow. The visit to his father's birthplace in Howbeg was of course, the main opportunity for the Marshal to see the largest number of his extended family:

"There I meet an elderly spinster who sheds tears of joy: she is my first cousin. Her brother arrives, an old man of 73, who has nearly lost his sight. However, he can distinguish my hair which he says is just like his. His wife follows. We are at the house of his elder son, who will follow him in the running of the farm. He has with him his wife, his children, and his brothers and sisters."

Other family connections, both close and more distant distant, were met that day, and the next day in Glen Corrodale. How did he relate to his father's birthplace? According to information provided by folklorist Alexander Carmichael, the Marshal was not only empathetic with his relatives, but also recognised the very location of his father's childhood:

Matheson, Doirnie, Kintail, which mention this most unlikely, but nevertheless enjoyable tale: "I use to hear both on the Mainland and in Uist that the Duke of Tirentim after parting with Napoléon Boneparte when he was made a state prisoner in the Elbe after the loss of his troops in Russia that he had never seen the Empourer afterwards and that he had taken the oath of allegenc to Lou[i]s Phillipic that he kept aloof from joining the Emperor on his return to France after his escape from his confinement in the Elbe.

"That he afterwards came into the confidence of the British Government privately, and that he had been in the millitary tent of the Duke of Wellington during the whole action of the British forces in Brussels in 1815 and knowing all the manuneries of the French army that he put up the Duke of Wellington to all the tactics of the French Army and that he had as much to do with the Battle of Waterloo to magnify the laurels of the Great Duke of Wellington as he had himself. This I use to heare from tratition but I cannot vouch for the correctness of the statement." See Carmichael WATSON MS 363, Fo 28.

"On coming in sight of the river he exclaimed "That is the river Hough. I know it from my father's description; many a salmon has he caught there." He sent for all his relations in the neighbourhood. When his blind old uncle was brought to him, he embraced him affectionately, saying: "You dear old man, how like you are to my own father."[132]

However, Carmichael is inaccurate, for the Marshal did not meet any of his father's brothers, who were long since dead, but instead only cousins. However, the local "Anglican" Minister, who was eighty-five years old, and whose wife happened to be Flora MacDonald's niece, remembered his uncles and assured him that he bore a great resemblance to one of them.

Meeting his Uist family had one major sobering effect for the Marshal. Of Clanranald descent as they supposedly were, he realised that their economic and social conditions were markedly different from those of all the MacDonald gentry he had met in London or in Edinburgh:

"All indicates that these relatives are not wealthy: their clothes; their house which is shaped like a hut, but much bigger, and is made of a large room and of a smaller one; the sparse furniture, which is roughly made. Here, one lives on potatoes, fish, milk, cheese, sometimes on meat (mutton), poultry, ship's biscuit and oatcakes, on water and whisky."

Generous as ever, the Marshal proceeded forthwith to grant them some financial assistance:

"I also ask questions to the young farmer [a cousin]. I am told that he is a good character. He pays 50£ a year for the rental of his farm to Mr Clanranald, who is the landowner. To give him some support, and provide him with a bit of financial ease, I pay a year's rental for his farm. Clanranald grants a 10£ pension to his father, MacEachen, and to his unmarried sister. I give the same amount, which I pay in advance, and which

---

132   Marshal MACDONALD, *Recollections*, Op.cit., p

they will receive each year, the 30th of June, in remembrance of my journey."

All in all, the Marshal was reported to have given two hundred sovereigns in various donations that day. Some time later, in Glasgow, he was to meet other relatives, in the person of John MacEachen, son of his father's brother Alexander, and all his numerous family – ten people altogether. John MacEachen (also written M'Eachin) lived in Greenock, and was obviously somewhat better off than those who had stayed in Uist. Knowing of the Marshal's visit, he had taken the steam-boat to head for the West Coast and meet him there, but engine failure thwarted his plans. He eventually caught-up with the Marshal in Glasgow, and the latter invited him for tea at his hotel with the whole family, and again the next day for breakfast.[133] There again, he provided his relatives with whatever direct or indirect assistance he could:

"I manage to get Mr and Mrs MacEachan to accept 50 Guineas to get presents [or: as a present?]. It is true they are my relatives. I promise to try my best to arrange to have their son coming back from the colonies, and to have him employed with the Customs in England. I also promise 20 Guineas to a young MacDonald from South Uist, who is also my relative, but in a more distant way, so that he may start some sort of business [?] in that island."

The Marshal's travel diary gives us a good insight into the situation of the MacEachens at the time: those remaining in Uist were farmers or joiners, living in "huts", in extremely modest conditions, whereas those who had left the islands joined the burgeoning middle class in the Clyde area, or went into employment in the colonies. We are a long way from the splendour of the Clanranald motto and coat-of-arms,

---

133   MACDONALD, M.D, *"A noble trait in the character of Marshal MacDonald, Duke of Tarentum etc."*, Op.cit. *This article has a copy of a letter written by the said John M'Eachin, Greenock, to his sister Isabel in South Uist, dated 20th of July 1825, which describes these events.*

proudly displayed by the Marshal on his own armorial. Had Neil not gone into exile after the '45 Rising, and had his son subsequently been born and bred in Howbeg, instead of pre-Revolutionary France, the Marshal's social prospects would, in all likelihood, had been fairly similar. Had he lived in South Uist like his first cousin, he would probably have been burning kelp for Clanranald, wondering how to pay the next rent to the factor, with emigration to the cities or the colonies, or enlisting in the army his sole prospects of any betterment.

Not that it would have been so easy to leave the islands. When, in 1804, Ranald MacEachen (another cousin of his) tried to recruit people from the Uists for the Canadian Fencibles, Clanranald forcibly prevented his tenants from leaving his estates, and had the unwelcome recruiting agent arrested and sent to Inverness gaol.[134] At the time, Clanranald, whose income was largely based on the kelp industry, needed the biggest workforce he could get to collect seaweed, and was not prepared to tolerate anyone depleting his stock of captive labour.

In retrospect, it seems that the Marshal's search for his Scottish roots rested upon somewhat of a *quid pro quo*.

In France, where his father had been transferred from the Prince of Wales's army to serve as an officer in the French army, MacDonald had been considered by the "Ancien Régime" to be of noble origin, even if it was a small and foreign lineage. With the Revolution, when all such titles and privileges had been abolished, MacDonald had, by his own merits, risen with great speed in the army ranks to become a commanding officer. Under Napoléon, he had been made a Marshal as well as granted the title of Duke of Tarentum in the aftermath of the battle of Wagram. This title made him part of the "noblesse d'Empire", a new form of nobility which the Emperor had created in 1801. Since only thirty-four titles of Princes or Dukes were granted out of the 3300 titles created by Napoléon, we can appreciate that he occupied one of the higher echelons of the new aristocracy.

---

134   John PREBBLE, **Mutiny**, Penguin Books, 1977, p 448-451.

In 1814, as the Empire fell, the restored monarchy found itself with two nobilities: the old one, which existed before the Revolution, and the new one created by Napoléon. With Article 71 of the Royal Charter, King Louis XVIII chose for political compromise: the new nobility were to keep their titles and the old to regain theirs. MacDonald then found himself belonging simultaneously to the old nobility, in a minor rank, and to the new one in a major position; not forgetting that he was also a general who owed his career to the Revolution. Being representative of the different elites of France, at different epochs, contributed to make him acceptable to all and it certainly played no small role in ensuring his position as Arch-Chancellor of the Légion d'Honneur. However, under a restored monarchical regime, emphasizing his links with the old aristocracy could do him no harm. MacDonald, who was always prone to advertising his descent from some ancient Scottish nobility (as we see from his common use of the Clanranald armorial, and its presence on many artefacts in his household) probably saw in this journey to Scotland the opportunity to do so.

In Britain, it was the other way around. He was received with all due honours because of the titles and ranks he had acquired under the Revolution and then under Napoléon, and which had been confirmed by the monarchy. Without them, his own social position would have been no more than that of the son of a *"Daoin'-uasail"*, or small gentry of ClanRanald, and it is most unlikely that such "threadbare nobility"[135] would have been enough to open the door to the higher circles of British or Scottish society. When he came to the Hebrides, he must have realised that while he, as the Duke of Tarentum, had been invited to stately homes and castles as an honoured guest, his most direct relatives would not have got through the door except with their cap in hand, and probably via the servants' entrance. Born in France, bred in the midst of a community of Jacobite exiles, the Marshal might have dreamt of his long distance connection with the household of the Lords of the

---

135 *To use an expression employed by John Prebble to describe his cousin Ranald MacEachen. See John PREBBLE, **Mutiny**, Op.cit.*

Isles; but the fact remained that, in strict social and economic terms, his family in Scotland was closer to the people who had made the Revolution in France, and sent the likes of Clanranald to the guillotine.

This *quid pro quo* could have led to some embarrassing moments, but this was not to be. For a start, the Marshal was a realist who could assess situations quickly, as well as a generous man who could appreciate that human worth was not necessarily in a title. Even though it did not deter him from his passion for heraldry and ancestry, his diary did not try to hide the social situation of his relatives, and was perfectly matter-of-fact about it. Moreover, in Scotland, a whole myth was in the process of being built about the Highlands, the Jacobite Risings, and the old clan society. The Marshal's main contacts, MacDonald Buchanan and MacDonald of Staffa, were amongst the most prominent exponents of this new fashion, the Laird of Staffa having been instrumental in bringing Walter Scott to undertake his first journey to the Hebrides in 1810.[136] Linking the Marshal to the higher aristocracy of ClanDonald was not such a difficult task for them, since the complex blending of ownership and lineage, hierarchy and loyalty, which characterised the old Clan system helpfully provided a suitably flexible framework. Last but not least, the fact that the Marshal's father had himself been an integral part of the Jacobite myth, sailing with Charles Edward Stuart "over the sea to Skye" in the company of the celebrated Flora MacDonald, made it all the more easy.

And after all, just three years before the Marshal's visit, had King George IV himself, of Hanoverian descent, not paraded the streets of Edinburgh amongst huge cheering crowds, all dressed up in full Highland regalia, thanks to the good offices of Sir Walter Scott and Stuart of Garth? In such a context, Marshal MacDonald had just as much legitimacy, if not far more, to consider the lands and the ancient castles of the Lordship of the Isles as part of his cultural inheritance.

---

136   Derek COOPER, *The Road to the Isles.Op.cit, p 48.*

A Frenchman's view of Scotland at a time of changes

In 1825, as the Marshal began his tour, Scotland and the Highlands and Islands were experiencing major changes. The very last glimpses of the old society were barely there, and they were fast fading away. As he visited Culloden, buttons and bones could still be found easily on the battlefield. In Tioram Castle, he had the chance to meet with a ninety-two year old MacDonald, who recollected having seen the Prince and his followers sailing away to France in 1746 (amongst whom was the Marshal's father), and who could describe the scene.

Thanks to the strong traditional culture which prevailed in the Highlands, memories of events which took place eighty years before were still very much in the people's minds, and the Marshal marvelled at how people could describe events related to the '45 as if the Rising had only happened yesterday. But if the transmission of history by oral tradition was still prevailing in the Gaelic speaking areas, elsewhere it was increasingly in the hands of antiquarians, of cultural societies and of exponents of historical romance, chiefly Sir Walter Scott.

Jacobitism not being a political or military threat anymore *"...the story began to take on a warm, attractive glow as a Highland romantic epic of heroism and villainy, of intrigue and bravery, complete with comely maidens like Flora MacDonald and handsome heroes such as Bonnie Prince Charlie himself."*[137]
The Marshal, who was well read, and had a substantial library, was well aware of the main works of literature produced about the Highlands and Highland culture, from MacPherson's Ossian to Walter Scott's novels. Though his diary made the odd reference to one or the other when visiting such or such a place, he was clearly not a slave to these authors, and certainly did not tour the area to see if the reality matched the books, like many other visitors would do. Nor was he an enthusiastic antiquarian: *"One has to see with the eyes of the believer,"* he noted sceptically when being shown Mary Stuart's Room in Holyrood, the Royal Castle of Scone, and the remnants

---

137   Arthur HERMAN, *The Scottish Enlightenment, Op.cit., p 293.*

of some Roman camp in Ardoch. The viewing of all sorts of relics did not soften his critical sense, and, keenly interested in Scotland's history as he was, he did not fall into the trap of romanticism, despite visiting the country's many castles and battlefields. At Holyrood, Mary Stuart's bed was *"worm-eaten and in tatters."* The collection of paintings depicting the various Stuart monarchs, he regarded as having been *"... painted at various epochs by daubers"* to the point that they *"would hardly be accepted nowadays as shop signs."*[138]

For all his enthusiasm for the past, his life-long experience of politics and war had made him pretty hard-nosed, and this extended to Jacobitism and to Bonnie Prince Charlie himself. When he visited the Battlefield of Culloden, the *Inverness Courier* reported:

"Field-Marshal MacDonald Duke of Tarentum, arrived at Inverness on Sunday, the 26th, and put up at the Caledonian Hotel. He was accompanied by an aide-de-camp, and by Mr MacDonald of Staffa. Previous to his arrival, he visited the Battlefield of Culloden. There "he expressed his surprise at the imbecility which dictated the choice of that spot for the position of the Pretender's army. No spot could be worse chosen for the position of an irregular body of men acting on the defensive against regular troops; and the wonder was increased, the General observed, when the neighbouring high grounds behind the water of Nairn afforded as fine a position as could be wished to obtain the objects and suit the circumstances of the Jacobite forces."[139]

When visiting the caves of Corrodale, where his father had

---

138 During his visit to Holyrood, he also dutifully searched for memories of the sojourn within these walls of the reigning King of France, Charles X, who had spent eight years in exile there between 1796 and 1803, when he was only the Comte d'Artois. Little did the Marshal know that, five years later, Charles X was going to be back in Holyrood, definitively evicted from the throne by another Revolution. On the French exiles in Holyrood, see A.J MACKENZIE-STEWART, **A French King at Holyrood**, John Donald, Edinburgh, 1995, 141p.

139 **Inverness Courier**, 29th of June 1825

been in hiding with the Prince, he recollected an anecdote which recalled that his father had been sent on a useless errand by the Prince to recover some knife, in spite of the risk if being captured. *"Thus, in this unfortunate situation, he still acted like if he was the King,"* commented the Marshal, apparently much more impressed by the dedication of the Highlanders than in Charles Edward Stuart himself.

His description of the drawing room Jacobitism of the good society, though not openly critical, conveys a certain sense of amazement. In Edinburgh, Lady Clarke, *"a Stuart enthusiast"* was handing out white roses because *"Prince Charles was under her roof the very day she was born in 1745, and left there a white cockade which she has always kept."* The dinner at MacDonald Buchanan's the next day, attended by Walter Scott himself and a whole group of similar enthusiasts, all parading kilts, tartans and white roses was held to celebrate the anniversary of the Prince's birth. There, a touch of authenticity was provided by three Highlanders from the islands, brought in to sing some old "gothic songs", which also surprised the Marshal, who commented in his diary: *"These songs are curious, the performers warm up, and seem to bicker amongst themselves as would do street or market porters engaged in a squabble."*

On his return journey, as he sailed on Loch Lomond, more of the same was provided: *"… the ladies having arrived of the customs boat we used the previous day, with the same flags. They are dressed in the Scottish way. Moreover, the boat is festooned, and the sailors decorated with heather flowers, which are the distinctive sign of the MacDonald Clan."*

But for all this flourishing of tartan, the old order had gone. As the Marshal noticed, customs and traditions were fast fading away as the Highlands became open to the outside world due to better communications:

"The wearing of the Highland dress tends to have lost ground considerably during the last twenty years, which is since the beginning of communication. Roads which are pierced with the new system of Mr Macadam are generally very well maintained.

86

So, the digging of canals, the multiplication of schools, the
[...] have civilised, and still civilize everyday by putting men
in contact with each other and through the exchanges arising
from trade."

Thanks to the work of John McAdam and Thomas Telford,
the Highlands had ceased to be impenetrable. Under Telford, a
thousand miles of roads and some 120 bridges had been built,
and travel times had been reduced to an extent that made it
possible for MacDonald to travel from Stirling to Arisaig via
Inverness in four days, with various stopovers to visit people
and properties.[140] The roads the Marshal found generally good,
and he marvelled at the skills of the coachmen – all the more
so when he and his servant Auguste narrowly missed a severe
accident when driving their own gig on the road to Moidart.

By 1825, travel by boat had also markedly improved access
to the Highlands. The Crinan canal across the Kintyre peninsula,
and the recently opened Caledonian canal along the Great
Glen made it possible to travel by steamship from Glasgow
to Inverness. MacDonald went down from Inverness to Fort
William sailing on the *Comet*, a ninety-four ton vessel, built
in Dumbarton. But maritime transport remained dangerous:
the very same *Comet* was to sink in the Clyde a few months
later in October 1825, when it collided with the *Ayr*, resulting
in the loss of seventy of its eighty-two passengers and crew.[141].
On various occasions, when on board HMS Cutter *Swift*, the
Marshal was provided with first hand experience of the risks
attached to navigation: storms in the Minch or in the North
Channel, rough seas and adverse tides in Moidart, difficult
landings in many places, etc. At times, things got nasty, and
the Count of Coüessin, his aide-de-camp, a Breton who was
more wary than him of the perils of the sea, found them to be
"nearly in danger." The Marshal, who had faced death many
times during his life, refused to worry about it and left it to
those with maritime skills to deal with the situation.

---

140   Arthur HERMAN, *The Scottish Enlightenment*, *Op.cit, p 318.*
141   *Elizabeth BRAY, The discovery of the Hebrides. Voyages to the*
Western Isles, 1745-1883, Birlinn, Stornoway, 1996, p 212-

Whilst Scottish history and his family relations were MacDonald's prime concerns during his tour, they were by no mean his only fields of interest. The Marshal was not only interested in military matters, but also extremely keen on "improvements", in the broadest sense of the term, and a special attention for farming, industry and architecture shines throughout his travel diary. This is hardly surprising considering that he was himself a large landowner with a 1,500-acre estate at Courcelles-le-Roy, the proprietor, not only of a castle on those lands, but also of various properties, and that he was also the occupier of the prestigious Hotel de Salm (seat of the order of the Légion d'Honneur) in Paris. His interest in buildings, infrastructure, and industries of all kind was to bring him to write a separate essay on the matter,[142] but the travel diary itself provides ample evidence of this curiosity.

MacDonald visited Scotland at a time of spectacular changes, both in that country's economy and its society; changes which were reflected accordingly in the evolution of the urban landscape. In Edinburgh, the building of the New Town and its extension towards Leith (which he considered to be Edinburgh's "third town") was still under way, but nearing its final phase of completion. With all the new streets and housing developments, the property market was in full bloom, and the Marshal remarked on the many "To Let" signs... as well as on the way one new project was obstructing another's view. The new public buildings or infrastructures, recently completed or still under construction or renovation, also drew his special attention: the Botanic Gardens, the Museum, and Calton Jail... The panoptic conception of the jail, revolutionary for the time, and its method of functioning, blending physical efforts with religious preaching, attracted his curiosity. In Glasgow, as could be expected, a visit to the textile industry was *de rigueur,* as well as to the Museum. Both in Edinburgh and in Glasgow, the Marshal contributed to the Museums' collections by giving them medals of the King of France's coronation, seemingly

---

142   *"Observations générales sur l'Angleterre, l'Ecosse et l'Irlande"* (*General observations on England, Scotland and Ireland*). *Centre Historique des Archive Nationales, Paris, 279/AP/36.*

to the curators' satisfaction – a clear indication that these institutions were still very much in their infancy, and had only a limited selection of artefacts –. Appreciative of the elegance and beauty of the monuments newly erected in these cities, MacDonald drew the occasional comparison with those of Paris or Europe. And when some – like the Nelson's column on Calton Hill – were dedicated to the celebration of a British victory over the French, he made a point of focusing on the panorama.

MacDonald had the opportunity of seeing Scotland at a time when the memories of its Jacobite past were still present, but also when its main towns were being embellished or industrialised, when its communications were revolutionized, when its romantic literature flourished and when a certain part of its population was fast acquiring wealth. Perhaps symptomatic of those changes, and of the advent of a new area, was the first hints of the appearance of commercial tourism. For all his customary generosity, the Marshal had severe comments to make upon the condition of his visit to Holyrood Palace, and on the corporation of tourist guides in particular:

"The visit (is) exploited by four women or more. They are young persons, new in their charge, who dish out explanations just as parrots, and are hard to follow. They are not slow in making some money from the visitors, who must have a well-laden purse and be prepared to dig into their pockets."[143]

But the Marshal's appraisal of this changing Scotland was not limited to its main cities and their monuments. It also covered the rural areas, especially those of the Highlands and Islands, with a degree of attention beyond the level to be expected from a political dignitary and high commanding officer. This is hardly surprising since MacDonald was himself a gentleman-farmer, who had become well acquainted with agriculture during his years of political disgrace, when he had

---

143   *Not that such evolution was limited to Holyrood: in Antrim, the population around the Giant's Causeway had already acquired the knack of following visitors, to sell them boxes of local stones as souvenirs.*

withdrawn to his estate of Courcelles-le-Roy. His interest in the matter was genuine. In 1812, the Prussian officers who were under his orders during the Russian campaign (and who were later to defect) were horrified to observe that he was almost more interested in agriculture than in military affairs.[144] They were probably right, for his travel diary is peppered with comments and comparisons on the condition and size of sheep and cattle, on grazing techniques, or on the quality of the land, etc., not to mention his curiosity regarding the making of kelp.

The social conditions of the Highlands and Islands did not escape the Marshal's attention, and his description of the habitations of the common people and those of the gentry perfectly illustrates the contrasting wealth of landlords and tenants. The former he found living in thatched houses which he described as *"huts"*, and which he qualified as *"wretched"* or *"miserable"*. In spite of such *"scene(s) of misery"*, MacDonald noted with surprise that *"no one is begging, but for some children"*, and that *"nevertheless their inhabitants are dressed well and warmly, and are very clean, especially on Sunday."*

The houses and castles of the gentry provided a somewhat different scene, and the Marshal kept noting that most of these properties were undergoing, or had undergone recently, extensive schemes of modernisation, or, as he puts it, of "gothifiction", in the style of the time. Inside the big houses, such as Scone, Inverary or Kinfauns Castles, he noted the presence of Beauvais tapestries, of old master paintings and prints *"like in Italian Palaces"*, of pianos and musical instruments of all sorts. Armadale Castle, residence of Lord MacDonald in Skye, was no exception, but with a Highland touch:

"The interior is all gothic. Facing the entry door, in the vestibule, a light staircase with a double ramp. On the first landing, a great casement window made of colour-painted window-panes [...], and in the middle, full-length, Somerlet, First Chief of

---

144   *See GRANT-SUTTIE, Op . cit.*

the Isles in the Highland dress, from which the MacDonalds descend."

Explaining the wealth of some and the poverty of others required an appreciation of the evolving economic scene, and in particular an understanding of the process which made landlords clear vast portions of their Highland estates of their tenants, to replace them with sheep. MacDonald was not blind to these changes, but he was given only perfunctory explanations:

"It is remarkable how all these hills and glens are depopulated. We are told that this is because of emigration to America, or because of the recruiting for the Army and India."

In the Hebrides, the scene was somewhat different because that process had been delayed by the highly profitable exploitation of kelp, with required a lot of manpower. When MacDonald visited the islands in 1825, the kelp industry was still there, but it was beginning to collapse. As Martin Rackwitz recalls in his thesis on the early travellers in the Highlands and Islands:

"The kelp boom provided the great proprietors with a constant flow of money, but hardly any of the revenues were spent or reinvested in the islands. The drain of money and lack of investment were to haunt the proprietors when kelp prices began to fall and the bubble finally burst. The reasons for the rapid decline of the kelp industry in the Hebrides after 1815, and its collapse in 1822, were manifold. After the defeat of Napoléon, the Hebrides faced renewed competition from high-quality barilla from the Mediterranean. Moreover, the import duties on salt and barilla were lowered, and in 1825 the salt excise duty was abolished. The exploitation of potash deposits in Germany, and the development of a cheap method of producing soda from salt, forced a slump in the prices for kelp from the Hebrides. After 1811 the price for a ton of high-quality kelp slipped from £20 to about £9 to £10 and remained

there until the early 1820s. Poor-quality kelp was hit hardest by the slump in prices, and by 1822 some grades were already sold for as low as £4 10s.

After 1822 the price for high-quality kelp also came increasingly under pressure. In 1824 prices slipped to £8 per ton, in 1825 to £7 and in 1828 to £4 15s. By 1834 the market value of a ton of high-quality kelp from the Hebrides had slipped to a meagre £3.[200] *At this level kelp manufacture was no longer profitable as wages were still at about £3 to £4 per ton."*[145]

The Uists, which were the main area for kelp production, were about to suffer heavily from this collapse. Clanranald, who was an absentee landlord, and actually an English Member of Parliament for a rotten burgh, had left it to his factors to run his estates. Enjoying a lavish lifestyle in London, he had depleted his fortune instead of reinvesting it in the islands in other activities. Threatened with bankruptcy, he was forced to sell the lands held by his family for centuries piece by piece when the price of kelp plummeted in the 1820s. He eventually had to dispose of the Clanranald heartlands of South Uist in 1837, and those of Benbecula in 1839, by selling them to Lt-Colonel John Gordon of Cluny. The new owner, who had no historical or family ties with his tenantry, found their numbers to be excessive now the demand for manpower had gone, and he had no qualms in getting rid of them. The Uist clearances were brutal. In the 1820s, by the time of the Marshal's visit, the population of South Uist and Benbecula was around 6,000 people. It increased to 7,300 in 1841, but plummeted to only 6,100 in 1861 as people were chased off the land, and forced into emigration, either to the mainland or overseas.[146]

MacDonald was not blind to the hardships endured by the people in the Highlands. As a landowner, he had himself seen the tenants of his own estates in France experiencing difficult times. However, his reaction had been markedly different from

---

145   Martin RACKWITZ; *Travels to terra incognita, etc., Op.cit.*
146   Francis THOMSON, *The Uists and Barra, David & Charles, 1974,* pp 106 and 110. See also http://www.histpop.org/

that of most Highland landlords:

"*Use the resources you will find in Courcelles*" – had he written to his daughter, when he was away campaigning during one of such periods of hardships – "*Give, take in my purse. I do not wish to see anyone in misery, either on my estates, on in the neighbourhood.*"[147]

However, the Marshal, either for lack of information, or by discretion towards his contacts in the Scottish gentry, did not see fit to investigate matters further; or if he did, he kept his impressions of the nature of the landlord/tenant relationship in the Highlands to himself. Moreover, it will be remembered that with no Gaelic and limited English, he had little means of communicating directly with the people, and henceforth could not really enquire into the exact causes of their dire condition.

If MacDonald saw Scotland at a time of dramatic economic, social and cultural changes, he also saw some of Scotland's more perennial features, starting with the weather. "*In the whole course of the above tour, the weather proved most favourable*" said a report of his tour.[148] The Marshal obviously had a different opinion. In his diary, the word "rain" is mentioned thirteen times, and the word "wind" more than thirty, in the majority of cases associated with the word "strong", or some perjorative connotation. As for the word "sun", it appears only once: in short, typically Scottish summer weather.

More pleasantly, the Marshal was greatly impressed by the hospitality he met everywhere, and especially the courtesy and deference of the people in the Highlands:

"*...the warm reception he met with in every place he shewed himself, was calculated to make a powerful impression upon feelings less ardent and susceptible than his; in whom they have excited sentiments of gratification and admiration of everything he has met and seen in Scotland, which border on enthusiasm, in the admiration of the people and the country in general, and in particular in the warmth of feeling and generous hospitality which the Field Marshal experienced throughout*

---

147   Quoted on http://www.loiret.com/
148   "*Tour of his Excellency etc.*", Op.cit.

the Highlands and Islands."

"He was particularly struck with the air and gait of the Highlanders, accompanied uniformly as he observed by a courtesy and address, and polished manner, which attracted his admiration not less than his surprise, and he frequently remarked to his fellow travellers, that, from the time he entered the Highlands at Dunkeld, until his return to Glasgow, he never met with any individual who did not put his hand to his hat or to his bonnet, and accompanied his salute with a very becoming and graceful attitude."[149]

As the diary tells us, the Marshal had to face on numerous occasions the sometimes formidable Highland hospitality. In every household, great and small, food and beverages were readily produced, most prominently, whisky. From modest thatched houses to castles, whether on land or at sea, he was more often than not greeted by toast, or even a succession of them. Even in Edinburgh, when visiting the 76 year old Catholic bishop, Mgr Cameron, he was surprised to see the visitors being offered a demijohn bottle of spirits. Things did not ease up as he went further north: the cruise on the Caledonian Canal with the *Comet* drifted from an exchange of toasts to a proper party, and his stay in Armadale Castle gave him the opportunity to witness some colourful high jinks: *"I learn the next morning that these gentlemen went back to the table till two in the morning. They have thrown a totally drunk Mr MacDonald in a dark closet, some of the youngsters having hidden his watch."*

By all means not a teetotaller himself, the Marshal was nevertheless well aware of the limitations imposed by his age and his gout. As a rule, as soon as he saw things "heating up", he withdrew – or so he tells us – to his quarters. Perhaps because of his military skills, he had the capacity to recognise a bear trap when he saw one.

MacDonald was also able to experience the generosity of his hosts. His ship was on various occasions filled with all sorts of fresh victuals, and he himself left the islands with, *"... a*

---

149   *Ibid*

little ratter dog, to which I give the name of Uist, [and] some potatoes, which I intend to plant at Courcelles...." In that field, however, he was able to reciprocate, and the diary provides numerous examples of him giving gifts of all sorts, not only to his relatives, but also to those who had looked after him. The list of his presents to the officers and crew of *H.M.S Swift* , as he parted with the ship in Inverary, is impressive, and as one would expect, was well appreciated:

"*I take leave of the crew, granting twenty guineas (500 francs) to the forty men, plus some smoking tobacco and ten bottles of whisky. To the rower of our rowing-boat, I give 6 guineas, to the steward and the kitchen boys 5. To the captain a vermilion snuff-box engraved with my name and "Souvenir to Captain Beatson", 12 bottles of sherry, 12 of Madeira wine, 12 of Port and three dozens of Porter. To the two officers, each a dozen bottle of sherry, and six of Madeira; plus a souvenir that I promise to send them from Glascow. I drink to the health of the crew which answers by three "hoorays" and drink in its turn. We get into the rowing-boat and after we have parted with the ship, we get a salute of fifteen gun shots. The echoes from the valleys repeat and propagate the sound, followed by hoorays. We answer, and the crew climbs to the ladders.*"

True to French tradition, MacDonald's diary highlights his interest for food and for women. Regarding food, his feelings appear to be rather mixed. "*Long dinner, fine fare, though in the English way,* " he notes cryptically, as he depicts the dinner at MacDonald-Buchanan in Edinburgh, where he meets Sir Walter Scott. His description of the one he had at Armadale Castle, where he expected to join the wedding celebration of Lord MacDonald's daughter, rather contrasts with what was reported officially.

"*The party then adjourned to the Castle, where a sumptuous entertainment was prepared for them.*"[150]

---

150   Ibid

But, according to the Marshal:

"*The sight of the dinning room gives us concern, and we share the same thought: the table is not set, and the only preparation being made is to serve some tea. Where are the provisions for a party, which the arrangements noticed upon our arrival, made us expect? We make some enquiries, and learn that this party was due to be held at the house of Mr MacPherson, nephew of the author and translator of Ossian, some forty miles away, and that it was postponed upon the news of our arrival.*

There are talks of using the leftovers from the dinner of those gentlemen for whom the tea had been made, as well as some beefsteak that one hastens to put on the grill, a chicken, the compulsory potatoes, some kails and a soup. All these things will be fine, as long as they are being served, but it is an old wifie who is in charge of preparing the dinner, and she takes it easy. At long last, we have our supper and dinner at the same time, as it is close to 9 pm."

Regarding women, MacDonald never fails to report a pretty face or a graceful expression, and he is especially interested to see them wearing tartan dresses or plaids. Their legs, however, do not meet with his approval:

"*Most of the women have rather strong legs and big feet, and this is certainly not due to having them naked, for I have noticed that they were very strong in higher society too. I am hereby talking of the Scottish women only.*"

The Marshal shares with other travellers to the Highlands, amazement at the sight of women walking everywhere barefoot, and putting their shoes on only when entering a house:

"*All travellers have criticized the fact that women and girls walk with their bare feet, holding their shoes in their hands, even within towns. They are right, and I share this view. This criticism is not directed to the people of society, or to the bourgeoisie, but to the better working-class people, where*

one may witness well and cleanly dressed persons, with white
dress, printed cotton (an even silk), hat with ribbons, shawl
and even a elegant veil but [..?]

I only saw one, at last, holding an umbrella in her other
hand."

Nevertheless, he kindly looks for an excuse for this outlandish behaviour:

"I have discussed this custom with various people, who were
equally critical of it, but who noticed that it had its use. When
the weather is wet, and tracks are muddy, shoes get wet very
quickly; so when women enter a house, they wash their feet and
put on their shoes, which are dry, thus preserving themselves
from humidity and its consequent illnesses."[151]

Leaving Scotland, MacDonald continued on his journey through England, Ireland (with a brief stay in Dublin), Wales and back to England again. As he sailed from England, he reiterated his intention, already expressed on a number of occasions in Scotland, to come back to the British Isles a few years later. He wrote in his diary:

"Farewell, beautiful England, charming country whose
inhabitants have welcomed me with so much care and
politeness. Farewell for two or three years. I'll come back to
see you at that time."

Though, to the best of our knowledge, he never came back, the whole trip had made a marked impression upon him. One specific point of his visit to the British Isles had drawn his attention:

"No inquiry there, nor any form of inquisition. Nowhere the
strangers we were have been asked for their passport. I have

---

151   *This point is also raised in Martin RACKWITZ; Travels to terra*
incognita: The Scottish Highlands and Hebrides in early modern travellers'
accounts c. 1600 to 1800, Op.cit., Ch. 8.1.1

been through the three kingdoms, through the islands: no constable or public officer to be seen; everywhere is safe. The people of England is proud of its freedom, of its independence. He benefits from it, but he pays. Everywhere wealth and cleanliness. It is an admirable country in every aspect."

This appreciation was perhaps somewhat naïve, for one is seldom asked for identification when travelling on board a British Navy vessel provided by the First Lord of Admiralty, and when invited by the highest gentry in the land. As for the prevailing "wealth", and the lack of police or "inquisition"; the Radical leaders of the aborted 1820 "Weavers'Rising" in central Scotland, John Baird and Andrew Hardie, would probably have held a somewhat different opinion. But they could not, for they had been hanged five years before, and as it happened, it was MacDonald's guide in the Highlands, Reginald MacDonald of Staffa, who had presided over their execution as Sheriff of Stirlingshire.[152] However, the Marshal's comment must be put in perspective as those of a man who had himself spent a large part of his life under the supervision of the Republican *Commissaires*, or of Napoléon's secret police.[153]

---

152   I am indebted to Donald William Stewart for that information. See Peter Berresford ELLIS and Seumas MAC A' GHOBHAINN, **The Scottish Insurrection of 1820** (1970: London, 1989), 29, 54, 149, 285.

153   Incidentally, a most bizarre story regarding Marshal MacDonald seems to have circulated in Scotland five years before his visit. In 1820, at the time of the "Radical Rising" (or "Weaver's Rising") which took place in the Lowlands, rumour had it that: "An army was said to be mustering at Campsie under the command of Marshal MacDonald, a Marshal of France and son of a Jacobite refugee family. This army was going, so it was whispered, to join forces with another array at Cathkin, under Kinloch, the fugitive Radical laird from Dundee." (Quoted on www.electricscotland. com/history/highlands/2no14.htm). Needless to say, MacDonald, who was then a Minister of King Louis XVIII, and not the Republican General of his youth, had nothing to do with this affair. But how did it come about that his name was circulated? Whilst this may be a pure coincidence, we must note that the Marshal's cousin, John M'Eachin, lived in Greenock, where some of the 1820 disturbances took place.

Section IV
A Scotsman in France, a Frenchman in Scotland?

Macdonald never made any mystery of his great fondness for Scotland, to the point that, under Napoléon, his fellow officers used to joke that: *"The Emperor was afraid to trust him within hearing of the bagpipes."*[154]

This jibe is unfounded, for he actually fought against British forces in Holland when an officer of the Republic, and did not change sides for all that. When in Spain in 1810, he may also have been sent to confront them had not he been recalled due to ill-health. However, the question may be raised as to how he balanced his French and his Scottish identities.

When he came back from his journey to the Hebrides, he kept close contacts with the land of his forefathers, as could be expected, and visitors from Scotland were certainly made welcome at his house. Sir Walter Scott, who visited Paris a year later, was treated with great kindness,[155] and offered all the necessary assistance in collecting information for his "Life of Napoléon Bonaparte" – though he may not have taken as much advantage of it as one might expect.[156]

More strikingly, it was widely reported (though he made no mention of it in his diary), that MacDonald brought back a special item from his father's home of Howbeg, in South Uist.

"...Before leaving the ruined house, he filled a stocking full of earth, and brought it to France with him. This earth, at his

---

154 *Quoted in CAPTAIN H. M. DAVSON, R.H.A , Napoléon's Marshals, Chapter 7, in The Journal of the Royal Artillery, Vol. XXXIV., No. 11.*

155 Sir Walter SCOTT, *Journal,* 3rd of November 1826.

156 *"I have been assured that Marshal MacDonald having offered to introduce Scott to some generals who could have furnished him with the most accurate, information respecting military events, the glory of which they had shared, Sir Walter replied, "I thank you, but I shall collect my information from unprofessional reports." Louis Antoine Fauvelet de BOURIENNE, Memoirs of Napoléon Bonaparte, Book 1, Chapter II.*

request, was buried with him."[157]

Whether this intention was carried to the end, and whether this wish was respected when he died in 1840, we do not know, but visitors from the Hebrides passing his grave at the Père-Lachaise cemetery in Paris may pause and wonder if perhaps there is not some soil from Tobha Beag laid there.[158]

MacDonald was also anxious to maintain the Scottish tradition in his family beyond his own lifetime. This was manifest in the painting of his four year old son, Louis Marie Alexandre MacDonald which he commissioned from the well-known painter Horace Vernet a few years after his return. The young boy is shown wearing a red tartan dress, and carrying, somewhat uncomfortably, "a Scottish sword of the MacDonald Clan" (probably an officer's basket-hilted sword). This initiative obviously bore fruits, for there are photographs of the 2nd Duke of Tarentum in full Highland regalia, at some later stage of his life. His own son, and grandson of the Marshal (and last of the male line) was to be named Napoléon Alexandre Fergus MacDonald – a most interesting combination of Gaelic and Napoléonic first names. Another granddaughter was called Marie Ines Eugénie Flora MacDonald, an obvious homage to the said Flora MacDonald, whose portrait was apparently adorning the family home.[159]

Nevertheless, for all his commitment to Scotland in general and to Clan Donald in particular, there can be no doubt that Marshal MacDonald considered France as his main country. This, he made perfectly clear in the introduction of his "Recollections", where he thus described his return home from Britain:

"My rapid journey has been brought to a satisfactory conclusion. The coast of France looked to me as the Promised

---

157   *Edinburgh University Library,* **Carmichael Watson MS 125,***fo.134. Also* **Tour of his Excellency etc.** *, Op.cit.*

158   *The grave is located Allée des Acacias, also nicknamed "Marshal's Alley" for the number of Napoléonic Marshals being buried there.*

159   *The aforesaid artefacts were auctioned in December 2005 amongst other Napoléonic Memorabilia by Osenat Sales Room, in Fontainebleau.*

Land. I have once more seen France, my beloved country!"[160]

A century after the Marshal's death, another French officer of note came to Scotland. As he visited Edinburgh in 1942, General De Gaulle, in a speech in which he made passing references to the Stuarts, to the *Garde Ecossaise* of the French Kings, and to MacDonald himself, declared that:

"I do not think that a Frenchman could have come to Scotland at any time without being sensible of a special emotion. Scarcely can he set foot in this ancient and glorious land before he finds countless natural affinities between your country and ours dating from the very earliest times. In the same moment, awareness of the thousand links, still living and cherished, of the Franco-Scottish Alliance, the oldest alliance in the world, leaps to his mind."[161]

Born in France of Scottish descent; a French citizen loyal to his nation, yet always bearing Scotland in his heart; buried in Paris, but with some Hebridean soil in his grave, Marshal MacDonald was certainly one of the most striking examples of this very ancient relationship.

---

160   *Letter dated 6th of August 1825, quoted in Chapter 1 of the "Recollections."*

161   · Speech delivered by General de Gaulle in Edinburgh, 23rd June 1942

THE HISTORICAL BACKGROUND TO MARSHAL MACDONALD'S VISIT: SOUTH UIST AND BENBECULA

by Domhnall Uilleam Stiùbhart

Although it is now nearly a generation since it was submitted, James A. Stewart's Edinburgh University doctoral thesis 'Clan Ranald: the history of a Highland kindred'[1] remains a model of its kind, an essential account of the final tragic and disastrous decades of the Clan Ranald estates, the beautiful, far-flung lands stretching from Moidart and Arisaig in the mainland *Garbh-Chrìochan*, west to the islands of Eigg and Canna – as well as, for a while, the Island of Muck – and further out still to Benbecula and South Uist in the Western Isles. Stewart not only explored the vast Clan Ranald archive itself, but also tracked down the papers of Robert Brown, the factor who, on behalf of the clan trustees, effectively oversaw and administered the estate from the beginning of the nineteeth century. His thesis delineates a basic historical framework for the period, outlining issues and events, as well as presenting vivid vignettes illuminating key turning-points.

Although Stewart's work has yet to be superseded, inevitably his judgments and interpretations have to be modified in the light of subsequent analyses, above all significant recent work by major historians such as Tom Devine, Robert Dodgshon, Allan I. Macinnes, and Eric Richards. It is true that a number of these studies at least are flawed, demonstrating a tendency to the somewhat skewed and reductive perspectives of the monoglot scholar, as well as suffering perhaps from a more general, and serious, lack of subtlety and balance of judgment. Their marvellously assiduous archival research is all too often undermined by the disappointingly thin and

---

1   James A. STEWART, *'Clan Ranald: the history of a Highland kindred' (University of Edinburgh, Ph.D., 1982).*

103

unsophisticated conceptual – not to mention imaginative – explanatory frameworks they deploy, in which the people of the Gàidhealtachd figure far too often as mere economic abstractions or routine stereotypes. In spite of such failings, however, these studies have been crucially important in liberating us from worn-out notions of a pre-modern Gàidhealtachd society that was crippled by conservatism, archaic, monolithic, unchanging, and ripe for destruction. They demonstrate how resourceful and innovative – and indeed how disputatious and divisive – Gaels could be when faced with an era of extraordinary upheaval and dislocation. Above all, they have focused our attention outwards, to look beyond the Highlands to wider British, imperial, and global networks and contexts for change. Nevertheless, James A. Stewart's work continues not only to raise questions, but also to suggest answers to more contemporary research agendas.

Recent years have also seen the coming to fruition of several significant projects which enable historians of the period to look beyond conventional textual documentary evidence. Firstly, the SEARCH project, under the auspices of the Department of Archaeology in Sheffield University, will, when fully published, allow us to set the period in a much wider perspective, drawing upon the evidence of surviving material culture remains, settlement patterns, and indeed the island landscape itself. Secondly, there is the ever-increasing plethora of books charting island genealogies, many of them compiled through the industry of the comainn eachdraidh (the local historical societies), with the assistance of Bill Lawson's *Seallam!* centre. When this ambitious series is completed and collated with the profusion of papers in the Long Island Estate archive at Aisgernis in South Uist, it will offer historians an unequalled opportunity to compile detailed demographic studies concerning the processes of croft formation and Clearance during the period. Finally, there is ongoing research into the oral tradition of the Uibhistich themselves, embracing not only a marvellous treasure-trove of songs, but also stories, historical narratives and anecdotes, place-names, customs and beliefs: a wide cultural framework considerably more heterogeneous, ambiguous, eclectic, perceptive, and sophisticated than some outsiders choose to believe. Given the sheer abundance of estate documentation, let alone other forms of historical evidence, as well as the likelihood of new textual sources being discovered in the future, the following fragment of historical narrative must be regarded as even more provisional than usual.

Marshal Étienne Jacques Joseph Alexandre MacDonald spent only three days, from 29 June to 1 July 1825, in Benbecula and South Uist, where his father Neil MacEachen was born and brought up. He visited the islands at a time of turmoil, when a people who for two generations had experienced massive upheaval were now on the very brink of catastrophe. Despite a series of major emigrations, population numbers in South Uist had, in common with the rest of the country, shot up dramatically since the mid-eighteenth century, from some 2,209 in 1755 to 6,890 by 1831. The root causes for this remain unclear, although clearly improved nutrition due to the new wonder crop of the potato played a part, as well as, possibly, increased immunity to the smallpox which had ravaged previous generations. The resulting population explosion fuelled the high levels of military recruitment which were so essential to a chief's status at the time, but its most immediate effect was to supply a workforce for an industry whose effects fundamentally reshaped the island economy, society, culture, work and settlement patterns, and indeed the landscape itself: kelp.

If one figures to himself a man, and one or more of his children, engaged from morning to night in cutting, drying, and otherwise preparing the sea weeds, at a distance of many miles from his home, or in a remote island; often for hours together wet to his knees and elbows; living upon oatmeal and water with occasionally fish, limpets, and crabs; sleeping on the damp floor or a wretched hut; and with no other fuel than twigs or heath; he will perceive that this manufacture is none of the most agreeable.[2]

2   William MACGILLIVRAY, 'Report on the Outer Hebrides', *Transactions of the Highland Society, New Series ii (1831), 301, quoted in STEWART, 'Clan Ranald', 527.*

The first record we have from Uist of the commercial burning of seaweed to make soda ash, a basic ingredient in the production of glass and soap, dates from 1751.[3] During the following decades the Uist gentry would develop the industry and begin to market the product using existing seaborne trading networks embracing Highland and Lowland Scotland, Ireland, and England. For the people of the islands, the expansion of the kelp industry involved even further-reaching effects than the great growth in the cattle trade a century previously. The clan gentry, and later the trustees and factors, had to learn to negotiate and maintain partnerships with commercial interests from outside, while within the island they had essentially to restructure the local economy and society in order to create extensive and cheap labour pools available to carry out when required the backbreaking work of harvesting and burning kelp during the brief summer and autumn season. In effect, South Uist and Benbecula were organised into a single vast kelping plantation, a plantation whose factors would not scruple at using force to impose their will.[4] This reorientation of Clan Ranald, and the new opportunities for profit and status resulting from the boom in the kelp industry, placed this society under unprecedented stress, sharpening existing rivalries between and among tacksmen and tenantry, sparking off new alliances and new enmities, and throwing individual talents and individual flaws into a harsher light. Matters would grow infinitely worse when boom turned to bust in the aftermath of the Napoléonic Wars.

Within the islands, the immediate effect of the population explosion and the rise of the kelp industry was increasing congestion within local townships. The profits of the industry were certainly not shared among the people themselves, who were unable fully to participate in the market. This was not only because of their lack of capital, legal power, or security of tenure. In an attempt to keep wage levels low, the estate

---

3   *National Archives of Scotland [NAS], GD201/5/1232/1/26.*
4   *For examples, see NAS GD201/1/338; /5/1231/1/44; STEWART, 'Clan Ranald', 543.*

trustees actively discouraged competition between tacksmen for kelp workers. As agriculture, fishing, and cattle-raising had perforce to be neglected for the demands of the kelp harvest, islanders found themselves increasingly dependent upon meal rations for survival, and fell further into arrears as a result. At the same time, at a less quantifiable level, we can surmise a loss of communal bearings, of communal cohesion as traditional social landmarks were swept away. The old tacksman class had more or less vanished by the end of the eighteenth century, with a new cadre of mainly protestant factors and farmers taking their place.[5] The chief of Clan Ranald was an absentee landowner quite ignorant of his lands and his people, while his property was now run by trustees almost all of whom were as unacquainted with it as the chief himself. Almost entirely dependent upon profits from kelp, the Clan Ranald estate was increasingly vulnerable to fluctuations in the British economy.

The end of the Napoléonic War in 1815 was followed by a general economic downturn across the country. The kelp industry was particularly hard hit, as imports of better-quality Spanish barilla flooded the market. Faced with imminent disaster, in 1816 the estate factor of Benbecula and South Uist, Duncan Shaw had decided to take a drastic step and split the traditional townships into crofts. This experiment did not flourish, and following a severe winter during 1821–2, the estate trustees decided to sell off all Clan Ranald territory except for the two Outer Hebridean islands, which still might offer some hope of making money through kelp. By the time of the Marshal's visit, the trustees were at loggerheads with the chief, administration was in chaos, much of the estate was up for sale, and Shaw was making plans to clear a thousand of the poorest tenants from their homes in South Uist and send them overseas.

❈ ❈ ❈ ❈ ❈

---

5   For later opposition to the employment of Catholic estate officials, see ibid., 549.

After the Forty-Five, the fate of the Clan Ranalds hung upon one misspelt letter. The chief's son, Ranald or Ronald the Younger, had been out during the Rising, had marched south to Derby with the clan regiment, had taken part in the last farcical charge of Clan Donald at Culloden, and had subsequently fled to France into exile. In the Bill of Attainder, a London clerk, unfamiliar with Highland names, wrote down his name as Donald. By a bureaucratic error, a single slip of the pen, *Dùthaich Chlann Raghnaill* was preserved for the MacDonalds of Clan Ranald. Ranald MacDonald the Younger, however, did not return to Uist until 1754, nearly a decade after he had left Scotland with the Prince. He found clan affairs mired in chaos.

By a legalistic quirk of fate, the Clan Ranald lands had not been lost to the government. Nevertheless, the surveyor for the Forfeited Estates, David Bruce, had inveigled Ranald's incompetent and peevish father, Ranald MacDonald the Elder, into granting him a factorship for the entire estate, assuring him that untold mines and mineral resources were ripe for the excavating.[6] A more perceptive member of the clan gentry, however, had already realised that it was not underground that future wealth was to be obtained, but rather around the shores. Alexander MacDonald of Boisdale (1698–1768), the chief's vastly more capable half-brother, persuaded Bruce to grant the factorship of the Clan Ranald estate to him, effectively carrying out a coup on behalf of his own family. As the younger Ranald apprehended, Boisdale's intention was to pay relatively low tack duties to Bruce, all the while creaming off for his own family the burgeoning profits from kelp.[7]

To make matters worse, the household of Ranald the Elder appears to have been a petty bedlam, a 'Domestic hell' into which the exile found himself plunged on his return, and from

---

6   *Ibid.*, 489–90; also NAS GD201/1/364/25; /5/62, 79, 106, 1143–4, 1147, 1217/84.

7   NAS GD201/1/252–6, 273; /2/17–19, 20–2; /5/61, 79, 101. *The previous year Boisdale had bought lands in South Uist from Allan MacDonald of Morar: STEWART, 'Clan Ranald', 499–500.*

which he longed to escape.[8] With the diligent assistance of the clan lawyer Roderick MacLeod, the young Ranald attempted to put matters to rights. Two years after his return, he officially assumed control of the estates from his father.[9] Boisdale, clearly in high dudgeon, relinquished his factorship, but at a price. In 1758 he received a feu charter for his lands in Uist south of Loch Baghasdail, as well as the island of Eriskay. Boisdale had in fact carved a small kingdom for himself and his descendants out of the Clan Ranald estates.[10]

The unwary might read this episode through the prism of a powerful folk motif wherein the rightful heir, having fought for the Good Cause and survived many an adventure through charmed luck, returns home to assume his rightful inheritance, putting the evil counsellors to flight. Matters, however, are rarely so simple. Forceful and charismatic, a remarkable entrepreneur, immensely strong, and by all accounts the best drinker in the country in his day, Alexander MacDonald of Boisdale still figures in oral tradition in Uist as Alasdair Mór nam Mart, Big Alexander of the Cows. By a mixture of sharp practice and a fine eye for the main chance, he had rescued the Clan Ranald estate from being either administered by government agents, or else abandoned to the inept and surely fatal management of his incompetent half-brother. Alasdair Mór nam Mart and his family would continue to loom large in Clan Ranald affairs for the rest of the century and beyond.

Despite the promise of his early years, it was not long before Ranald the Younger was overcome with despondency. Estate finances were entrammelled with long-standing debts and the interest charges they incurred – especially those contracted by Penelope, the spendthrift dowager Lady Clan Ranald, the widow of Ailean Dearg who had fallen at Sheriffmuir – and doubtless exacerbated by the punitive destruction inflicted upon

---

8   NAS GD201/5/1217/8.
9   NAS GD201/1/246–9; /2/13; /4/68–9, 79; /5/78, 82–3, 1217/7; *for the rôle of Roderick MacLeod, see NAS GD201/1/258, 261–2, 266; /4/49–55, 57–63, 65–72, 74–8, 80–1, 84, 86, 88–91; /5/48, 60, 65–6.*
10   NAS GD201/1/364/7–9; /4/71, 75–6, 82, 85, 85A, 87; /5/1015–21; *Clan Donald iii, 291–2.*

the estate by government troops after Culloden. Overwhelmed by the ever-pressing need to provide for other members of his family, by the apparent impossibility of ever reforming the Clan Ranald estate, and by the recent death of an infant son, in 1763 Ranald came close to selling off his entire property. Only a £6,000 loan from the Bank of Scotland preserved the estate – for a while at least. It was clear, however, that management of the property would have to be placed on a firmer footing. The following year Ranald granted a commission and factory over the Clan Ranald estates to the Edinburgh lawyer William MacDonald.[11] The year after, a concerted effort was made to secure the future of the property, with a board of tutors appointed to administer *Dùthaich Chlann Raghnaill* in the event of Ranald's son John succeeding during his minority.[12]

During these years the kelping industry was growing steadily. As we have seen, the tight schedule of the work, entailing brief periods of intensive, exhausting labour, required that tenants neglect agricultural tasks. It also compelled them to work during what had hitherto been church holidays: not just religious events, but times of feast and celebration for the entire community. In the late 1760s, following the death of Alasdair Mór nam Mart, his heir Colin MacDonald of Boisdale, a man renowned 'for his autocratic manner and intemperate behaviour,'[13] was determined to stamp his authority on his estate. At the same time, a newly-arrived Irish Dominican, Father Matthias Wynne, was equally zealous in protecting, as he saw it, the rights and position of the church against encroachments by the estate. In 1768, after Boisdale, a protestant, had coerced his tenants into working during Michaelmas, Wynne peremptorily ordered him out of the church. Faced with this humiliating challenge to his power, around Michaelmas the following year Boisdale:

---

11   *Clan Donald ii, 361; STEWART, 'Clan Ranald', 489–92; see also NAS GD1/8/16–17, /27–8; /5/111–12, 133, 142, 1228 [9 Mar 1763]. A draft tack of 1764 gives Benbecula to Alexander of Boisdale: NAS GD201/2/34–6.*

12   *NAS GD201/1/269.*

13   *Kathleen TOOMEY, 'Emigration from the Scottish Catholic bounds 1770-1810 and the role of the clergy' (University of Edinburgh, Ph.D., 1993), 94.*

... summoned his tenants to the number of 1000 souls to inform that unless they renounced their religion and swore an oath never to communicate with a Priest again, they would lose their houses on the Island; and those who did not eat meat in Lent were scourged.[14]

Although mass resistance among the tenantry, and the threat of emigration, subsequently forced Boisdale to relent, over the next few years he dramatically raised rents, victimised those who resisted him, and employed a church schoolmaster to attempt forcibly to convert the children on his property. In reaction to such drastic measures, Captain John MacDonald of Glenalladale (1742–1811), brother of Father Hugh, priest of Moidart, raised with Bishop John MacDonald a scheme he had clearly already been considering for some time. As a result, in May 1772 Glenalladale organised a major emigration of Clan Ranald tenantry over the Atlantic to St John's Island, present-day Prince Edward Island, where disbanded Fraser's Highland veterans had already been settled since the time of the Seven Years War, and where he himself had purchased two lots the year before.[15]

This dramatic quarrel over the economic direction and religious complexion of the Clan Ranald estate demonstrates that the aging Ranald was now sidelined, and had effectively lost control of his own property. Glenalladale's father had been the factor of the mainland territories of *Dùthaich Chlann Raghnaill*; indeed, it could be said that it was his exertion as legal procurator for the chief in 1748 which had preserved the property for the family.[16] In 1760, the year before his death, he had been appointed factor of the entire Clan Ranald estate.[17] Although the threat of emigration had forced Colin MacDonald of Boisdale to desist from his most aggressive

---

14   *Ibid.*, 97: SCA BL3/221/9, *Bishop Hugh MacDonald to Bishop George Hay.*

15   TOOMEY, *'Emigration from the Scottish Catholic bounds'*, 94–7; Stewart, *'Clan Ranald'*, 500–3.

16   NAS GD201/1/364/4–5; *Clan Donald ii*, 358.

17   STEWART, *'Clan Ranald'*, 500.

policies, the departure of his rival Captain John of Glenalladale overseas meant that it was he who was now unquestionably the dominant personality among the clan gentry. Following the Glenalladale emigration, the chief was pressured to grant a factorship to Boisdale over the entire estate except his ancestral lands of Benbecula for twelve years, or until such time as the estate debts were finally paid off. Boisdale was even granted the privilege of choosing his own tenants at will.[18] Rents were raised, and shorter leases granted, in a pattern reflecting economic changes throughout the Gàidhealtachd.[19]

Ranald MacDonald, Captain of Clan Ranald, died in 1776, leaving his second wife Flora Mackinnon and a son John. His widow took the heir to Edinburgh for his education, and thereafter lived there or indeed on the Continent, apparently at no small expense to estate finances. The Clan Ranald property itself was administered by a board of tutors, guardians appointed by the previous chief, among them a number of lawyers and MacDonald relations of the family.[20] The tutors made strenuous efforts to maximise income from the property, commissioning a judicial rental, and attempting to reduce the number of tenants in receipt of a pension. Now that there was no longer a chiefly household in *Dùthaich Chlann Raghnaill*, there was no need for feudal casualties, which were converted to cash payment. In 1777 tenants were forbidden to use querns to make their own meal; henceforth, they would have to take it to estate mills to have it ground at a charge instead.[21]

The crucial rôle played by tutors and trustees in managing the Clan Ranald estates and many other properties across the western Gàidhealtachd reminds us that the usual account by historians of an old cadre of hereditary chiefs being swiftly superseded by a new arriviste élite in a brief series of major land sales during the early nineteenth century may be rather

---

18   NAS GD201/1/364/22; /5/1022; also /1/281–3; GD50/216/43; STEWART, 'Clan Ranald', 492.

19   STEWART, 'Clan Ranald', 494. *For further actions by the estate at this time, see NAS GD201/1/283–4.*

20   STEWART, 'Clan Ranald', 497, 543.

21   Ibid., 497–8, 520–1; NAS GD201/1/295, 351/12; /2/50–2; /5/1233/2, 15.

too simple. The administration of property by trustees whose primary duty was to act on behalf of creditors and indeed themselves made the dismemberment of clan lands considerably easier, the more so given that Highland estates were increasingly in demand as badges of rank, or even as collectors' items, at the time.

John MacDonald of Clan Ranald was educated outwith the island, travelled to the continent on Grand Tours for several years, and had little more to do with his native land.[22] He died in November 1794, best known for having divorced his first wife Catharine MacQueen, daughter of the famous hanging judge Robert, Lord Braxfield, in a notorious scandal.[23] His second wife was Jean, none other than the daughter of Colin MacDonald of Boisdale. Their son, Reginald George (1791–1873), was only three years of age at his father's death. A new group of trustees was chosen under the direction of Hector MacDonald-Buchanan, W.S., a younger son of Colin of Boisdale, half-brother of the new chief's mother, and factor, commissioner, and agent on the Clan Ranald estates.[24] MacDonald-Buchanan, it should be noted, was also the half-brother of Ranald or Reginald MacDonald of Staffa (1778–1838) who was to show the Marshal around the Highlands during his visit. Also on the trust was Archibald MacDonald of Sanda (d.1796), whose mother Penelope was the new chief's aunt.[25] Nevertheless, although some members of the clan gentry were involved, in general this particular group of trustees was Lowland in character, with little or no experience or knowledge of the estate and the people they were charged with administering. One major exception, however, was Robert Brown. First appearing in the record on 16 December 1797, this clearly remarkably able, energetic, and influential man was employed as factor for the duke of Hamilton, and retained the

---

22   *Clan Donald ii, 362.*

23   Leah LENEMAN, *Alienated affections: The Scottish experience of divorce and separation, 1684–1830 (Edinburgh, 1998), 43, 121–3; also* NAS GD201/1/313; /5/183, 189, 191–2.

24   *NAS GD201/5/195, 200–2.*

25   *Clan Donald ii, 362–3.*

Hamilton connection even though living at Nunton/Baile nan Cailleach in Benbecula until 1811.[26]

As we have seen, many older families of tacksmen on the estate were gradually being squeezed out. The estate administration increasingly preferred to cut out middlemen altogether and to deal directly with tenants, a matter of growing concern given the vast profits to be made from kelp. In addition, it was becoming more common to stipulate that improvements be undertaken as part of the terms of tack renewal.[27] We should be careful of being too uncritical when we read the many contemporary critiques of tacksmen by 'improving' authors with an axe to grind: many tacksmen's entrepreneurial and managerial skills, not to mention the cultural capital they wielded among the tenantry, were ably demonstrated in the emigrations they organised and led, and indeed in their success overseas not just in carving out new farms and townships, but also in the ease with which they negotiated local systems of authority and assumed positions of influence after they arrived.

In the Scottish Gàidhealtachd, however, shorter tacks meant that those who held the land grew ever more reluctant to risk undertaking major improvements. Nevertheless, population pressure led to a clamour for tacks, with competitive bidding leading inevitably to rack renting, which led just as inexorably to further indebtedness.[28] Wage competition, on the other hand, was frowned upon by the trustees: indeed, the tendency of older tacksmen to take the part of tenantry in disputes meant that they were objects of suspicion – witness the probably not entirely serious recommendation in one of the board's minutes that old tacksmen be confined to one farm alone.[29] It should of course be stressed that tenants were by no means an undifferentiated mass without their own share of rivalries and disputes.

The decline of the tacksmen meant that the estate management were paying ever more heed to the tenantry

26   STEWART, 'Clan Ranald', 545–8.
27   Ibid., 507.
28   Ibid., 510–11.
29   Ibid., 515, 518, 520; NAS GD201/5/1233/31/25–6.

themselves, especially given their rôle as a cheap labour pool for the kelp industry. The beginning of the French wars at the end of the eighteenth century, with the cutting off of Spanish barilla supplies, brought about increased reliance on domestic kelp supplies. Given that Uist kelp was among the best quality seaware in the country, the industry came to dominate the island economy. As we have seen, this strenuous and gruelling work was extremely labour-intensive, and transformed the island economy. Firstly, it prevented tenants from full involvement in agriculture, stock raising, or fishing. In addition, seaweed was not being used to manure the ground. These facts, when combined with the effects a rapidly rising population, meant that dearth and indeed famine were becoming more and more frequent, with the tenantry dependent during the winter and spring seasons on imports of meal rations from the south. One remarkable corollary of the kelp industry was the unusually high number of horses in Uist, kept in order to transport loads of kelp from the shores. This might explain the continuing importance of the *oda*, the yearly horse race and procession, in the island during the period, and also why its demise exactly coincided with the collapse of the kelp industry.[30]

The Clan Ranald trustees appear to have made deliberate attempts to keep their tenants' wages as low as possible, not only to ensure that they continued to work at kelping, and that debt levels on the estate were kept as low as possible, but also to try to stave off emigration which would otherwise eat away at island manpower reserves.[31] Ever since Glenalladale's emigration of 1772, the departure of disaffected tenantry and the activities of emigration agents were a constant source of anxiety to those administering the estate. A good example of this can be seen in their efforts at the beginning of the nineteenth century to curb the activities of one agent, Ranald 'son of MacEachan of Howbeg' – possibly a close relation of Neil MacEachen – which culminated in his arrest in 1804.[32]

---

30   Alexander CARMICHAEL (ed.), *Carmina Gadelica ii* (Edinburgh, 1928), 337–8; STEWART, 'Clan Ranald', 524–9.

31   Ibid., 529–30.

32   Ibid., 532–3; also 516–17.

For the tenantry of the period, emigration was not so much an attempt to preserve an ancient, clan-based way of life overseas, but rather an escape to freedom, a means to achieve social advancement, to allow entrepreneurial ambitions free rein.

Although ostensibly passed for humanitarian reasons, the Emigration Act in 1803 was intended to curtail high levels of emigration by pricing the passage out of tenants' reach. Not only would the islands be a plantation; they would also be a prison. The advocacy of Robert Brown, factor for Clan Ranald, was crucial in promoting the bill and getting it passed. Nevertheless, despite government legislation, despite the trustees' attempts to entangle tenants in their leases, not to mention direct threats that they would refuse to look after infirm parents of tenants who had left the estate, emigration continued to be an issue.[33] Indeed, it is clear that, just as happened with Colin MacDonald of Boisdale in the early 1770s, the fear of losing manpower overseas prevented too much undue pressure being applied by the authorities. Thus, for example, when crofting was introduced to the estate in 1817, the new system was confined to Benbecula at first out of a concern that the people of South Uist would thereupon follow the example of their southern neighbours in Barra and leave the island altogether.[34]

For a while at the beginning of the Napoléonic Wars, the estate appeared at least to be flush with profits from kelping. The Island of Muck was acquired in 1799, while six years later the trustees were able to buy the superiority of all the Clan Ranald lands from the duke of Argyll.[35] The last Captain of Clan Ranald, however, was spendthrift, wilful, incompetent, and chronically ill-suited to his rôle. Reginald George MacDonald, in the words of the editors of *Clan Donald*, was 'not too well equipped by nature for contending with the altered conditions'[36] – nor well equipped, for that matter, to earn money elsewhere. He did have talent, however,

---

33   *Ibid.*, 537–43.

34   *Ibid.*, 535–6; also 537.

35   NAS GD201/5/240; *Clan Donald ii*, 363; STEWART, 'Clan Ranald', 529.

36   *Clan Donald ii*, 363.

in making full use of available sources of credit. Educated at Eton, Christ Church, and in a succession of Continental Grand Tours, Reginald never once visited his ancestral estate during his youth – indeed, it appears likely that he was deliberately prevented from doing so by his own tutors.[37]

Reginald George MacDonald's one brief opportunity to manage the estate unencumbered by trustees, between June 1808 and September 1811, was a financial disaster, with his debts shooting up dramatically from £47,000 to over £90,000.[38] Reginald's marriage in 1812 to Lady Caroline Anne Edgcumbe (1792–1824), daughter of the musical connoisseur Richard, second earl of Mount Edgcumbe, entailed further ruinous expenses, possibly exacerbated by the fact that he subsequently became one of the M.P.'s for Edgcumbe's pocket burgh of Plympton for the next twelve years.[39]

The same year as the chief's marriage saw a further major famine among the people of Uist.[40] Kelp prices were already falling. The end of the Napoléonic Wars in 1815, accompanied by the abrupt termination of military service for many, and an ensuing peacetime economic depression, hit the people of Uist hard. With the resumption of competition from Spain, the repeal of salt duties, and the introduction of new chemical processes, the kelp industry collapsed, while rent arrears soared. No alternative sources of income were available from the property itself or for that matter from investments, and the Clan Ranald estates faced imminent disaster. On 24 February 1816 the factor for the islands, Duncan Shaw, for the first time suggested that, in order to improve the land and to encourage the industrious and the indolent alike, the communal townships, 'the same mode practised in the Western Isles time past all memory', be broken up into crofts, with strips of land lotted and let to individual tenants.[41] The experiment did nothing

37   STEWART, 'Clan Ranald', 552–6.
38   Ibid., 549–50, 557–8.
39   Ibid., 558–9.
40   Ibid., 560, 561.
41   NAS GD201/5/1228/2; STEWART, 'Clan Ranald', 565. Shaw had already been instructed to restructure township souming four years previously: NAS GD201/5/1217/36. It should be noted that here is an example

117

to stave off famine over the next few years. By 1822 tenants' earnings, never very high, were but a fraction of what they had been during the boom years of the kelping industry.[42] In a desperate effort to claw back arrears, the trustees 'instructed Shaw to round up and sell off as many cattle as he could from the tenantry – a move which only exacerbated matters still further.[43] Shaw's solution was to reemploy as many tenants as he could in a massive programme of public works, building sandbanks and seeding them with marram grass in order to stop sandblow inundating the machair, draining the lochs on the west side of the island, and building roads out to the east – in other words, creating the landscape of South Uist as we know it today. All the while, he was hoping for a resurgence in kelp prices, which was not to come.[44]

By this time too the trustees and the clan chief were at loggerheads. Relations had never been easy, but with crisis looming, mutual recriminations ensued. By 1822 the trustees saw no alternative but to sell off the mainland portions of the Clan Ranald estate, along with Eigg and Canna (Muck had been disposed of some eleven years previously).[45] Reginald George MacDonald was incensed. Although he had previously been accustomed to live in the Highlands at Appin House, as soon as he attained his majority, with a rôle as a Highland chief to live up to, he had decided to build a mansion on his ancestral lands in Arisaig. He selected the grounds without consulting either factor or tenantry, evicted some of the latter, and even forced the local priest, Father John MacDonald, to quit his residence, a move which 'irritated the minds of the people in a great degree indeed.'[46] Faced with the imminent loss of half of his estate, the chief attempted in vain to break the trust, claiming to have entailed his property during his brief majority, thus making it impossible for the estates to be

of crofting townships being created after the kelping boom collapsed.

42   STEWART, 'Clan Ranald', 567.
43   NAS GD201/1/352.
44   NAS GD201/1/338.
45   NAS GD201/5/1228 [13 Dec 1822]; STEWART, 'Clan Ranald', 575. The sale of Arisaig had first been mooted in 1817: ibid.
46   STEWART, 'Clan Ranald', 562; see also NAS GD201/4/102/207.

sold off piecemeal.[47]

At the beginning of 1824 Reginald had a major falling-out with his tenants in Arisaig. The factor of the mainland portion of his estate, the Catholic John MacDonald of Borrodale, informed the trust that Clan Ranald had turned the priest and his congregation out of the local chapel, but had then, somewhat inexplicably, decided to take part in the traditional New Year shinty match with his tenants. Borrodale found them refusing point blank to take part in any game, and planning to retake the chapel by force if necessary. He eventually talked them round 'and accordingly I marched them all to the ground where Clan soon joined. The day was bad but the amusement went on.' Borrodale later discovered that the people had intended to return two notes of credit their chief had given them as soon as he arrived, then to play a separate match of shinty among themselves, some players with 'turned coats'.

> I saved him from that disgrace & ... you surely would conclude he would have Thank[ed] me. He never yet took the least notice of it altho' he was fully informed (not by me) of the whole. ... Who can support such a man, I say that no man can.[48]

It was not just in Arisaig in which the tenantry were becoming restless. On 26 February 1825, the island factor Duncan Shaw suggested that a jail and courthouse be erected for the district, not just because of the suffering of the people in the face of continuing dearth, but:

> As we propose soon letting a considerable portion of your estate in sheep-farms, you are most materially interesting in suppressing thefts.[49]

---

47   STEWART, 'Clan Ranald', 550; NAS GD201/5/333–7, 341–2, 352, 354, 356–7, 361–2.

48   STEWART, 'Clan Ranald', 563–4; also ibid., 517; Scottish Catholic Archives [SCA] OL1/3/9, Bishop Ranald MacDonald to John MacDonald of Borrodale, 1 Mar 1824.

49   STEWART, 'Clan Ranald', 568–9.

In Shaw's eyes, although Benbecula and the northern district of South Uist were still potentially viable as kelping areas, for great swathes of the rest of the island clearance was now the only option. Some townships and farms would be put entirely under sheep, while others would preserve a residual kelping population who could also labour on the new farms when required.[50]

This, then, is the dispiriting background to the Marshal's visit in 1825. It is possible that he was encouraged to visit Scotland not only by reports of George IV's famous King's Jaunt to Edinburgh in 1822, but also by a tour made by his friend Macnab of Sancerre to the Isle of Skye, during which he visited John MacDonald of Borrodale.[51] The Marshal's diary suggests that he was very ill at ease with sea travel across the 'perfidious element' – 'the desolation', as he describes it – hence the short time he spent in the island of his ancestors, an island whose economy was by then suffering rapid decline, indeed hovering on the brink of collapse, an island whose entire population had recently been turned out of their traditional communal townships and resettled on crofts, with many hundreds about to be evicted once more as their homes were cleared for sheep farms. It is no wonder that so many people turned out to see the Marshal, in the hope that the scion of a well-known tacksman family would surely take pity and show charity to the ravaged people of Uist. For chief and trustees alike, the resulting pantomime must have been a strain indeed. It was probably a relief that the Marshal spent so little time in the land of his ancestors. Occasionally we see other less celebratory sides of recent estate history: Clan Ranald's badly-situated little 'castle' in Arisaig; the locked church nearby; the importunate crowds thronging the Marshal during his visit to Uist; maybe

---

50   See NAS GD201/1/335, 338, 354; also STEWART, 'Clan Ranald', 571–3.

51   SCA OL1/3/4, Macnab of Sancerre to John MacDonald of Borrodale, 1 Apr 1822. The origins of the Marshal were already of interest to John MacDonald of Borrodale following Napoléon's exile to Elba in 1814: see SCA OL1/2/6, Robert Brown to Borrodale, 19 Nov 1814: 'I have often heard the late Mr Ranald McEachen the Clergyman of South Uist speak of his friend Mr McEachen who had gone to France in the year 46'.

even the ominous presence of the local militia.

Two years later, under Duncan Shaw's sheep farming scheme, the estate began to clear a series of townships in South Uist: Geirinis, Driomoir, Gròigearraidh, Stadhlaigearraidh, Sniseabhal, Peighinn nan Aoireann, Staoinebrig, Cill Donnain, Àirigh a' Mhuilinn, Aisgernis, Dalabrog, Cille Pheadair – and Tobha Beag.[52] Two years after the Marshal's visit to his ancestral village, the people who had greeted him there were summarily evicted from their own homes and sent over the Atlantic.

The trustees had already begun to dismember the Clan Ranald properties. In 1826 Arisaig, where Reginald George MacDonald had his mansion, was sold to the trustees of Lady Ashburton for £48,950, along with the superiority of Bornish for £350. Dr Hugh MacPherson purchased Eigg for £14,500, while Donald MacNeill bought Canna for £9,000. In 1827 Col. Cameron bought Kenchreggan for £8,000; fishing rights on the River Sheil were sold to Alexander MacDonald of Rhue for £300, while the remainder of Moidart was bought by Major Allan MacDonald for £9,000. In 1838 the islands of Benbecula and South Uist, the remainder of the estate, would be sold to Col. Gordon of Cluny for £96,000.[53] Cluny had been in competition for the property with none other than Patrick Sellar. All that remained to the last chief of Clan Ranald was the ancestral stronghold of Caisteal Tioram, and the nearby island Eilean Riosga. For the rest of the nineteenth century, the people of Benbecula and South Uist would suffer misery and oppression as wretched as in any comparable rural area in the country. It is an irony of history that it was the French wars prosecuted with such success by Napoléon's generals which made South Uist the way it was when the Marshal MacDonald visited it in 1825. Their defeat spelt disaster for the island's economy and for its people.

---

52   STEWART, 'Clan Ranald', 572.
53   NAS GD201/1/340; /5/391; Stewart, 'Clan Ranald', 575–8.

FIELD NOTES BY ALEXANDER CARMICHAEL CONCERNING MARSHAL MACDONALD

1. *Edinburgh University Library [EUL] Carmichael Watson [CW] MS 108 fos.13*[v]*–14: probably from Donald Macintyre, Dòmhnall mac Néill, 84, Tobha Beag, 6 April 1877.*

Duke of Tarentum

Came ab[ou]t 45 yrs ago. When he came to sight of Faoghail Hough he said A this is the river my fath[er] told me he used to be a breacach [*trout fishing*]. There was a crowd & he went up & kiss an old man & said O seo m'athair – Alx Maceachain & Neill d[itt?]o sons of the two brothers – Raol was Alex son. Gave £20 to the old man, £20 to his sist Isabel ni Raoil nic Fir Houbig. Gave also £20 to John Maceachain Iocar. He left £20 to ea[ch] of the two first while he lived. Took fill of a stocking of earth from 'Tota na Bracha' below which is ?Am Mùr on the flat near the river.

Duke Tart middle sized smart man high sight [sic]. [*later addition*: Swarthy complex[ion] About 5-10 or 5-11.]

2. *Ibid., fo.14*[v]*: written later, possibly May 1877.*

Duke of Tarentum

Came to Uist abt 46 [*years ago*]. Left 10lb a year to his cousin Alast & Isebel each as long as they lived. His nephew a ??count along with him. He had 2 sister. Had one son – No English – I can't speak to you but Ill send you my son – He then got an English tutor to his son. The son died & his pro[perty] claimed by a man fr[om] America.

Raol had a son John ~~who had a son Tomas~~ who was a cooper in the Customs Greenock who had a son Thomas who went to Quebec Probably this was the claimant. He came to Paris to see the Duke who behaved kindly to him. Duke sharp – knew his relatives by sight. He wld be abt 70 or 75. The late Angus Fletcher Edin[burgh] corresp[onde]d with him.

Angus Macintire & Kenth Beaton were taken away from Croic Pheugh? Paton was put out at Assynt & money given him to take him home. Macint[yre] Was ?keunpr? In France 15 yrs. & came back to Uist.

3. *EUL CW 363 fos.9–10: Notes by AC concerning Marshal Macdonald, probably in 1890s, probably from notes made from old Niall MacEachainn, and memories of him.*

Marshal Macdonald

(1) Niall Maceachain mac Eachain mac Iain mac Eachain mac Iain mac Alastair mac Iain mhic Raoghail bho Arasaig. Be Raoghal bho Arasaig a chiada fhear a Chlann eachain Hough-big.

(2) Niall mac Eachain mac Alastair mac Iain mac Raoghail bho Arasaig. Alastair athair Néill athair a Mharshail. Bha Niall aige mac Raoghail. Be seo chiad fhear aig an robh Houghbeag. Bha Alastair aig Raoghal. Be Alastair Mor Hough big a theirte ris. Bha ceathrar nighean aig Alastair Mor – nighean dligheach agus te no dha dìolain. Theireadh Alastair Mor Domhnallach ris fhein a deigh a Mhorair is cinnteach.

Ghleidh Clann Eachain eile ris an ainm ghnathaichte.

Neill Ranald John and Angus Ranald being the father of Alastair Mor the father of the Marshal. Raoghal Houghbig – This Raoghal was the first called of Hough beag. Raoghal had no son except Alastair Mor.

The Maceachains were a sept of the Macdonalds and came to Uist from Morair. Neill Maceachain had been studying for the priesthood in the Scots College at Douay near Paris. But as his namesake and kindmans the late Neill Maceachain said – Thill Niall dachaidh gun dol fo lamhan easpaig idir. Bha cuid do bhoidean na sagartachd ro chruaidh leis ri ghabhail agus thill e dachaidh gun an gabhail idir – Neill came home without going under the hands of a bishop at all. Some of the vows of the priesthood were too hard for him to take and he came home without taking them at all...

4. *EUL CW 363 fo.28: note apparently, according to note by AC, by Capt Alexander Matheson, Doirnie, Kintail.*

I use to hear both on the Mainland and in Uist that the Duke of Tirentim after parting with Napoléon Boneparte when he was made a state prisoner in the Elbe after the loss of his troops in Russia that he had never seen the Empourer afterwards and that he had taken the oath of allegenc to Lou[i]s Phillipic that he kept aloof from joining the Emperor on his return to France after his escape from his confinement in the Elbe.

That he afterwards came into the confidence of the British Government privately, and that he had been in the millitary tent of the Duke of Wellington during the whole action of the British forces in Brussels in 1815 and knowing all the manuveries of the French army that he put up the Duke of Wellington to all the tactics of the French Army and that he had as much to do with the Battle of Waterloo to magnify the laurels of the Great Duke of Wellington as he had himself. This I use to heare from tratition but I cannot vouch for the correctness of the statement.

A MARSHAL OF NAPOLÉON IN THE HIGHLANDS & ISLANDS OF SCOTLAND

Note on the origin of the document, on its transcription and on its translation. By Jean-Didier Hache.

The Centre Historique des Archive Nationales, in Paris, holds a number of documents related to Marshal MacDonald, his life, and his family connections. These documents, which will be found under file 279/AP/36, have been bequeathed to the French National Archives by the Massa family, which was directly related to the Marshal.

The origin of this relationship lies with Sylvestre Regnier, Duke of Massa, Count of Gronau and Peer of France (1783-1851). Massa had married Anne Charlotte MacDonald, who was the Marshal's first daughter; Anne Charlotte's mother being MacDonald's first wife, Marie Constance de Monloisir, who died in 1797.

The Massa family files contain a number of interesting papers which show the family's keen interest in its Scottish roots. These include, amongst others, a birth certificate of Neil MacEachen, delivered by the Paris Scots College in relation to an obscure matter of military pension; some modern correspondence with MacDonald of Clanranald (by that time living in the South West of France); and two manuscripts directly related to the Marshal's visit to Scotland and the Hebrides in the year 1825.

One of these, obviously in the Marshal's own hand, is entitled "*Observations générales sur l'Angleterre, l'Ecosse et l'Irlande*" (General observations on England, Scotland and Ireland). It is hardly legible but by a confirmed archivist or paleologist, for it must be said that, in comparison with the Marshal's handwriting, the average doctor's prescription looks like an exercise in calligraphy. From what we could make out of it, this document is essentially a work of economic

127

geography, and does not deal with what is of interest to us here; namely his own family history and his relation with Scotland and the Scottish people.

But in the same box of files another document may be found. It is the Marshal's travel diary proper, entitled "*Voyage du Maréchal MacDonald en Angleterre, en Ecosse et en Irlande. 1825*" (Travels of Marshal MacDonald in England, in Scotland and in Ireland. 1825). The manuscript available in the French National Archive is not in the Marshal's own hand, but is a transcription from the original made by his own grand-daughter, the Countess Mathilde de Massa. Thankfully, her handwriting is perfectly clear, and readable without any sort of difficulty.

We must posthumously praise Mathilde de Massa for her initiative; as well as the Massa family for having the foresight to make this interesting document available to the public, via the French National Archives. We must also thank Mathilde de Massa for her dedication, for deciphering the Marshal's diary was obviously no easy task. Even her familiarity with her grandfather's handwriting, and her own sagacity, were defeated on many occasions as the numerous blanks, points of suspension and question marks which are scattered throughout her transcription bear witness. Not only did the Countess perform this thankless exercise, but also, aware that future readers of this document could be unfamiliar with Scotland's geography and history, she took care to include a number of explanatory footnotes to enlighten them, or simply to clarify the text. I have retained them in full in this English translation.

Let it be said that the Marshal's travel diary, while pleasant enough to read in French, lays no claim to literary excellence. Had it been so, I would have left the task of translating it to a native English speaker, and preferably to a specialist of early XIXth century literature. But, as Mathilde de Massa says, in one of her footnotes: "*We must point out that the Marshal was noting very quickly these details and impressions, which often lack in cohesion, and are written as flying notes*". So, this travel diary is what it purports to be: a succession of sentences, rapidly written during the course of a journey, with the charm of spontaneity, but with little regard to the harmony of tenses or to the homogeneity style. The punctuation is equally awkward, with successions of semicolons during whole pages. Without betraying the meaning of the text, I admit to having made some minor adaptations to make it more accessible to XXIst century readers.

Another problem lies with place names. The Marshal took great care to mention as many as possible of the nooks and crannies, islands and headlands he visited or passed by. But he had little English and no Gaelic, and was not always able to check their proper names. Many place names are written approximately, if not phonetically, and their spelling occasionally changes from one page to another. Mathilde de Massa herself, confronted with the additional problem of the Marshal's handwriting, was not always able to identify the exact name of some locations. Similar mishaps also happened with people's names.

I have adopted the policy of retaining the Marshal's spelling unchanged, and of leaving it to the reader to make the necessary corrections when such corrections were obvious (e.g.: "Eigg" for "Eig", etc.). Only when people or place names were too unintelligible have I indicated their proper appellation in a footnote; at least when I have been able to do so. The same problems, and the same rules, also apply to people's names.

The editor of this book, John Randall, has taken the bold view that having a Frenchman translating the text would give a "French feeling" to this translation, and help to convey the Marshal's vision of Scotland. I hope this trust has not been misplaced, and am thankful to him and to Alayne Barton for checking and correcting my work, and weeding out its more obnoxious errors and Gallicisms.

Abstracts from the

TRAVELS OF MARSHAL MACDONALD IN ENGLAND, IN SCOTLAND AND IN IRELAND. 1825

From the transcription written by Mrs Mathilde de Massa, grand-daughter of the Marshal. Centre Historique des Archives Nationales, Paris, 279AP36.

> Except where otherwise indicated, footnotes are assumed to be from the Marshal's granddaughter, Mathilde de Massa, who transcribed the Marshal's diaries, and so are the [comments] or [?] within the text which are marked in bold and in brackets. However, the *text and footnotes in italics* are the translator's own comments.

Marshal MacDonald begins his journey on the 1st of June 1825, in the company of the Count of Couëssin, his aide-de-camp and husband to his niece (herself a grand-daughter of Neil MacEachen), and with Auguste, his servant. They cross the Channel to reach Portsmouth and, travelling through the West of England (Salisbury, Bath, Bristol, Clifton, Oxford, Windsor...), slowly make their way to London.

In Windsor, the Marshal visits Milady Lucy Stuart, an old acquaintance he had last seen in France, some thirty four years before, at the time of the Revolution. Going through Hampton Court, Richmond and Ripley he reaches London on the 11th of June, where he stays at the Brunswick Hotel.

The visit has been mentioned in the press. On the 13th, he visits Westminster, and is introduced to the House of Lords and the House of Commons by the Speakers of both Houses. A number of Lords (Melville, Montrose, Athol and Beresford), come to speak to him. The Marshal, himself a member of the French Parliament, is much surprised by the fact that the British parliamentarians do not wear any sort of uniform or costume indicating their position, and that they are "... sitting or lying on their benches with hardly any decency."

During his stay, the Marshal is feted at a grand "family" dinner gathering the crème de la crème *of the MacDonald aristocracy in London: Sir Archibald MacDonald, Lord Clanranald and General MacDonald (Adjutant to the Duke of York). Also present are Lt-General Murray (Commanding the British Forces in Ireland), General Major Doyle, Sir John Sinclair and the Duke of Sussex (as Count of Inverness).*

The Marshal leaves London for Scotland on the 15ᵗʰ of June, and follows the Eastern route: Cambridge, York, Durham, Newcastle... He reaches Berwick and the Scottish Border on the 18ᵗʰ of June.

18th of June 1825

Berwick

From the top of the last slope, one may make out the two steeples of Berwick and, gradually, the town itself. We cross the bridge. Five or six little ships lie there, half afloat, since the tide is low. It is seven in the morning, and the town looks dreary, with few shops open and few people in the streets. We change our horses and go to Dunbar for food.

The countryside between Berwick and Dunbar is all even drearier and monotonous than that which we saw at the last stage posts: meagre cultivations, barren slopes, with small woods and isolated trees here and there, which the northern wind has crippled before they could develop. We go up and down, our path haphazardly following a narrow gully which widens and narrows intermittently. We see some peat bogs for the first time. As we go up, we witness the sea breaking against a rocky coastline, with gun batteries, towers and blockhouses scattered from place to place in order to defend the coast.

Dunbar.

Five or six miles from Dunbar, the country livens up again: the fields are better cultivated and more productive, the grazings are full of cattle, and there are some fine country seats with their parks, some in the gothic style, some modern. As we reach the town, we notice one of these country seats, built in the prevailing fashion, on the left hand side, and, near the first houses, a new Church in the gothic style, light enough for its small size. Both buildings may be recognized by the reddish colour of their stones in the Spanish [style?]. The façade of the Duke of Lauderdale's castle, built in the modern style, is located at the end of that street. The castle is supposed to overlook the sea, but I have not visited it.

The harbour is of little importance, with a few ships, and the sea breaks right at the foot of the houses. It is to that small town that Queen Mary Stuart withdrew after her unfortunate wedding with Bothwell.

We leave for Edinburgh. The mountains on the left become more remote; the plain, which is well cultivated, widens up. After a short distance we reach the village of Prestonpans, famous for the first battle which was fought and won there by Prince Charles Stuart, nicknamed "the Pretender". The position is well chosen on both sides. The Highlanders, weaker in numbers, but well determined, crossed over the stream and the swamp during the night, and rushed onto the English, breaking through them and causing great carnage. The rout was horrendous and the victory total.

The road is full of charm, like the beautiful drive of a park. Country houses and their parks may be seen now and then. The sea appears, first close by and then further away again, hidden by broken ground as we come near the Gulf of Edinburgh. One can see the coast on the other side, and two enormous rocks at the Gulf's entrance. Addington, a small town with a mediocre number of houses but with a fair number of trees. Musselburg, more lively.

Here we are in Edinburgh. We cross two railway lines. The sea is breaking near the road. The stones have a [...] bluish colour, and are used for the buildings and the roads alike.

Edinburgh

We enter the city at 2.30 pm. We can see in the distance Arthur's Seat and Salisbury Craigs or rocks, Carlton hill, Admiral Nelson's monument, Leith, the high and the low part of the city, the castle, and, as we come in, Holyrood. We shall visit all of this in detail after getting rid of the black dust which has covered us since yesterday, when the wind turned from the North. That wind is cold and bitter, and we have kept the coach windows closed, and so have had no fresh air to breathe for two days. It is true that our path heads continuously northwards.

Visit to Monsignore Cameron, Bishop of Edinburgh. We would have liked to get information about the Hebrides from Bishop MacDonald, but he has left two days before for his Bishopric, in the island of [...] in Loch Linnhe[1]. All the islands of the Hebrides pertain to his diocese, and he knows them perfectly. We shall go and visit him so that he may accompany us, as he promised in Paris, for in these islands only Gaelic is spoken.

Mgr. Cameron, an old man of 76 years, was sitting at a table upon which was an enormous bottle, of the type we commonly call a "Dame-Jeanne"[2] and had as guests a Lady and two Gentlemen whom I took to be Bishops[3]. He was warned of my visit by his Coadjutor, whom I met and left in Paris. I had also met Mgr. Cameron in Paris, and recognized him by his nose.

He reminded me that I had invited him to dinner, but that he had been unable to accept because of his departure. He told me that the first Mass tomorrow (Sunday) would be at 9.am, and we intend to go there.

Chapel of Holyrood. At the Palace's entrance, stands a Scottish guard, with its red uniforms and tartan trews. We are shown into a dark, square-shaped yard, around which is

---

1   *This island is likely to be Lismore, historic seat of the Bishopric of the Isles.*

2   *Dame-Jeanne: Demijohn*

3   In England and in Scotland, the Catholic clergy wore secular clothes.

a [...] simple looking building, decorated with turrets on each of its external angles. Over the façade stands a little dome, culminating in a crown (See map and description). We enter via the Chapel's kitchens [?], through a small door. One is, first of all, brought to notice the Arms of Scotland, on a wooden shield carved 700 years ago, and then one observes that the Chapel's ceiling, far too massive, has caved in. There are pilasters of various heights, supported by small columns in the Gothic style. The transept crossing at the back is whole, without any stained glass windows.

A vault, shut by a padlock, contains the remains of the Scottish Kings, as well as those of various other people, including Darnley,[4] murderer of Rizzio and secretary to the unfortunate Queen Mary Stuart and the Duchess of Gramont, wife of the present Duke, Captain of the Guards of the French King Charles X.[5] These graves are scattered in the Chapel, and one treads over them.

In another corner, stands a side Chapel. This, so we are told, is the site of the confessional used by Queen Mary Stuart. As we leave the Chapel, raising our eyes, we see the walled door of her tribune. This is where I bought a brochure with a description.

Another guide brought us to visit the galleries where the portraits of the Kings of Scotland are stored and [...], painted at various epochs by daubers, and which would hardly be accepted nowadays as shop signs.

Then we visit the apartments which were once occupied by Monsieur, the present day Charles X.[6] They look shabby, and the furniture even more so. The view is grim. We have asked about and searched for the door upon which the word "Monsieur" was written, which a visitor claimed to have seen in 1824, but in vain, as the guide does not know anything. The

---

4   The Queen's husband. He died himself of a violent death.
5   She apparently died during the emigration. *[the "emigration" de-scribes the period between the French Revolution and the end of the Na-poléonic Empire when the French monarchy had to live in exile].*
6   « Monsieur » *is King Louis XVIII of France's brother. During the emigration (see previous footnote), he lived in exile in Holyrood surrounded by a small court.*

room, which was used as a kitchen for this apartment has been changed into a Throne room, where the present King George the IVth held Levées, when he visited Edinburgh. His Majesty stayed a few miles from the town.

From there, we go to the apartment of the unfortunate Queen Mary Stuart, which is small and dark. Both the tapestry on the Queen's bed and the furniture come from the Gobelins, at the roots of such art. All of it is worm-eaten and in tatters, and so is the cover over her bed, though it is still white enough.[7] We see a work-box made by her own hands, a flat basket, and portraits in various costumes.

As we leave the Palace of Holyrood, the Scottish Guard forms up and the sentry presents arms. More than likely the local servant, who follows me, would have told them who I was.

The visit to the Chapel and Palace is organised in four sections, exploited by four women or more. They are young persons, new in their charge, who dish out explanations just as parrots, and are hard to follow. They are not slow in making some money from the visitors, who must have a well-laden purse and be prepared to dig into their pockets.

We visit the main districts and streets of the Old Town, with the purpose of going up to the Castle, but I am affected by some rather strong colic which compels me to return to the hotel. However, it diminishes and ceases nearly as soon as we have crossed the bold and high bridge which links the two towns. There was once a loch there, which has since dried up and become a fine meadow, but the building craze which has seized Paris and London as well as Edinburgh, has brought on the building of fine houses on its surroundings, amongst which are some squares well planted with trees.

We have walked the three big and magnificent streets which run in parallel in the second town, all three from different architects. The streets are large and spacious, [...] and take the shapes of squares and gardens, either for the pleasure of the eye, for the enjoyment of the inhabitants, and also for their health

---

7   Apparently made of silk ?

with the circulation of vast amounts of air. The parallel streets are uniform and flat, but the transversal ones follow a sharp slope. The pavement is laid with beautiful flagstones. All the openings and all the streets benefit from theatrical views of the old town and of the rock upon which the Castle is built.

The main streets are Queen Street – where I am housed –, Princes Street and George Street. The latter is superb. At its Western end lies an elegant church with fine architecture, and on the other side is a beautiful circus with a garden and, planted in its midst, a column with grooves just as high as that of the Place Vendôme, but without any ornaments.[8] At the top is a walkway with a statue of Lord Melville, who is supposed to crown it.

A few years ago, houses in Queen's Street were very expensive, but nevertheless highly sought after, for their view was towards the north, to the Highlands of Scotland, Leith, the gulf of the Frith of Forth,[9] the shores and the monument to the Navy. Since then a range of houses has been built which has obliterated this superb view.

19ᵗʰ of June

We have begun this day by hearing Mass. Another small church, a Catholic one, and the only one in Edinburgh which is also a cathedral. A very simple, low building, without spires or steeple, built in the gothic taste. Bishop Cameron was expecting us at the gate and, having offered us the Holy water, brought us to a pew located in the Choir. The altar is decorated by a wooden panelling sculptured in the gothic style, with a little painting, rather poor in quality, depicting the descent from the cross. No nave, and in consequence, no cross with the choir; a pretty little organ-chest in golden copper on the other side, while closed pews fill up the whole building. The priest who celebrates the low mass does so conscientiously, which means

---

8   A Paris monument, the Vendôme column was built with the bronze from the guns captured by the French army at the battle of Austerlitz, and crowned by a statue of Napoléon.

9   Sic. The Marshal regularly confuses Frith and Firth.

at length. There was a fair crowd, including many soldiers led by a non-commissioned officer.

As we went out, the Bishop introduced me to a number of persons of rank bearing my name, who later came to visit me. The weather is overcast and cold, with small rain which continued, increasing in strength till three o'clock, thus preventing us from going out. Mr. MacDonald Buchanan (who sent me, in 1814 or 1815, an abstract of my family's genealogy), and his brother, Mr. MacDonald of Staffa, came to see us. They gave us the information which I needed to go to South Uist, where they were born. The latter offered to accompany me, which I accepted. We decided to rendez-vous at Fort William, on the Caledonian Canal, on our way back from Inverness, which we must visit.

The former begged us to come to dinner with his family on Wednesday the 22nd, with Sir Walter Scott, who has been away from Edinburgh for the last few days, on urgent business. I was planning to leave the town on that very day. Sir Walter Scott, knowing from London that I was planning to stay for only three days, had asked me not to leave. The desire which I had to meet this famous author brought me to comply with Mr MacDonald Buchanan's request.

We went to visit Lady Sinclair and the family of Sir John, whom I met in London,[10] and who wrote to her to invite us. He asked for herself and her daughters to be dressed in the Highland garb, to invite dancers from that country, and to offer us lunch, dinner or tea as we may wish. I preferred the last option, and only with her family, between 8 and 9 o'clock in the evening.

From there, we went to visit Sir William Arbuthnot, former Lord Provost of Edinburgh. I had been acquainted with his brother in Paris in 1814 or 1815, and met him again in London. Lady Arbuthnot insisted that we stay for dinner, but I refused, and only accepted tea with her family. Her situation is similar to mine, for she has recently lost a dear daughter, but it could not be worse than mine, since the loss of my dear and lamented

---

10   At Sir Archibald MacDonald's dinner.

Ernestine is for me the cause of poignant pains.

Visit to the MacDonalds. The elder, Buchanan, introduced us to his daughter whom I mistook for his wife, of whom he had not told us anything, and to a young and charming Miss MacDonald, very pretty, with a white complexion, magnificent fair hair, a slender waist, tall enough and beautifully shaped, but all these agreements wasted by a rather nonchalant and contemptuous expression. Also, we were introduced to three Scotsmen born in the same island as my father, South Uist.

A third town is being constructed below the second one, on the way to Leith. Various parts have already been completed. It will be even more beautiful than the second one, and far superior to it. It will be decorated by a magnificent circus or crescent on a similar pattern. This architectural innovation (just as the indentations of the place Vendôme) is in very good taste. We saw the first ones in Bath.

I asked who would live in all these houses in the second and the third town, having noticed the presence of many signs marked "To Let". They are busy building and decorating, but the street's poor pavement is being neglected. However, I have noticed in some of the streets of the third town that some parts are built like roads in such a soft and thin way, much as Regent Street in London. It is to be hoped that this system is generalised.

20th of June.

We were supposed to begin our errands today at around 11 o'clock, but I was told that a Scottish regiment was due for inspection at the Castle a 10 a.m, so we made arrangements to attend. However, because of the delays with our breakfast and our carriage, as well as some visits which occurred, the regiment had already been disbanded when we arrived; the officers and sergeants having to go the races in Musselburgh to do some recruiting.

The Castle is built in various stages right on the crest of the rock, rendering it formidable and threatening to the three towns, which it could destroy should there be a revolt.[11] The position is picturesque as seen from below, from the North, South and East. The Western side is spoilt by the building of a large construction which is used for barracks. Climbing through the Old Town, which is also picturesque from these three sides, we saw some old houses, as well as some new ones with eleven storeys. We went round the terraces and platforms, and the view is remarkable on all sides. One can see the mountains of Stirling and Loch Lomond, the Gulf of Edinburgh, and a far stretch of land, with many diverse panoramas.

I did not care much about the military details, but, out of politeness, raised a few questions to the Interim Commander, as well as some about the Scottish regiment to the Major who had the courtesy to accompany us.

We were shown a small room where James the First was born,[12] and, below, in a room lit by four lamps, and surrounded by an iron cage, lay the Crown, Sceptre and Rod of Justice of the Kings of Scotland, which were found 6 or 7 years ago in a big wooden chest buried a few feet below the location of this iron contraption. These precious items, hidden for more than a century, had been sought after for a long time, and their discovery was made possible, partly thanks to legend and partly to notes which had been left in the Archives Room.

As we left the Castle, we went past the charity institution which cares for and teaches the sons of Scottish sailors who have been killed or badly wounded in battle. It appeared to us that these children were gathered on some meadows for an inspection of some sort. Then we passed the Hospital. We entered the Museum, which also hosts the University. Elegant buildings are being raised, and old ones, which are an obstacle to the latter, are being razed.

The room on the ground-floor hosts stuffed animals, and

---

11   In 1745, Prince Charles-Edward army did not manage to take it [the Castle].

12   John Stuart, son of King Robert, was kept as a prisoner in England as from the age of twelve by Henri the IV, Duke of Lancaster. His captivity lasted [...] He was an enlightened and accomplished Prince, protective of the lower classes in his Kingdom, and who died murdered through a conspiracy in his own Kingdom.

above that are horned-species, especially those of Scotland. Above is a gallery where, in the recesses, the smaller bird species have been classified, but I did not climb there. I forgot to say that the large ones are stored with the animals. The ones with the richest feathers are in a room on the left. The professors [...*here a few lines of the manuscript are missing*].

It is in that room that I offered him four silver medals of varied sizes. One depicted the coronation of Charles X, who lived in the Holyrood Palace during his exile, under the title of Monsieur, the second showed his coronation and the third one, his enthroning. On the obverse of each was a profile of the King. The fourth medal showed the first scene, but was very small.

The professors have been very touched by this gift. These are the first medals given to the Museum, and a beginning for its collection. The Museum room is new, elegant and well decorated with grooved pilasters with ornaments. It is a miniature museum, which will obviously grow up with time.

From there, we have walked around some areas of the two towns, have visited shops and made some purchases. Then we went to see the jails, which have been built according to some new model which makes the guardian's surveillance easier. The part we have seen can hold three hundred prisoners. It is used for offences such as vagrancy and robbery, and there were 120 prisoners that day, both men and women; more of the latter.

The body of building is circular, with a number of floors. Sexes are separated and prisoners work with their hands. Each parlour contains three or four persons. These rooms draw their light from the yard, itself lit from above through stained-glass. Facing this circular building, in its midst, is a small, similarly shaped room, lit by small and narrow openings such as loopholes, from which the guards may see the prisoners without being seen. At the bottom of the yard is a round wheel which is turned by recalcitrant prisoners who do not wish to work. This punishment is insignificant, and they are looking for some ways to make use of it.

Behind the circular building, and on every floor, there is a small corridor. Beyond it are the cells in which the prisoners are locked every night, one per cell. The only furniture is a bed, with a bible on it. I forgot to say that inside the yard, right in its midst, lies a pulpit where a chaplain officiates every Sunday.

As we left the jail, we went up Calton Hill on foot, the carriage path being obstructed by the proposed constructions. The old observatory and the new one are on the North and West of the hill. A rather heavily built column, made even more massive by [...] is dedicated to the memory of Admiral Nelson's victories. I must say that I was much more interested in the view, than in this column, which is there to celebrate our maritime defeats and disasters. It is the view from that hill top that makes up the Edinburgh panorama that I'll see in London. All the viewpoints are admirable. Holyrood and its ruined chapel are in the background, as is the Old Town, and Salisbury and Arthur's Craigs.[13] On a slope of the latter, a footpath has been cut, in order that one can climb to the top more easily.

The rain has surprised us as we climbed down Calton Hill. We have walked past the door of Sir Walter Scott, who is away, and from thence gone to Mrs MacDonald's, sister of Mr. MacDonald Buchanan and Mr. MacDonald of Staffa. There we have found a young and charming Miss MacDonald, their niece, whose father, a Colonel in the Artillery, is presently posted in Ireland. We have come home for dinner quite tired. A delegation from the Highlander's Society for Agriculture, Industry and Trade was introduced to us by the French Consul, Mr Mafrelot. I kept the latter for dinner.

At 9.pm we went to Milady Sinclair to spend the evening and have tea. She and her daughters were dressed as Highland women, with dresses, shawls and hats of silk or wool. Miss MacDonald was there; and so were Sir William and Lady Berkeley; Sir William being director or inspector with the Customs; two of their daughters, one of whom was very pretty; the mother, who is niece to the Earl of Liverpool, and other Ladies and Gentlemen whose names I cannot remember. At 10.pm, we were brought into a dining room for supper, where

13   Rocks.

there was everything, except the tea for which I had been invited. Miss MacDonald played Scottish airs on the harp, with Miss Sinclair on the piano forte.

As we were about to leave, around 12 o'clock, the Sinclair Ladies asked me to write my name in an enormous in-folio register, so as to have a piece of writing from me. I did so, with a sentence describing the evening's agreements, which seemed to please the family a lot and, which, so I was told, will delight Sir John Sinclair upon his return.

I think I mentioned that I met and left in London one of the members of the Highlander's Society for Agriculture, Industry and Trade. He sent me a lithographed map of Scotland printed on canvas to help me in my travels. I had no need for it, having one already, but I was told that a refusal would offend him, so I thanked him for it.

21st of June.

Visits start early, with Lieutenant-Colonel MacDonald of Clanranald, uncle of Sir Archibald. He saw me in Paris in 1787. Then comes Captain Wright of the English Royal Navy, who has been asked by Lord Melville to put a Cutter of the Customs & Excise at my disposal for my trip to the Hebrides.

I visited the Law Courts, once the seat of the Scottish Parliament. I was shown into the main hall, which is filled with people in motion, not unlike the Stock Exchange. They are litigants, petitioners, lawyers, clients, visitors. In a corner is a judge in full regalia, who listens to the development of a court case's first hearing.

The ceiling of that room is remarkable. It is made of wooden boxes [...?] detached by groups and holding each other [...?]. I am shown into two Chambers where five Judges are sitting, and their President asks me to sit beside them. I stay for a few moments. There is some pleading going on, and I don't understand a thing.

From there to the library, where there are some low lying unlit rooms, probably just as obscure as most of the books they contain. Then, a very beautiful ship-shaped gallery, well

143

lit, but where the architectural features occupy the space which should belong to books. I am shown a number of manuscripts from the XIVth century, and in another room, two other manuscripts from the Xth, all well written. The former are written in story-teller's ink, with large gold and blue majuscules. Last but not least, the Charters of the Scottish Kings, and an undated, autographed letter from Queen Mary Stuart to her mother-in-law,[14] written in French in the diplomatic style, as it is an official letter.

Some travellers have said that Edinburgh's new towns resemble Athens, but they look more like the Parthenon. This town has produced, and still produces now, some great men and many scientists. Leith, where we are going to, must be its Piraeus. It used to be a village full of fishermen, but today, it has the beginnings of a town,[15] linked to the others by a long street which was once only a track. The harbour has docks and many ships. There are plans for it to become a military harbour. Most of the trade is with the Baltic and the North. Whale fishing employs a lot of sailors.

Newhaven & Edinburgh

Further out lies Newhaven, where one goes for sea baths. There is a multitude of small houses with their gardens for Edinburgh's rich merchants. In a few years' time, Leith and Newhaven will become one with that famous town (Edinburgh). In the latter location is the first suspended bridge, a kind of jetty over the water which facilitates the boarding of the steamboats which continuously criss-cross the sea. This bridge, built for pedestrians, is about 500 to 600 French feet long. It is supported by pillars and attached to the shore, the first part being more prone to oscillations than the rest. I went right to its end. Three stairs lie at the bottom of the platform to facilitate

---

14   Her mother, the Dowager Queen Marie of Lorraine, Regent of Scotland during Mary Stuart's minority.

15   The Marshal considers Edinburgh as being composed of three towns, the old one and the two new ones. He uses alternatively the singular and plural to describe it.

boarding, and they are used according to the wind's direction.

Coming back to town, we stopped at the new Botanic Gardens. Blossoming rhododendron prevails. This garden is not finished yet, but perfectly drawn in that style which the English cherish, and kept to the point of perfection with a great variety of flowers and shrubs. Fair sized trees have been transplanted there with the use of machines, and seem to have settled well. There is a great hall for lectures on botany, and greenhouses for the exotic plants from both the East and West Indies. Two greenhouses are kept for the various species of heather from the Cape of Good Hope: they are infinitely varied and have flowers of all shapes and colours.

From this garden one has a delightful view of Edinburgh. It is one of the most magnificent panoramas that one may see, and it is more than likely that it will be eventually reproduced as a drawing.

I finished my day with a real tea at Sir William Arbuthnot's. Met there Sir Liston[16] [?], who had come to see me in the morning, as well as Milady, both very pleasant and full of wit. He is well known for his merits, and for his embassies at Constantinople and The Hague, where they met Mr and Mrs de Sémonville,[17] and General Andréossy, of whom they spoke with great eagerness. I also saw Sir David Nederburn, friend of the Countess of Gontant, and Lady Clarke, a Stuart enthusiast, whom I had met that morning. Prince Charles was under her roof[18] the very day she was born in 1745, and left a white cockade there which she has always kept. She gave me two white roses from a bunch she held in her hand, and reminded me that tomorrow was the very anniversary of the birth of that unfortunate Prince, an event which she celebrates every year.[19]

---

16 Obviously the British Diplomat Sir Robert Liston (1742-1836).

17 Mother-in-Law of Marshal MacDonald, who had betrothed in second wedlock her daughter from a first marriage, Mlle de Montholon, widow of General Joubert.

18 At her mother's, probably ?

19 Niall MacKenzie, in a critique of the first edition of this book, remarks that this interpretation is erroneous, since the Prince was born on the 31st of December. This celebration might have commemorated the birth of the Prince's father, since the Old Chevalier was born on the 10th of June

There were also other people whose names I cannot remember, except Miss MacDonald Buchanan Robertson of Kinloch Moydart. Milady Arbuthnot does not speak French.

22nd of June.

22nd of June.

I spend all the morning writing, receiving or making visits. Miss Louisa Isabelle MacDonald, daughter of the Artillery Colonel, and niece of Mrs MacDonald Buchanan and Staffa, sends a sketch-book of autographs which is all white. They say it is a third volume. I write two phrases, but I cannot remember what they were.

At 7 o'clock, dinner at MacDonald Buchanan's, where I meet Sir Walter Scott. He is 55 years old, but looks 60. His face is handsome and fresh, but cold. Head as that of Titus, sparse hair, white, same as the eyebrows; small and witty eyes, height 5 feet and 6 to 7 inches. He limps, from an accident sustained during his youth.

We swap a few compliments. He speaks French well. I was told that he does not admit to the authorship of any of the books published (since) under his name, and I am advised to speak only vaguely about it. I think that I even did not mention anything. That very day "The Crusades", by the author of Waverley[20] were published. No one in Edinburgh doubts that he is the author of this new descriptive and romantic style that we all know.

We move to the table. Five to six men, and half as many women, all in the Highland dress, and more of both kinds arrive after dinner. It is the anniversary of Prince Charles Edward's birth, and all these people wear a white rose.[21] Long dinner, fine fare, though in the English style. We remain at the

---

1688 Old Style, which translates into 20th of June according to the Gregorian calendar. However, a two day gap still remains to be bridged. See *Scottish Gaelic Studies*, Volume 25, p 359.

20   History of the time of the crusades. [probably "The Talisman", which was published in 1825]

21   This memory survived 40 to 50 years after the death of Prince Charles Edward. The Cardinal of York, his brother, last representative and heir to the line of Stuart died in 1807 during the Napoléonic Empire.

table 3 hours and a half. After the sweets, the ladies withdraw, bottles are passed around and things start to get animated. Sir Walter Scott then becomes lively, and takes part in the merriment. Three Highlanders from the islands are brought in, and they sing some old gothic songs. The guests provide a supporting chorus, and Sir Walter Scott distinguishes himself. These songs are curious, the performers warm up, and seem to bicker amongst themselves as would do street or market porters engaged in a squabble.

At long last, the coffee is brought; we rise and join the ladies. There was quite a crowd in the sitting-room. I am introduced to the newly arrived, most of them MacDonalds, men or women, in the Highland dress. The men wear the regular garb of their name, the women silk or tartan dresses or scarves. One of them touches the harp,[22] the other plays the piano. The singers from the Highlands are brought back, and after the first song, a repeat of the one heard at dinner, I withdraw at 11pm to have tea with Milady Nederburn, whose husband is the director or inspector for the mail post. She has been a friend of the Vicomtesse de Gontant for twenty years.

Strawberries are served, the tea being taken. Only five to six people. They offer to visit the park and the castle of Hopetoun tomorrow, and to have lunch with us there. I agree.[23]

23rd of June.

We leave Edinburgh at 7 o'clock. Our travel companions are ready and with us. Sir David Nederburn climbs into the coach with me; Couëssin in Milady's calash with a young man, Mr Dundas [?] , nephew of Lord Melville, and a young lady recently arrived from Paris, where she was a pensioner at the Sacré-Coeur's convent to learn French, which she speaks passably.

Sir Charles [**Sir David?**] points out the viewpoints, the

---

22   Old expression.
23   The Marshal was leaving Edinburgh the next day. One will re-member that he had postponed his departure to have dinner with Sir Walter Scott. The castle of Hopetoun must have been on his road.

castles and the country houses and provides me with their names, which I do not memorize. He has little French. We cross an immense park and pass by a castle named Dalmeny, which is a construction dating back from the times of James VIth and Ist of England. It belongs to Lord Rosberry. It is located near the Frith of Forth.[24] The view is magnificent. It can be seen from Leith. Broken ground, beautiful trees, culture [...] charming road, which we leave to enter the park of Lady Hopetoun. In a similar position, the castle is a beautiful palace. We enter. Her Ladyship, in deep mourning, welcomes us. She lost her husband in Paris, 18 months ago, and an expression full of melancholy stamps her face. She is the sister of Sir David Nederburn. She introduces me to 7 or 8 children, amongst which are two girls of a young age. All have red hair. Then she introduces us to another Lady, Lady Falkirk, who has two daughters with her, about 5 and 9 years old.

Our arrival causes Lady Hopetoun some sensation. We leave her to visit the premises. There are fine rooms, many paintings, some of which are remarkable. We have lunch and take our leave.[25]

Linlithgow

We visit Linlithgow, which is a posting-house. We are shown the Town House, recently built, and a modest building. A full-portrait of General Hopetoun is exhibited [...], a mark of gratitude by the local inhabitants. The Church, praised by the parishioners, has nothing remarkable.

We are led to the ruined castle of the Kings of Scotland, destroyed in 1745 by the English troops. It is there that Mary Stuart was born. We are shown the room as well as the apartment. One has to believe this and see it with the eyes of the faithful.

We get through Falkirk. Within a mile from the town, on the left hand side, the field where the Battle of Falkirk, won by

---

24   *Obvious distortion of the "Firth of Forth". As will be seen later in the text, the Marshal confuses the Firth and the Forth.*

25   The Marshal leaves with Mr Couëssin to continue his journey.

Prince Charles on the 28th of January 1746, took place is being pointed to us. Further away on the right hand side, on a hillock, is the ruined tower where King Robert the Bruce stayed.

Stirling.

We discover Stirling, and its castle, on an elevated position, in the style of Edinburgh's. There we find Lieutenant-General Graham, the Governor, who has been warned of our visit. He comes to meet us and greets us warmly. He introduces us to his wife and daughter, and invites us to dinner, which I decline. From the terrace of his apartment one has an exquisite view of the Frith flowing through a plain, or rather a large basin through which the Frith winds. In the background lies the chain of high mountains of the Highlands, ended on the left hand side by Loch Lomond.

In that plain, from the point where we stand, one can see, a short distance away, three hillocks of basaltic rock, covered with coppice woods, as if thrown by hand at the foot of a chain of mountains, and in the midst of it all, Sir Abercromby's castle. In the far distance, on the right hand side, at the end of this beautiful range, we can see the castle which is inhabited by the General Count of Flahault.[26]

We take leave of the governor and arrange to rendez-vous with him in a fortnight, at Ross, on the banks of Loch Lomond where he will come [where he comes from?] at Mrs MacDonald Buchanan. He provided me with some explanations about the Battle of Bannockburn, in the XIVth century, which still lingers in the memory of the Scottish people who won it over the English.

Mr MacDonald Staffa, our guide for the islands, arrives from Edinburgh. He is very busy with a gathering of some seven to eight hundred highlanders who will congregate tomorrow to celebrate, with a banquet and with games, the anniversary of the battle won by Wallace, general of the King of Scotland. He arranges for a piper, a driver and a [...] of children dressed

---

26   *Ex-General of Napoléon, who married Mercer Elphinstone in 1817.*

149

in the Highland way to pass under my windows.

Staffa would like to keep me to witness this celebration, but I intend to leave for Perth and spend most of the day and night with Mr MacDonald Saint Martin, a few miles away from this town. The road from Edinburgh is remarkably pleasant. One frequently meets with the Frith of Forth. This countryside is undulated, wooded, [...], with magnificent viewpoints.

24th of June

From Stirling to Perth.

Departure for Perth at 6 o'clock. We are entering small mountains. It is still the Lowlands of Scotland. The countryside changes in outlook, and is little wooded. Clumps of green trees are scattered here and there, but the land is nevertheless cultivated, with some rather sad-looking thatched cottages.

As we leave the village of Ardoch, a Roman camp from Agricola's army is pointed out to us. Entrenchments and ditches can be clearly distinguished: they could perfectly belong to the last centuries, and be Saxon, Danish or English, but we believe in this centuries-old tradition and faith.

The woman who normally shows these venerable antiquarian relics and provides explanation was not at her post, so we only saw them from the coach, but they are right next to the road.

Since Stirling and especially during the last ten miles, we have met with some Scotsmen dressed in the Highland way, on their way to the celebration on foot or horse, as well as women dressed in their plaids.

Two miles from Criffe, on the left hand side, the castle of the old Dukes of Perth, whose role was so great in the 1745 revolution, is pointed out to us. This castle belongs today to Lord Guild [?] who has married a grand-daughter of the last Duke. This castle is called Drummond Castle.

We lunch at Crieffe, small town through which the Av... [?] flows. Our host takes us through his garden across a hilly pasture. He shows us some viewpoints, and tells us about the

150

loch which bears the same name as the river, which can be seen running through the mountains. Behind them lies this loch which is famous because of the strife between the Breadalbanes and the MacNabs regarding some graveyards on the islands.

As we leave Crieffe, we follow Sir David Beard's park, the castle being pleasantly situated at the foot of the mountain. Milady has given her permission for the travellers to cross the park, but we did not make use of it.

Before entering Perth, we see, with the eyes of the believer, the so-called Royal Castle of Schonne.[27]

It is said that the Romans of Agricola, when seeing Perth, exclaimed "Ecce Roma". There might be some resemblance with the surrounding of the Tibre River.[28] The city was built a mile further away on the hill, but there are no remains of it left. The new town on the Tay is pleasantly built in the vast plain which surrounds it.

Perth

No relays to the number of seven [?] till Inverness, and it will take three days to get there with the same horses. I am dumbfounded. I had been assured that these 115 or 117 miles could be crossed in two days. I urge our host to send horses in relay, or to have some sent from Inverness. He is suddenly inspired and says that stage-coaches do not work on Sunday. He is going to write to his friends to give us relay horses. This suits us perfectly well: the steamboat will leave on Tuesday for Fort William on the Caledonian Canal. By arriving on Sunday, we shall have the Monday to visit the battlefield of Culloden.[29]

I had an invitation from Mr MacDonald St Martins,[30] lawyer in Edinburgh, but, without my knowledge, plans had been laid

---

27   Read Scone.

28   *It must be recalled that the Marshal (then a general) was for a while governor of Rome during the campaigns of Italy, under the French Republic. He is consequently in a good position to make comparisons between Perth and Rome.*

29   Culloden, the fateful battle where fortune eschewed Prince Charles Edward Stuart.

30   A few miles from Perth.

for me to remain in Stirling to see the games; getting to Perth only that night, and spending the day after at St Martins'. It was fine to lose without any necessity, half a day in the first one of these towns, but this honest gentleman was consequently only expecting me the next day, despite the fact that we were due to sleep at St Martins. I preferred to have a bed prepared here (in Perth), the more so since one has to walk back on its own tracks from St Martins, which is 5 or 6 miles from Perth. Being told of my plan, this gentleman nevertheless received us cordially. He had invited a few of his friends for the next day, and I am annoyed with this inconvenience.

Schomme Castle.[31]

Before going to his place, we go to visit Schomme, which belongs to Lord Mansfield, who married the daughter of the Archbishop of York. This castle has been completely rebuilt anew, and one can only see a part of the older one inside. One hundred and three master suites. Beautiful rooms used as dining rooms. Lounges, one with fabric hangings from Lyon, and upholstered furniture from Beauvais. Some paintings and portraits by masters. A statue attributed to Cannova. A musical gallery, though with a low ceiling, and narrow, and at one of its extremities a fine organ-case.

Large library with many books. Milady has her own. Browsing through some of the shelves, I noticed the works of the wise Delphine, and the *Almanach des gourmands* [32] right above Mme de Sévigné. I leave my visiting card in Milord's apartment.

Fine views over the Tay. In the park, two small pieces of artillery, at each end of a terrace, above the external wall.

We make our way back to Saint Martin right at the entrance of the city [of Perth], not far from a long bridge high up over the Tay. Located five or six miles from Perth on the road to

---

31   *See footnote supra*
32   The Gourmet's Alamanach. The "wise Delphine" probably refers to a book from Mme de Staël, romantic writer and opponent to Napoléon, which was published in 1802.

Aberdeen, Saint Martin's house is a square building, built by the father of Mr MacDonald, who was well acquainted with mine. His portrait is in the sitting room, which is well lit with fine carpets and some heavy wall-hangings.

The master of the house, Mr MacDonald Saint Martins, greets us with great cordiality. Some time later, we proceed to dinner. There are four of us. He had introduced us to one of his friends, the others he had invited for the next day only. I am much annoyed with this mishap which deprives me of the opportunity of meeting them. Our host, as an open-hearted Scotsman, leaves us free to make our own arrangements. He has had beds prepared for us.

As we leave the table, he shows us his house, and his library, in which there is a gun given to his father by Prince Charles.[33] He shows us a sword which his grandfather bore, and which killed many Englishmen, or so he believes. We then visited his park, with well kept kitchen-gardens, fine fruit-walls and one of the green-houses is already providing some red grape, which is ripe enough and has a very nice taste, as well as white Muscat wine.

At 9.30 in the evening, we take our leave. I promise to return to see him if I make a new trip to the Highlands, which I intend to. Our host seems to be about 50, with a tall size and a fine figure.

We return to our inn: a Free-mason was on sentry-duty at the door of a large sitting-room where a fair crowd was gathered to celebrate the summer's Saint John's day, which is the association's high day. I took great care not to make myself known, being the Deputy Grand Master of the Society in France.[34] Our host, who is a member, comes in decorated with all the paraphernalia. He seems to have carried quite a few toasts. He hands me a card from Sir David Nederburn, who invites us to go for lunch the next day to Lord Grey.[35]

---

33   Prince Charles Edward (the Knight of Saint Georges), nicknamed "the Pretender" by the English.

34   Which was then only an open ("liberal") association, and which is still so in England where the Grand Master is a Prince of the Royal family.

35   *There is a confusion – either in the original text, or in the transcrip-*

We accept after the hostel owner Mr Kengrew [?] has told us that it will take us 7 hours to be driven to Carnacavdock, with two-and-a-half hours to freshen the horses at Dunkeld and Blair, and back in Perth at 11 o'clock. Anyhow, we are expecting MacDonald of Staffa, who stayed at Stirling to chair the celebrations of the battle of Bannockburn,[36] which was fought near that town.

25th of June

We make our way to Kinfauns Castle. We follow the left bank of the Tay and enter the park, two or three miles from the town. Sir David Nederburn welcomes us as we alight from our carriage. I am very surprised to enter a house which appears to be so small, with a little door and little staircase. The masters are at prayer. We enter the sitting-rooms which cause me some surprise. They are decorated like Italian palaces with many fine paintings and prints. The whole place looks like a museum. In the largest one there are harps, piano, music and a fine library. The masters arrive and we get acquainted in the most open manner.

Lord Grey[37] is a man aged over 60, small, with a cool, thoughtful and philosophical appearance as he is described. He has two daughters at home, the younger one being pretty enough, the elder very much marked by small-pox.

Milady is a 50 years old woman, and her manners are open, light and cheerful. The whole family speaks little French, the younger daughter more than the others. A friend of their daughters speaks it rather well.

This family has spent seven months in Paris, living close to my own place at the Hotel of Villars......[?]. I had met Milady

tion – between Lord Grey, English Statesman and Prime Minister – and Lord Gray, a Scottish aristocrat, also involved in politics. The Marshal is visiting the latter.

36 Which freed Scotland from the yoke of England. The arrival of Donald, Lord of the Isles, on the battlefield carried the day. King Robert the Bruce, holding his hand, told him "My hope is constant in thee!". These words are the motto of Clan Donald.

37 A Statesman. (see note above).

at the Countess of Gontant's. We renew our acquaintance. We have lunch. Though Lord Grey has many servants, he pours the tea himself, and goes to another table to cut a large slice of roast-beef, which is the basis of our lunch. We talk about the Scots. The dining-room is of fine proportion with many paintings and prints.

As we leave the table, Milady shows me the Lord's workshop. He is [...?] a mechanic. We go to visit the new castle, where work was begun five years ago. It is in the hands of painters and decorators. The external part is in the gothic style, with fine stones of a dark hue. There is a tower in the middle, in the back of the main building. On the left wing, there is a square tower which is less elevated. On the right wing, a heavy and elevated tower.[38]

The entrance will be covered under the curve of an arch. A wag has already said that it will be quite an expensive umbrella. Entrance staircase. First and second halls. Fine ground floor, from the back and from the front.

Milady's boudoir is very large, with a large casement-window jutting out. Milord's cabinet is already partially furnished in the Gothic decorative style. Fine furniture. Statues from Canova. Many busts and statues, purchased during a tour. Fine chimney in marble from Carrare [...]. Sculptured woodwork in the apartments, and the ancestor's coat-of-arms and alliances everywhere.

We did an external tour of the new castle[39] and of the old one.[40] The latter is going to be razed to the ground, and the new one will enjoy its magnificent views. It overlooks the Tay, being quite elevated on the mountain. A small vale, or rather an opening, separates two ranges of rocky mountains which are both picturesque and wild. In front lies the plain, in a basin surrounded by mountains on two or three sides.[41] On the left

---

38   *The transcription of this phrase is uncertain, and peppered with question marks.*

39   Kinfauns Castle.

40   It seems that the relatively small house in which Lord Grey was living then was not the old castle, probably inhabitable. The house where he welcomed the Marshal was probably a temporary dwelling.

41   Graded apparently? *(Uncertain transcription)*

hand side flows the Tay. Three or four vessels sail down it, one of them a steamship. They seem positioned to enhance the perspective.

We wish to leave. Our hosts invite us to walk with them down a fine lane, to a point half-way down the slope, which has viewpoints similar to those seen from the castle, at the end of which lies a delightful thatched cottage which is used by Mylord's factor. At our nearest end is a charming sitting-room decorated with wooden roots, which could be mistaken for petrifications. Very fine view from the casement-window. At last, we part with each other, with a sincere exchange of cordialities from both sides.

The weather is threatening. The rain begins to fall the moment we meet the carriage which was awaiting us at the foot of the hill.

Before entering Perth, we notice to the right of the Tay some fine barracks, which were built for the French prisoners who were remanded there, of which there were some 7000. Further on, the bridge shows its profile and looks light and elegant.

We learnt at Lord Gray's Castle that there were horses in Dunkeld and even at a number of other stations, amongst them Blair. We mention this to our host, who seems rather embarrassed by his ruse to have us bypassing two of these with his own horses. We do not insist over this matter since he has written to the Inverness road, asking them to provide us with those of the stage-coach, which does not work on Sunday.

We leave Perth by half-past-twelve. The road follows the right bank of the Tay for a while. We can see School Castle [?] with its red sandstone, whose low trees and [...] could make one believe that it is a ruin. We enter a pass. The road goes up and down, and the countryside becomes more stern. The rain starts again, but it is just a shower. We keep following the pass which gets narrower. Mountains rise, some with slate and basaltic rocks, others covered with green trees. We descend upon Dunkield, a small town where we cross the river over a fine bridge. This town is surrounded by very high mountains and located in a small basin. It is well built, with an air of prosperity. This is where the Duke of Athole has a castle and where he normally spends three months of the year. He is expected in eight days. I met him in London, at the House of Lords. He is an old man of seventy years, with failing eyesight.

We ask to be driven to that residence. The entry gate is crenellated. We write our names in a visitor's book, as in all the castles we have visited. I am shown the name of the young Viscount de Bourbon-Bousset, husband of the charming Idalie [?]. The gardener is showing us around. On the left hand side are new stables, very fine and in the gothic style, which makes one anticipate something grand for the habitation; but not at all, for it is a house [...] on the external side. The Duke must destroy it, and build something in a style similar to that of the stables in its place.

I thought that we would see the inside of this house, which is located in the midst of a charming garden, diverse and full of flowers. Indeed, after viewing the latter, the gardener takes that direction, but instead shows us a ruined church, an erstwhile catholic cathedral which had 37 successive bishops.

We are taken to the hermitage to see the waterfalls. We walk for quite some time, following the left bank of the river. Rain appears suddenly. We take shelter under a cover facing an embankment. I am very tired, and have a rest. The gardener wants to call for a boat to take us to the other side, to the cascades, but the rain increases. I ask to return by the shortest route, but the pitiless gardener, indifferent to my poor and gouty feet, wishes us to have an idea of this beautiful, but lengthy and narrow, park. He takes us around a circuit of considerable size eventually bringing us back to the gate from whence we started, leaving the castle on the right hand side, which he does not show us. In spite of my ill humour, I have him tipped generously, and leave two cards for the masters of the house. Amongst those fine trees which I noticed, was a superb chestnut tree.

We continue our journey with the same horses, which will take us to Calnacardoch[42] where we shall sleep. As we leave Dunkield, we are shown the [Duke of Athole's] park across

---

42   *Dalnacardoch perhaps ?*

the road. We keep climbing in a narrow glen. The mountains are like those surrounding Dunkield, intended and wooded in a variety of ways, with many new plantations. All this land, for thirty miles, belongs to the Duke of Athole. We climb up and down. We reach Blair, indicated on the map as a burgh, which has apparently only one inn and a hamlet. In front of us, at the foot of the slope, are relay horses which we do not use since ours have been rented to take us for 46 miles.

As we follow our route, we notice, on the left hand side, a church which is being built for Blair and which could become something. Further on, on the right hand side, a castle, white as snow, and a park. It is the Duke of Athole's hunting lodge. The country is sad, the hills less wooded and more rocky, becoming eventually woodless.

We reach Calnacaradoch Inn at eleven o'clock at night. The mountains are flatter and barren. Little night, or hardly any at this time of the year, the more so since we have the new moon.

26th of June

We take some fresh horses and leave at 6 (in the morning). We still have 69 miles to do before we reach Inverness. Relay at [...] and Pittmuir, where we have lunch. This village is not on my map, whereas isolated inns are indicated. The scene of that country is that of rustic desolation, wild, totally barren till Pittmuir. A short distance from that place, on the left hand side, is the castle of Mr MacPherson, the author or translator of Ossian. It is inhabited by his descendants, and overlooks barren hills.

Relay at Vie... [...] Freeburn; of the first place, the still barren hills begin to..[...].[43] All along the road since Dunkield, miserable huts are scattered along the road here and there, a scene of misery. However, no one is begging, but for some children. The people who work on the road live in tents, for the lack of habitation.

---

43   *The transcription is incomprehensible.*

I was forgetting to say that the postillions have shown us a stone in a field, after a narrow pass, which marks the spot where Viscount Dundee[44] was killed in [...]. Sir Walter Scott mentions it somewhere in one of his novels.

The road becomes broader and smoother. We descend for a long time and rather rapidly, going round a mountain. The track is well cut, but the bridge at the bottom of this valley is not broad enough. Postillons in England and in Scotland are bold, but very skilful. Slopes have to be pretty steep to take them at pace and [...] lock. Since I have left France, the brake-block has only been used two or three times.

We have arrived at the Freeburn's Inn. Beautiful team of horses, those of the pole are superb, with their new silver-plated harnesses. We keep going down, go through a pass and climb up again, the valley broadens up and we reach a vast plateau. The mountains recede on the right and left, and we are met with rain now and again. Facing us is a very fine view, with the mountains in the distance, which seem blue, contrasting with the nearest ones, which are covered with black pines mingled with green fields. We keep moving forward and begin to descend, discovering the vast Gulf of Murray facing us, with some mountains in the background and Inverness on the left. The Battlefield of Culloden must not be far off on our right, and the coachmen point it out to us in the distance.

Before reaching this point, we thought we would have to go through the town first, but I notice that it would be a waste of time. I ask the coachmen to take the first road to the right, and tell them that the extra journey will be paid for. We ride for about three miles, and here we are on this very ground which has deprived the House of Stuart, extinct anyhow, from the Kingdom of Scotland forever.

The Cicerone is there, and we tread upon this land soaked

---

44   The famous Graham of Claverhouse, terror of the Prebyterians under Charles the IInd, and who, having taken arms again in 1691 (?) for the Jacobite cause, at the head of most of the Highland Clans, was killed as he won the day over the partisans of the house of Orange; a victory which his death left fruitless.

with the blood of so many MacDonalds.[45] Perhaps am I walking on the same portion of land where my father stood? He was a companion to Prince Charles Edward, and he never left him. We are in front of the Sea and of Aberdeen from whence the English army had landed [?][46] and was arriving with the Duke of Cumberland. These events and their details are all too well-known for me to need to describe them. The conductor explains them in the Gaelic tongue, and shows the location where the Prince stood during the action and the direction he took when he withdrew.

Under our feet is land which has been overturned by sightseers in the hope of finding something. Mr MacDonald of Staffa picks-up a rusty button and even some bones.

Facing the sea, we have on our left hand side the castle which gave its name to the battle. Its field is vast, naked and the land is poor; a chain of mountains lies to our right, pointing in a horizontal direction; a ravine lies below; on our left, the Murray, and behind us, Inverness, where we are going. It is a small town, well-enough built, which seems to be growing. The Caledonian Canal commands the other side of the river.

The packet leaves tomorrow at 4 o'clock in the morning for Glasgow. She will take our carriage to that city, while we will stop in Fort William to proceed by land to [**Torra...**] where I arranged to rendez-vous with the English Excise Cutter which was laid on for our disposal.

In Inverness, I meet Mr Danenant [?].He comes to pay me

---

45   They shed their blood for the Stuart cause in all the other battles at different epochs, the Chief of Clanranald being killed at [...], but at Cullloden, a point of honour prevented them from acting; they did not get the right flank of the army, which was always their position, and sacrificed a cause which was dear to them to their wounded pride. *[it is unclear in the manuscript if the first part of this footnote was written by the Marshal himself, or by his granddaughter, as follows]*
The Marshal's father was attached to the person of Prince-Charles Edward. There is some confusion in the Marshal's mind when it comes to the story of Scotland in these modern times. This can be sufficiently explained by all the great events to which he was himself associated during his career, as well as by the loss that he had just incurred [*the death of his 3rd wife],* and which would have been enough to disturb his memory.
46   *Sic. See Mathilde de Massa's footnote supra.*

a visit, and will leave tomorrow with the stagecoach for Perth and Edinburgh. After dinner, that is, past nine o'clock, we went for a tour of the town in a carriage. Nothing remarkable; this is Sunday, all the shops are shut in Scotland, and the observance of that day is strict. We have noticed in our trip, especially today, that Highlanders go quite some distance to attend Church, and that they never fail to do so, whatever the weather, in all seasons.

It is remarkable how all these hills and glens are depopulated. We are told that this is because of emigration to America, or because of the recruiting for the Army and India. The huts, which are scattered here and there, seem really wretched, but nevertheless their inhabitants are dressed well and warmly, and are very clean, especially on Sundays.

The wearing of the Highland dress tends to have lost ground considerably during the last twenty years, that is, since the beginning of communication. Roads, which are pierced with the new system of Mr Macadam are generally very well maintained. So, the digging of canals, the multiplication of schools, the [...] have civilised, and still civilize everyday by putting men in contact with each other and through the exchanges arising from trade.

The wearing of tartan plaids seems to be kept by the women of society, and there are men who have similar coats, but more generally they have a single colour pattern of brown and blue. As for the people, one may still see children wearing the petticoat but hardly any with tartan; as for breeches, waistcoats or jackets, they may be seen here and there. In twenty years, there will be nothing left of it.[47]

All travellers have criticized the fact that women and girls walk with their bare feet, holding their shoes in their hands, even within towns. They are right, and I share this view. This criticism is not directed to the people of society, or to the bourgeoisie, but to the better working-class people, where one may witness well and cleanly dressed persons, with white

---

47   (*At the bottom of this page, a note from Mathilde de Massa*): We must point out that the Marshal was noting very quickly these details and impressions, which often lack in cohesion, and are written as flying notes.

dresses, printed cotton (and even silk), hats with ribbons, shawls and even elegant veils but [..?]

I only saw one, at last, holding an umbrella in her other hand.

I have discussed this custom with various people, who were equally critical of it, but who noticed that it had its uses. When the weather is wet, and tracks are muddy, shoes get wet very quickly; so when women enter a house, they wash their feet and put on their shoes, which are dry, thus preserving themselves from humidity and its consequent illnesses.

Most of the women have rather strong legs and big feet, and this is certainly not due to having them naked, for I have noticed that they were very strong in higher society too. I am hereby talking of the Scottish women only.

27th of June.

Here we are, in the Packet or "Steam Boat", and they are opening the Canal locks. We then enter Loch Neiss which is 24 miles long, and 3 miles wide at its broadest point. About half-way, we see a ruined castle on the right hand-side, and then further away, on the left, a waterfall whose spray may be seen two miles away. The weather is very poor, and no one disembarks to visit it.

We reach Fort Augustus, and the poor weather still prevents me from leaving the packet. The Captain commanding the fort comes to see me. His fort is disarmed. The packet salutes it when entering and leaving the locks, above and below the fort.

Shortly afterwards, we see the house of MacDonnell of Glengarry (I left a couple of cards for him and Milady to the commanding officer of the fort mentioned above). It is simple and modest, a short distance from the old castle, burnt during what is being called the rebellion of 1745. A few miles further on is the tower of the seven heads, as described by Mr Charles Dupin.[48] I think as he does. It is a small tower which, seen from

---

48   Charles Dupin, a French mathematician and Member of the Academy, is the author of a book relating his travels in the British Isles between 1816 and 1819.

the steamer, has the shape of those which can be observed at the top of cathedral towers, especially the one in Yorck. Below, a vault-like entrance, and beyond, a well-built little house.

We have reached the first lock out of seven, before reaching Fort William. We come ashore at that lock-gate, at Neptune's Inn, two miles from the Fort. I must take the road to Araisack, where the cutter is awaiting me. My carriage will go to Glasgow. I take leave of the Scottish travellers. We had our lunch with tea. We have dinner, and I ask for wine to be brought. I raise my glass to the Ladies' health, the Gentlemen raise their glass to mine, to Couëssin's, to that of a Captain of Artillery and to Mr Staffa's. I raise my glass to the health of King George the IVth and it is returned to that of Charles Xth's. I can see that things are warming up, and I desert the table.

Mrs Reed [?] speaks good enough French. She speaks to me, and we engage in conversation. She points out Ben Nevis, in front of the house where the inn is located, that is the dominant [?]. It is the highest mountain in Scotland. It can be seen clearly. Some parts are covered with snow. She tells me that without that snow, this mountain should change ownership, but it never fails to have some.

At the inn, I find a man who has arrived from Arasaik,[49] where he has seen the cutter. The lady who speaks French offers the use of her small carriage to carry my parcels, and a fair number are handed to her. We shall catch up with them the next day, and meanwhile have a good night at the Neptune.

The route followed by the steamer is constantly between two chains of mountains, some of which are wooded. The greatest number, especially those near Fort William, are indented with rocks and bare. Some valleys, which are called Glens in the Gallic language, cut across them. Some huts are scattered here and there, especially facing the south, and henceforth protected from the north, but they look just as miserable as those which we saw between Stirling and the first relay before Inverness.

---

49   Read "Arisaig"

The evening promises to be fine, the mountains have shed the fog. We need fair weather, since we do not have the use of a covered carriage anymore for our land travels.

28th of June.

28th of June.

The morning is superb; that is at 5 am. Ben Nevis and the other mountains are cloudless and the sun is shining brightly. Loch Eil is smooth as a mirror. In the far distance, as if viewed through a sighting glass, one may see the Island of Lismore, and even Bishop MacDonald's house – but as for myself, I cannot see it –.

At 6'oclock in the morning, two gigs, which are some kinds of ...[?] are brought to us. Two people will travel in each one, and we shall drive ourselves. A servant will ride behind us to bring them back from Araiseck to Neptune's Inn.

After having had a first lunch with tea and coffee, we leave by going up Loch Eil, on a fine track which follows it for some miles. This valley is pleasant. We make our way between two chains of mountains, without any form of climbing, and about three and a half hours later, we arrive at the Inn of Glen fenin [?],[50] some twenty miles away from Fort William, at the head of another loch, Loch Sheil. At its mouth, and close to the shore, a small chapel has been built and, next to it, a round tower which is tall and crenellated around its top. It is a memorial to the gathering of all the Chiefs of the Clans, and of their vassals, who served the cause of Prince Charles in 1745. This is where he planted his standards after his landing at Borrowdale. Ten miles further, there is another inn above Loch Maylort.[51]

As we leave the first of those inns, we begin to go up and down, still by a fine road, but the bends are too short and too narrow. Our horse takes fright. The servant rushes forward and holds it back. That would have been my undoing, and that of Auguste,[52] who had taken care of the reins!

---

50   Read "Glenfinnan".
51   Read LochAilort
52   The Marshal's servant, who was with him in the gig, apparently to save him from driving. Mr de Couëssin and Mr MacDonald Staffa must

164

Looking back, one may still see Ben Nevis, as if it was very near. Extraordinary optical effect.

The country becomes more rustic and wild. Barren hills, torrents and waterfalls, falling from the mountain tops right across the road. The valley floors are peatbogs. Some huts are scattered here and there. Meagre cultivations, the main crops being potatoes, which are the staple diet of these poor highlanders. There are small fields of beans, barley, and oats, from which are made the thin girdle-cakes which the lords themselves do not disdain to have served at their table. I tried those of Lord Grey, near Perth. One may find them good, if one is so inclined. They are bland, probably made without yeast or salt. The mountains, in common with all those seen since Stirling, provide grazing to the numerous flocks which wander on their slopes, some owners having up to 5000 [**heads of cattle perhaps?**[53]]. Horses and cattle are on their lower parts, sheep mostly above. The males and the females have twisted horns, those of the former being stronger. Lambs, which I would have guessed were a year to eighteen months of age, are only six to eight weeks old and look fat as our sheep in the Berry.

These sheep seem to be a little wild. Their faces and four legs tend to be black, with a white stripe above the nose. I hardly saw any sheep which were totally black. The wool is smooth and flowing. Shearing has not begun. Their fleeces yield more or less three or four of our pounds, and their flesh has a very good taste. They are left *[to graze]* for three or four years on these hills, then they are sent to the market, and thereafter they go to the lush pastures of England. They stay outdoors all the year round, however, when there is too much snow, they are brought down to these small valleys and given a little grass and salt. They can graze grass under the snow, as long as it is not too thick. These hill-grazing sheep are the richest property of the farmers and landowners. One wrings from the land only what is necessary for the subsistence of the inhabitants, namely potatoes.

---

have been in the other gig.

53   We recall what we have said previously about the Marshal's abreviations.

While the horses are cooling at the second inn, we walk down a slope, to ride again once the horses have caught-up with us. The country gets wilder and wilder during the next few miles, but the road is still fair. The hills begin to be covered with woods. At last, we enter the property of Mr MacDonald of Clanranald.[54] The hills are more and more covered and the track is as the sweep of a park, with woods right and left. A mixture of trees, where the green prevails.

Borrodale and Arisaig.

We soon spot Borrowdale,[55] and stop there. We are at the house of a gentleman bearing the same name as me, called Glen-Alladale. The lady speaks French,[56] and has preceded us, to inform of our arrival. Further down this road, we meet some onlookers. It is Mr MacDonald who welcomes us with his son, a fine young man of thirty, dressed as a highlander and as strong as Hercules. A few miles from that habitation, we had met another gentleman of that name, riding a horse, who lived in another valley.

The Borrowdale MacDonald introduces us to his family, who are in their best attire: four young ladies, and their mother, who has been suffering from rheumatism these ten years, and has not been able to stand or walk for all that time. The young ladies are dressed in the French way. They have been brought up in Edinburgh, and are musicians. In the sitting-room, there is a lot of music and many instruments: a tambourine, a flute, a piano, a fiddle. I cannot remember if there was a harp.

The patriarch has refreshments brought in. I raise my glass to the family's health. They are Catholics. Here are their names and ages: MacDonald Borodale is 73 years old; his wife, Jean MacNab, 50; the older son Angus is 30; his younger brother

---

54   The Clan from which the Marshal originated : MacDonald of Clanranald.

55   *Like on many other occasions, the spelling of place names varies in the manuscript (e.g: Borrodale, Borrowdale, etc.).*

56   The lady met at the Neptune's Inn, and who took care of the Marshal's parcels.

Alexander is 18, and at College in Glasgow; John, the third one, is 16, and Donald the fourth one is 11. The older daughter Clementina, their sister, is 25; Catherine, the second one, 23; Margaret the third one is 19 and Jean, the fourth is 17.

The patriarch is a farmer[57] for Clanranald. His house is pretty, located at the bottom of a small cove, facing the Gulf of Ayl...[? **Probably Eynort**[58]]. This is where Prince Charles landed, and where he embarked with my father, on a small rock, on the left of the confluence of a small mountain stream, a short distance from the house. It is the patriarch's grandfather who was host to the Prince for a few days. In remembrance, the Prince presented him with a silver snuff-box, which he had had made in the country and upon which the testimonial, which was read to me, was engraved; and the elder of the sisters showed us a little lock of his fair hair,[59] and gave me some of it.

We take our leave of this interesting family. Two of the young ladies are very pretty, the two others fair.

Borrowdale is only two miles from Arisaik, and Clanranald's castle is half-way. The elder of Mr MacDonald's sons is our guide. He has been ordered by Clanranald to take us there, and to do the honours of his castle. We arrive there by a special way, and are greeted by the porter. While our apartments and the dinner are being prepared, we go to Arisaick to see the ship which will take us to the Islands and which has been awaiting us for four days. I had requested it for the 27th or 28th, so I am not late. We also want to make some provisions, but I am

---

57   A small explanatory note. At this time, Clanranald still kept the prestige of a Clan chief descending from the King of the Isles. His parents, who had little fortune as is generally the case with the inhabitants of these mountainous and island districts, were priding themselves with fulfilling an office or some employment in the little sovereignty. The famous Flora MacDonald, a family relation, married a MacDonald who was a factor of the Chief's estate.

58   *More than likely the Sound of Arisaig and Loch nan Uamh.*

59   Fair hair which he inherited from his mother, Princess Clementina Sobiesky, a beautiful Polishwoman. The elder daughter of Mr MacDonald Borrodale was named Clementine, probably in remembrance of Prince Charles Edward.

well disappointed, for instead of finding a large burgh, there are only a few scattered houses, a Catholic Church whose key cannot be found to show it to us, and a wretched inn.

We cannot see the ship either, as it is anchored a few miles away behind a headland. The captain has gone to dinner with a friend, and a message is being forwarded to him.

For the first time we see kelp, this marine stem which is used to make soda for soap, by being burnt[60] in an iron box three feet broad, ten to eleven feet long, and two feet high. One [...?] the box, and as the weed gets burnt up, more is added till the box is full. The material produced by this weed is liquid as mortar, and ash-grey in colour. It is mixed up and crushed to make it compact, and the soda is made. It is then put into barrels for transport.

We return to the castle: it is a rotunda with two rooms jutting out, built eight years ago. It is not very high. A ground floor with some rooms above; a double wooden staircase, but it is only provisional. A fine entrance hall, decorated with wooden pillars painted in white. This castle is very badly positioned, having no view and being surrounded by a chain of rocky hills, though with some woods. The bottom of the basin is a peat bog, with a small loch at its end, with no park or garden. This location must be very unhealthy, whereas some distance from there, half-way up the slope, one would enjoy a fine view over the sea.

Our captain arrives. He is a very fine looking man, thirty-eight years old, a brave sailor. He speaks only English. I explain my itinerary to him, which he understands. We agree to leave the next morning at seven, and after having explained the places which I want to see, I leave it to the captain to be master of his course. He will decide according to the wind.

29th of June

The weather is atrocious, and it is pouring rain. However, the captain comes to take us. He is accompanied by half a dozen

---

60   In the margin of the manuscript is a note from the Marshal's hand which is illegible.

MacDonalds. We will find twice as many on board his ship, half of them women who come by sea from various parts of the coast.

In spite of the rain which continues with strength, we depart, me in my open gig, the others walking. All those who had come in the morning accompany us.

We are only a mile distant from the rowing boat, and three from the ship. The wind is strong, and suitable for South Uist. Here we are on the perfidious element, and it rolls heavily; we find our ship and are soon aboard. The captain takes us down to the lounge and shows us the cabins which we shall occupy during that expedition. We are saluted by a salvo of the 12 guns which the ship carries, followed by three hurrahs' from the crew and the people on board. The captain introduces us to his three officers and 40 sailors. The anchor is being weighted, but we notice two rowing boats filled with visitors and ladies which are coming towards us. We await them, and send one of the ship's rowing boats to tow them alongside. They arrive, and after some exchange of compliments, the captain asks all the visitors to retire. We bid each other farewell. The ladies have brought fresh butter, eggs, cream and cakes. We greet them with the firing of a few guns and a triple hurrah and we wave at each other with hats and white handkerchiefs for as long as the rowing boats can be seen. Amongst the ladies is Mrs Reed, who speaks French, and had preceded us to Arisaig, where she left the parcels which we shall find on our return from the Isles.

We are now under sail and heading for the Hebrides with a fair wind and choppy seas. We leave the Isle of Skye on our right hand side; on the left hand side those of Eig, Rum, Sandy and Canna; further beyond and on the left hand side Barra and Erisky. The wind changes, we are on the high seas, and running tacks. We have dined, are tired, and retire to our berths at 9 o'clock. Some moments later, the wind becomes favourable again, and we hear the anchor drop at 10.30 at Skipport, where there are no houses. It is one of the best anchorages in Britain and in the Hebrides.

Mr MacDonald of Staffa, our guide and translator for the

Gaelic tongue, which is the only one spoken in the Highlands and the Hebrides, writes an express letter to have a gig and some horses delivered to the Creagorry Inn, some ten miles from here.

The 30th of June.

We put the open boat to sea at 6 o'clock in the morning, and will be rowing these ten miles. The messenger comes back just as we set out, bringing us Mr Shaw, Clanranald's factor. We take them onboard, as well as a pilot named MacDonald of Araisbeek [?]. The Captain wishes to be given permission to have a deer shot on the island. There are many of them, and he is granted it easily. Another pilot arrives, and MacDonald, who is a good shot, is sent hunting with one of the ship's officers and a few good hunters.

We have left one hour too late, and the tide is withdrawing more and more. We can see the sea bottom, and soon the boat touches the ground. Sailors jump into the water and enable us to go some distance further. At last, we cannot go forward any more, for the water has vanished altogether. On our right hand side, we have run along a long island whose name I cannot recollect, then that of Viay [?][61] and further Ben [...]; on the left South Uist, with the Atlantic on the other side of it.

Sailors carry us to the shore, where we await the gig and some small horses which are named poneys. They arrive, but there are some missing for Auguste[62] and the drivers. However we depart.

The purpose of my journey is to see the house where my father was born, the cave where he hid with the Prince Charles for three weeks, as well as what is left of our family. We are told that there are only eight miles to run, but we find that there are at least 15. No road. We follow our course along the strand, with some huts on the right and left similar to those on the mainland. Piles of kelp may be seen, similar to the small heaps

---

61   Read Wiay. The « Ben » located further might in fact be Rueval.
62   The Marshal's servant.

of manure in our fields. There are sheep on the hills and horses and cows on the lower ground. Shortly after having left the ship we see a small house on the left hand side, built with stones. It is said to be inhabited by an interesting family. Having gone further along the strand, we see another stone built habitation, which is the inn already mentioned.

Mr Clanranald's factor bears heavily on me to accept a night's hospitality at his house, but I do not agree. After having seen my father's birthplace, I want to return to the ship so that we may go the next day to the cave, and then to Armadale, which is Lord MacDonald's castle in the Isle of Skye (south), and then across from Arisaick to Loch Eylort, to Mr Robertson MacDonald.

We move along; a road begins, then diminishes into a track, and we cross an immense wasteland. In the distance, we see a house of some style but do not come near it. The end of our long journey is a further two miles away. We get there at long last, through a country which seems desolate.

We are welcomed by a quantity of MacDonalds, large and small. There I meet an elderly spinster who sheds tears of joy: she is my first cousin. Her brother arrives, an old man of 73, who has nearly lost his sight. However, he can distinguish my hair which he says is just like his.

His wife follows. We are at the house of his elder son, who will follow him in the running of the farm. He has with him his wife, his children, and his brothers and sisters. Everything indicates that these relatives are not wealthy: their clothes; their house which is shaped like a hut, but much bigger, consisting of one large room and another smaller one and the sparse furniture, which is roughly made. Here, one lives on potatoes, fish, milk, cheese, occasionally meat (mutton), poultry, ship's biscuits and oatcakes, with water and whisky to drink. We are offered some of the latter, and have a toast. Another MacDonald hands me a note, written in French, from a Major MacDonald (retired) who assures me that the bearer is also my cousin. I ask him some questions. He has lost his father and [...] and wishes to go to the colonies. He is well-dressed, even elegantly so. I am told that he is a joiner or carpenter by trade.

He has me discussing his plan to go to the colonies with him and I support him [...]⁶³

I also ask questions to the young farmer. I am told that he is of good character. He pays £50 a year for the rental of his farm to Mr Clanranald, who is the landowner. To give him some support, and provide him with a bit of financial ease, I pay a year's rental for his farm. Clanranald grants a £10 pension to his father, MacEachen, and to his unmarried sister. I give the same amount, which I pay in advance, and which they will receive each year, the 30th of June, in remembrance of my journey.

The house, previously known as castle, where my father was born and where he lived, has been burned and razed to the ground in 1745 by the English troops, as have all the other houses and habitations of the nobility and gentlemen who followed the cause of Prince Charles.⁶⁴

I am told about this expedition, and about my father, who always accompanied the Prince. These events are so present in the inhabitants' memory that it seems that they just happened yesterday.

The parish priest arrives. He is an elderly man, and was at the seminary of Valladolid, where he stayed for nine years. He has two thousand parishioners, but they are as scattered as the huts. However, some of them are gathered in clusters, and form a few hamlets. In Gaelic, he has a number of advantageous comments about the conduct, honesty of mores, and probity of my parents conveyed to me.

The weather turns to the worse and it rains. A lot of people

---

63   Unclear in the text.
64   The use of the term "castle" by the Marshal to describe his father's house raises the issue of a possible confusion. Neil MacEachen's house in Howbeg, which might well have had its roof burnt down in 1745, like many others belonging to Jacobite sympathisers, is a dwelling of some substance, but certainly cannot be described as a "castle". The only castle nearby to have been destroyed by fire is that of Ormacleit, which belonged to Clanranald. However, it was burnt down in 1715 and not 1745, and, so says the tradition, by accident and certainly not by English troops, absent at the time.

have gathered. They have been told of my arrival by the papers, and, the day before, letters from Mr Clanranald and from Mr MacDonald Buchanan had arrived, addressed to Mr Shaw, who was with us and the Captain of our ship. The whole west side of the island was in movement.

I am urged to leave. I bid farewell to my relatives and we shake hands in sign of friendship, and I even shake hands with people who are not related to me.

Two miles from there, I stop at the Anglican Minister, a respectable old man of 85 years. He has with him his wife, a daughter and two sons, I believe, one of them a very handsome man, dressed in the English way.

This old man had known my uncles. He finds that I have a great resemblance with one of them. His wife is Flora MacDonald's niece, and knew her quite well. She was married shortly after the Prince's departure, to a MacDonald I believe, from the Isle of Skye. She was enthusiastic about her devotion to the Prince. Had a lot of children. I am shown two of her portraits, which bore a strong likeness. This Minister is called Monron [?].[65] He has refreshments brought to us, with cheese and biscuits.

We take the road again. The wind is very strong. Once again, we cross what I called "the desolation". The sea was high, and I wanted to seize that opportunity to go back to our ship, the open boat having moved some miles further. But there are already fears that we may not be able to cope with the sea, which has become very agitated, and the current is against us. I am told of the situation and I leave it up to the Captain to decide once we reach the open boat.

From far away, we notice a large gathering. Mr MacDonald Staffa, who commands the militia in this island, has gathered them from a distance of 6,7 or 8 miles around. He has taken care to bring in the open boat the barrel of whisky we bought at Arisaik, as well as some smoking tobacco.

Upon our arrival, we are saluted by a triple salvo of hurrahs.

---

65   Probably Munro.

I say a few words, and have the whisky and tobacco distributed to them. They are sitting in a circle at random; men, women and children. I raise a toast to their health, new salvo. There are more arriving all the time, and we see others in the distance.

We hold council about our departure, and decide that it would not be sensible to return to our ship (we are some 8 or 10 miles distant from her), and that instead we must go to Mr Shaw, whose invitation I had declined that very morning. He seems delighted, but first we must cross a stretch of sea to go to the island of Benbicula, 9 miles distant by land and sea. The crossing will be hard, but we have nothing with us and cannot stay in the huts which are around us. We are taking our leave at the very moment when [...] arrives, in which a very pretty young lady, very well dressed.

We face the sea and, by strength of oars, we land at a mile's distance from the house where we are due to spend the night, and where a good fire, a good bed, and a good supper are awaiting us, as well as the lady of the house and her sister. They are from the Isle of Skye, and Mr Shaw from Perthshire. We travel this mile on foot, and are very well received at 9 pm, the supper being served at 10 in spite of our hosts being warned of our arrival.[66] Orders are given to leave the next morning at 6 o'clock sharp. We will need one hour to reach the inn, where the open boat will be, and to catch the tide, or we shall have to dine and sleep there.

1st of July.

We are up at 5 am, and have coffee and tea. The ladies, who have hardly slept, have breakfast with us in spite of the early hour. The gig and horses had come during the low tide, everything is ready, and we take our leave of the lady of the house, who is very nice, with very good manners , and from her sister Flora, Mrs Laud,[67] very pretty, and from the house, very well furnished, named ...tourn,[68] which was a nunnery

---

66   *Unclear.*
67   *Probably a bad transcription of McLeod*
68   *Nunton House.*

in the past.

We arrive at the inn. The wind rapidly takes our open boat to the ship, and we set sail. Mr Shaw, who has accompanied us, leaves us.

The wind is fair and we leave the harbour of Skipport and set off at a good speed, leaving the Hebrides behind us. We are bringing back with us from South Uist a little ratter dog, to which I give the name of Uist, some potatoes, which I intend to plant at Courcelles,[69] and the roe which had been shot the previous day.

Before we move off, we must see the cave where Prince Charles and my father hid for three weeks. We head in that direction, the ship drops sails, and we board the open boat which carries us to the shore.

Our guide did not know the exact place, but we hail some countrymen whom we spot and who come to meet us. Half-way down the slope, we distinguish a rather well-dressed woman. We land at the end of a little crescent-shaped bay, named Corrodale, which is surrounded by rocks. In front of us lies a rather high mountain, and above is a small rock which looks like a big brioche, and which is used as a landmark by sailors. To left and right are mountains made of basaltic rocks, partly covered with moss, heather, grass and sheep. Mountain streams are rushing from them. The landing is difficult. Countrymen come down, and lift us from rock to rock right up to a little plateau where huts have been built. We make enquiries and find that we are not far off from the place we seek.

We are frightened by the road which we have to take to reach the caves. There are two of them at that place, which the Prince occupied alternately. The countrymen know all the details and circumstances perfectly, through tradition. They all want to tell the story at the same time, and a fair number of them are gathering. I was not aware that they had been forewarned of our arrival from the hinterland of the island of South Uist, from which we travelled the day before.

---

69   *Courcelles-le-Roy, the Marshal's country home.*

Climbing onto another hillock, we discover the entrance of the first cave. It is a long way and we have to climb. We decide to go, and in a short time we are there. It is a recess where five or 6 persons may lie down, and, bending a little, one may stand there. When the Prince was there with my father and, I believe, two companions, the entrance was closed by blocks of grass-covered rocks clad with moss, so that the troops which were all over the island went nearby a number of times without realizing the presence of a cave which deprived them of a head worth a reward of thirty thousand guineas. Nearly all the inhabitants knew that hiding place, and no one was tempted by that sum nor betrayed the Prince.

After remaining in the cave for ten minutes, we collect some stones, while others are brought to us from the other one. As we leave, I am handed a letter from a Mr MacDonald, inhabitant of that island, who express his regrets that he was unable to come to (Howbeg?). He had been told that I would visit the place where he lives. I was unable to reply to him, having neither ink nor paper. It is in these caves that Flora MacDonald, famed in history for her generous self-sacrifice, came to visit the Prince, and took him to the Isle of Skye, and from there to Borrowdale where he took the ship to France[70].

It is in this cave that I was told an anecdote which I often heard from my father in my youth. Here it is. The Prince needed a knife, but it had been forgotten. He asked my father to find one. My father pointed out to him the risks of such an errand, but he insisted and made it an order. Thus, in this unfortunate situation, he still acted as if he were the King.

I cannot remember if my father left the cave and found the knife. What surprised me is that Mr MacDonald Staffa, our travel companion, told me that he had heard this anecdote from his own father. I do not know if the island's inhabitants know it.

As we leave the cave, I am introduced to the young lady whom we had spotted from the sea, and am told that that she is a daughter of Mr MacEachen, my first cousin. She is 27

---

70   Inaccurate. The Prince's wanderings were much more complex, and Flora MacDonald was only with him part of the journey.

years old, married in that district, already has eight children and is expecting. Her husband is in Glasgow. He is a clever man, and is into business.

At last, we leave the cave. I take the young lady's hand and slip her a gold coin. She thanks me profusely. We return to the open boat and to the ship, which sails for Armadale, Lord MacDonald's castle. We knew that a party was due to be held there on the occasion of his daughter's wedding which was celebrated in London some days after my departure.

We headed between the islands of Skye, on the left hand side, alongside which we sailed, and those of Canna, Rum and Eig, following the same route we took to go to South Uist. We must double round the headland of Sleat and tack. We manage to do so, albeit slowly. We are only four miles from the Castle, which one can see clearly with a field-glass. A number of open boats are rowing, making tacks to reach the same place. We have no doubts that a party is taking place and that we are awaited. We take the decision to put our open boat to sea, and to row towards the castle. We can see a fair number of people on the coastline and close to the castle, which we can only see in parts because of the trees.

We land, and are welcomed by a triple hurrah. Mr MacPherson, the manager, is accompanied by seven or eight MacDonalds, two of them in the Highland dress. He lives 40 miles from there and, having received the Lord's orders, has been waiting for me since the 28th. We cross a beautiful new part of the park, when I discover about 150 men drawn in battle order. A bagpiper in the Scottish dress comes towards us and seems to act as a guide. Our cutter salutes the castle with its artillery, and is answered by detonations of [...] which have been prepared.

These 150 men are workers who are busy getting rid of a rocky ledge and flattening it. The hurrahs start again on both sides. We reach the castle, which is adorned by two turrets of unequal shape: this is the first part of the castle, which was begun by the present Lord's brother, and which he inherited a year ago. The interior is all gothic. Facing the entry door, in the vestibule, is a light staircase with a double ramp. On the first landing is a great casement- window made of stained glass window-panes [...], and in the middle, full-length, is Somerlet,[71] First Chief of the Isles in the Highland dress, from whom the MacDonalds descend. Above and below are the Lord's Coat-of-arms which differ from mine only by the galley being in one quartering and the fish in another. In mine, the fish is under the ship, and in the next quarter there is a pine tree, above which is an eagle with its wings spread. Also, his motto is "By Land and Sea", whereas mine is "My hope is constant in thee."[72]

On the right of the vestibule is a fine dining room without other outlet, on the left a sitting-room of similar proportions, one [illegible] decorated, the doors and window-panes of these rooms being very nicely decorated in the gothic style. These rooms have a view over the gulf and right across the mountains of Glengarry.

On the back of the stairs, on the right hand side is the library, rather dark and gloomy although it opens onto the garden. On the first floor are vast sleeping rooms with large bathrooms. Those are, I believe, the apartments of milord and milady.

The sight of the dining room gives us concern, and we share the same thought: the table is not set, and the only preparation being made is to serve some tea. Where are the provisions for a party, which the arrangements that we noticed upon our arrival, led us to expect? We make some enquiries, and learn that this party was due to be held at the house of Mr MacPherson, nephew of the author and translator of Ossian, some forty miles away, and that it was postponed upon the news of our arrival.

There is talk of using the leftovers from the dinner of those gentlemen for whom the tea had been made, as well as some beefsteak that was hastily put on the grill, a chicken, the compulsory potatoes, some kail and some soup. All these

---

71   Somerlet [sic] was running the Isles and the West of Scotland in the XIth century. He was concluding treaties with the Kings of Scotland. One of his sons (the elder?) revolted against him, and was knifed by his brother Ranald, from which stems the MacDonalds of Clanranald.

72   Words said by King Robert the Bruce to the chief of MacDonalds upon his arrival on the battlefield of Bannockburn.

things will be fine, as long as they are being served, but it is an old wifie who is in charge of preparing the dinner, and she takes it easy. At long last, we have our supper and dinner at the same time, as it is close to 9 pm.

We have barely sat down at the table when a reinforcement of guests arrive. They are Mr MacEachen, the Doctor, Lieutenant-Colonel MacDonnell, Angus MacDonald Corrodale (or rather Borrodale?) in the Scottish dress, and whom we already met at Clanranald's castle in Arisaig, and at last, MacDonald of Ross [?] and his son, the latter in the Scottish dress, and whom we also met in the same place. All these people have been sailing since 9 am, and are starving to death. Toasts are raised, we have tea, followed by whisky. As (...) I escape and go to bed. I learn the next morning that these gentlemen went back to the table till two in the morning. They have thrown a totally drunk Mr MacDonald in a dark closet and some of the youngsters have hidden his watch.

The 2nd of July.

Our Captain has given the signal for departure at 6 o'clock. We are ready, but the tea and coffee are still being awaited. The tide threatens to withdraw, and we must hurry. I see the castle's plans.[73]. It will be magnificent when completed. I have a brief glimpse of the gardens, the park, the stables and coach-houses. We board the rowing boat, and the hoorays take place in lieu of farewell. As we reach our ship, we receive a similar salute to the one we got upon our arrival. The wind is against us, and we tack to double around Arisaik headland. We enter Loch Moidart to pay a visit to Colonel Robertson, son of the author of Charles Quint's History. Our ship drops anchor. The people who arrived during the dinner in Armadale are with us. The tide begins to rise, but there won't be enough water for us to travel with the open boat. First of all, we see the ruined Castle of Clanranald, named Castle Tioram, which is located on a rock. One of the Claranalds once burnt this castle

---

73   Lord MacDonald's castle in Armadale

down to avoid it falling into the hands of Cromwell's troops. About forty inhabitants are around it and welcome us with the customary acclamations.

We land at the foot of the castle and survey it, inside and out. Nothing curious, not even the view from that side. There we meet an old man, aged 92, whose name is Alexander MacDonald. He enjoys all his capacities, but for an eye, whose usage he lost four years ago. He saw, so he says, the Prince Charles, the day two French frigates fought against an English vessel of the line. He says that the Prince was a fine man, with very fair hair. A number of people were with him, but he does not have their names: I wanted to know if he had seen my father. I gave him a gold coin, and we parted from both the old man and the ruined castle, whose inhabitants have a lot of stories of visions to tell, and believe in them.

At the castle's foot, on the East side, lies the Catholic Church. It is a miserable hut,[74] isolated, covered with thatch like the others, and somewhat improved. We did not feel tempted to see the inside.

On our way to the castle, we left behind us a pretty little house [?], or apparently looking so, being located on the side of the slope with its surroundings well planted. This house is occupied by Mrs MacDonald of Glen Alladale. The tide does not reach far enough to allow us to go to the gulf's end to Colonel Robertson's. We take the decision to visit that lady, who receives us with joy. She is an aged widow, and she offers us refreshments, which we accept, raising a toast to her health, and then we take our leave.

The tide is just right, and we are on our way to Moydart. We reach land. A fine track takes us to the castle, located at the tip of the gulf, at the mountain's foot. We have a mile and half to walk. After a few steps, we see the Colonel who comes to greet us. He had heard of our departure from Arisaik, and was not expecting us any more, but that very afternoon he had been told that the cutter was in sight.

---

74   One is tempted to believe that a more suitable church was destroyed by the Independents acting under Cromwell's orders. Since the castle was not rebuilt in the same place, neither was the church.

End of the loch, culture [...?], a mile till the house, bridge across the torrent, mountains in a semi-circle, wooded, end of the world, tent [...?] small house. I was told in Edinburgh that the [**main?**] house was being repaired. The lady of the house comes towards us. Friendly reception. Eleven children. Two pretty young ladies, Mary and Catherine, are introduced to us. Three others of different ages, and a clever little boy. Three other boys are in office, and two older girls away.

They want to keep us for the night. We make our apologies, saying we want to return to our ship before nightfall. A dinner is being served, that we rush. Portrait of the author of Charles Quint's history. We take our leave. A full-length portrait of myself and a bust. We reach the open boat just in time, and leave the people who have accompanied us since Armadale with Mrs MacDonald of Glen Alladale

We were to see Castle Tioran again. It appeared isolated, clearly cut out, and the ruins seemed to produce a much grander effect than before, blending with the mountains and having their colour.

We have to leave from an inside bay to reach the one where our ship is anchored. The sea is rough, with a heavy swell, dangerous because of the rocks. The Captain, who steers our open boat, is worried. He urges the rowers. The tide is going out, and the wind is against us, which causes violent chocks to our open boat and makes us go up and down. Couessin, who knows about the sea, thinks that we are nearly in danger. However, I stay calm, and so does Auguste. We are followed in the distance by another rowing boat who will take our pilot back. We cross the bar not without a struggle. The sea is getting worse, and we crave for our ship, which can be seen in the distance. In spite of the rowers' strength and courage, we do not seem to be making any progress. The wind rises. We may capsize, or the ship may drag its anchor, for the mooring is poor. At long last, we reach the vessel.

After three to four hours of worrying and dangerous navigation with oars, the cutter's yards were dropped to give less catch to the wind, should it increase. The weather is threatening, and the sea still rougher. We are surrounded by islands and rocks. However, the barometer does not drop any further, but such is the fury of the Atlantic that these waters enter and cross each other between these islands through all the possible ways, and the waves strike them with force. We spend the night in this condition which is a source of anguish for the sailors; but as for ourselves, we sleep peacefully and leave it to the Captain to protect us from all danger.

3rd of July.

Fog and rain cover all the surrounding areas. We weigh the anchor. The wind is strong and against us. We must run short tacks to avoid being exposed. I go upon deck and cannot see anything but rough seas. The rain compels me to go indoors. We have to make the headland of Moidart, and succeed in doing so at last around noon. The wind seems to change in our favour. We are off to Staffa to see Fingal's caves. The captain has not left the deck.

Here is the island of Coll, which we must leave on starboard, then the one of Tiree. We can spot Staffa beyond a headland, but far away. The wind is very strong, but the weather has cleared up enough to enable us to distinguish things.

That morning, we saw, during a rift in the clouds, a number of ships heading north. Our ship provided them with a point of bearing. Its tall mast, which carries a huge sail, suffers, and a medium-sized one is brought to give it some relief. We come down for dinner at 5.30.

As we leave the table, the wind has abated. I had stayed below, and am called upon deck. The vessel had hove to, and I can see in front of me the Island of Staffa. MacDonald Staffa, who owns it, along with some other islands further East, expresses his joy.

The rowing-boat is ready, and we climb aboard to get to the island. We see her from the front. It is half-a-mile long, and has the shape of a light [...], both ends being elevated, and the middle part lower.

I forgot to say that, at about two miles away, one can see

in the distance a rock whose top is shaped like a bonnet. So it is called – and nobody could tell me why – the Dutchman's cap. It is used as a landmark for bearings by the sailors who sail in the Atlantic.

Our rowing-boat faces the roughness of the sea, and we come close to the island. We circumnavigate it from the left. In front of us is what looks like hewn and sculpted pillars, black as iron. In the middle, an elevated seat called Fingal's chair. Below, from right to left, in a croissant shape, are what looks like roughly hewn seats. On the far left, three caves which are vast in their elevation, breadth and depth; in the middle a portal jutting out like that of a cathedral. The sea enters under these archways, and pounds the entrance with great strength. It would be dangerous to come close to it at this stage. Always shaped as pillars, the stones seem set into one another in an uneven way. This arrangement is only perceived when close-by.

We go back to the middle and find a small, calm haven to land and climb onto the island. One has to walk upon the sharp points of the rocks, and then on less uneven ground. On our right hand side, towards the back, beyond a ravine is the shell of a house. There are some cattle and some sheep, amazingly big for their age; lambs aged between six weeks and two months are fatter than our own when they are two years old; cows, calves and heifers in the same proportion, and two little mountain horses.

We climb to the top where a heap of stones is situated. From all around this island and from its summit the view is magnificent. We had brought a bottle of whisky with us and, there, we raise our glass to the health of Mr MacDonald Staffa, the landowner, who is with us, and also give some to the sailors. A second rowing boat has followed us. We ask the sailor to catch a sheep and a lamb. The brown wool is as soft as that of a goat. In that country, it is used to make stockings which are rather rough, but soft and velvety. Ten miles further away to the South-West of Staffa, one may see the island of Icolnkil.[75]

---

75   *Iona*

One may distinguish very clearly a ruined church with a tower. That was a cathedral in which the Kings of the Islands were buried, and there are about forty of them resting there.

We come back to the boat and, with a fair wind we go nine or ten miles away to drop anchor in a good harbour in Loch Laig.

We hold talks about tomorrow's route. My aim is to go to Lismore. We have to go back on our tracks. We propose, if the weather allows it, to go from Lismore to Ireland, to see the Giant's causeway and Mrs MacDonald, born MacDonald of Glennadale, Countess of Antrim, in her castle located in the bay bearing that name. If the wind is against us coming back, a steamboat leaves everyday for the island of Cantyre,[76] the crossing being only ten miles long. From there to Campbeltown, on the same island, the town where our captain lives, and where his ship has sometimes to remain for repairs. Then from that location we shall go to Inverary, either via Ireland, or via Oban, facing the island of Kerrera, and thereafter by land.[77] I leave it up to the Captain to take the decision.

4th of July.

We weigh the anchor at 6 o'clock in the morning. We must come back on our tracks. We could circumnavigate the island of Mull by the south to go to Lismore, but navigation is hazardous. We prefer to do it from the north, to enter the Sound of Mull. The weather is uncertain, the wind is light. We pass by the Island of Staffa once again, and remain quite some time in front of it for lack of wind. We move forward a little bit, leaving on our right the islands of Tuadh et Ulvah,[78] on the left Tiree and soon after, Coll. In front of us are Muck, Eig, Rum, Sandy, Canna and Skye and on the left, on the northern horizon are the Hebrides. At last, we get round the Isle of Mull and enter

---

76   Obviously Kintyre Peninsula.

77   This most bizarre route suggests some confusion. Whether this is due to an error in the transcription, or to the Marshal himself, is unclear.

78   Likely confusion with the name of Loch Tuath, where are located the islands of Gometra and Ulva.

the Sound of that name, leaving Loch Sunart on our left.

We come close to the coast of Mull and can see a pretty little town, high and low, Torbermorry, with a safe harbour where three or four ships sheltered yesterday morning due to the threatening weather. I am told that in this little harbour, which is also used as dry dock by the ships which navigate around the Scottish islands, a warship of the famous Armada took refuge and was burnt by the English.

The mainland is on our left hand side. The wind, while still weak, gets better. We set in full sails. The tide is also with us. We can see, here and there, right and left, some houses which seem pretty, but few trees. Some ruined castles which used to belong to the MacDonalds, and which were destroyed either in 1745, or by Cromwell's troops, or during the feudal wars between the Highland Lords. Consult Mr MacDonald Buchanan's book on the genealogy of the MacDonalds.

For some time, we can see Lismore. We enter Loch Linnhe, where three tides meet. The sea is rough. The wind is in our favour, and we come round that island by its headland, where a magnificent panorama of mountains appears around us: Fort William on the left, Oban ahead of us, on the right the great channel which goes into the Atlantic, and behind, the Sound of Mull. The ship does not dare come near the South coast of Lismore. We hove to, and get down into the rowing boat to pay a visit to Bishop MacDonald. We have four miles to make. The open boat's sail is hoisted, and there we are in the small harbour. The Bishop, at the end of the pier, welcomes us. There is only an inn and a lime-kiln there. The Bishopric or Episcopal Palace is a very small house, more than modest, and beside it is a small chapel which is the cathedral. The Bishop has a dozen pupils. Clumps of trees surround the house. A little kitchen-garden, badly kept, in which there are some fruit trees. A herd of cattle and some sheep graze nearby. To honour and welcome me, the prelate had the house whitewashed outside, and oil-painted inside. We go up a little room like elsewhere [?] a visiting-room which looks like a dining-room. We cannot stay there because of the smell [of paint], and a casement-window which gives on the sea is opened.

Berigoniam, an old capital of Scotland, is across from us. All that is left is a ruined castle called Deuf...[?];[79] on the right hand side, Oban.

Miss MacDonald, the Bishop's niece, a tall enough person, does the honours. Wines are presented, tea is served. I have warned the prelate that I am going to Ireland, and that I would make use of the turn of the tide in an hour's time. He wants to detain me, but I insist. In any case, the house is not bearable, and we have agreed to this excursion to see the Giant's Causeway.

We take our leave. The Bishop had taken care to send cream and butter to the rowing-boat. We return to the Cutter, and sail to Ireland. If the wind turns, we shall go to Cambletown, in the South of the Cantyre peninsula.

5th of July.

The past evening had been sweet, the wind had softened, and the rising tide had made us lose a bit of our advance the following night. We come close to the Sound of Jura. On the right hand side is a very dangerous passage between the Island of Scorba and that of Jura. A violent and whirling current, called Gary Vrakan[80] drags the biggest ships, which may be swallowed up or broken on the rocks which these waters hide. Everyone is very keen to get away from it. A tack pushes us into the Sound of Jura, and the Captain shows his contentment. The wind is strong, and favourable to us, but there is a lot of fog, clouds and drizzle, which do not enable me to see the whirlpools but from far away. At noon, there are some periods of fair weather which open and close, but they end at 2 o'clock. Same weather. We waste one of such weather breaks visiting a small boat which is suspected of smuggling, but which only carries potatoes.

We are right across the headland on the West-South West of

---

79   *Likely reference either to Dunolly, or to Dunstafnage castles, the area being supposedly the seat of the capital of the Kingdom of Dalriada.*
80   *Read Corryvreckan.*

Jura, in the Sound of Islay, which is spelt Ayla.[81] Afterwards the wind is poor, and it is doubtful whether we can reach Ireland that night.

At 4 o'clock, the wind rises and becomes very strong. The sea is in a violent turmoil. We see the coastline of Ireland, the tip of the headland of Bangor, then the Giant's Causeway, but all this in a rather confused way because of the remoteness, the fog, and the drizzle. At 6 o'clock, the weather worsens. We have to reach a harbour and get some shelter, but the wind becomes squally, and we begin to worry. One dreams of a strong breeze which could push the ship, as it is experiencing very rough conditions. The night falls, and we are surrounded by rocks. At long last, the wind steadies, and at 10 o'clock, we enter into the small [harbour] of Bush, which is not very safe, and we drop the anchor, which may not be enough. We tie-up our ship for more safety.

6th of July.

County of Antrim.

During the night the sea has remained just as bad. In the morning, we land a party which is sent to Coleraine to fetch some carriages to take us to the Giants' Causeway. A steamer on its way to Londonderry passes by. It has experienced very bad weather in the waters we have just left, and has been compelled to take refuge by the island of Acseray (or Alisa).[82] The carriages are spotted, and we get into the rowing-boat. The sea is choppy. The Giant's Causeway, which is ten miles away, juts out into the sea for three to four hundred feet.

We experience some sort of pleasure from being on the land, and being driven by carriage. These are postchaises which are hard and unclean. We follow the coastline at a short distance. The country is cultivated and well-populated. About half-way,

---

81   *We have hereby taken the liberty to correct a mistake in Mathilde de Massa's transcription, which confuses the French word «îles» (islands) with the name Islay , and makes the text unintelligible.*

82   The island of Ailsa, in the Gulf of the Clyde.

we stop in front of a house which is modest and rather tidy. An excellent woman, aged 70, agile and in good health, invites us cordially to come in. I am introduced to her. She takes my hand, expresses her joy, and says that the MacDonalds of Scotland and Ireland are always welcome in her house: the County of Antrim, where we are, is full of them.

We continue on our route after the good wife has forced us to accept refreshments and try her whisky.

We cross the small river of Bush at the village of Bushmill. We take a guide, and are followed by many people who offer us, against payment, some small boxes containing stones [..?] of the Caves and of the Giants' Causeway.

We descend from our carriage and walk towards a small bay to see this cave. The sea is pounding and entering it with a din. We are obliged to get into it from the side, and to jump with great difficulty from one slippery rock to another. Here we are. The cave opening is an archway facing the sea, and it is a fine sight. A shot is being fired, and the cave reverberates with the noise for a long time and in a very resounding way.

We come back on our tracks. We have to climb up the coast, and come down again in another, deeper bay, to see the profile of the Causeway which happens to end in a third bay. With a good track, half-way up the slope, one may reach its end at the foot of a small promontory.[83] I am frightened by the distance which we must cover to reach that third bay. My feet refuse to go any further, being too exhausted by the distance that they have already covered to go to the cave. I urge my companions to go there on their own, and remain sitting at the end of the second bay, from where the Causeway can be seen from its side very well. Near to the top one can see some natural pillars formed like the pipes of an organ, while, lower, the surrounding rocks seem to have been chiselled like columns. My companions return and praise my decision to have stayed put: they have seen nothing more than I, besides that the pilasters shaping the columns show an octagonal stonework which has exactly the same measurement on its eight sides.

---

83   *The transcription appears to be erroneous and this translation is subject to caution.*

The weather has improved. We discuss again the possibility of going to Glennarm, to Mrs MacDonald, Countess of Antrim. I am told that she is at home, and will be delighted to see us. It is only 40 miles away, and the Cutter will come to take us there.

After collecting some stones, and having bought some small boxes which contain more of them, as well as having given a tip to those people who are following us so that they may drink to my health, we return to our carriage at one o'clock, and here we are, on our way to Ballycastle, our first relay. We follow the sea, more or less. The country is well cultivated, fairly hilly but with a nice road.

The Irish are a fine species of men; the women dressed well-enough, like in Scotland, walking with their bare feet, with enormous legs and big feet.

We dine at Bally Castle. Rather mediocre Burgh. A bad postchaise, and a small carriage which is shaped like a curricle, except that we are sitting on the sides, facing each other. The coachman is sitting on a small elevated seat, the two wheels being below.

The country becomes more hilly. No vegetation. Mountains of peatland, covered with fog. On a number of occasions, we have to walk to provide some relief to our horses; then we have to set the breaks, as at long last we descend into a valley. Greenery returns, cultivations, inhabitants… We follow this valley and reach Luskendale, our second relay, a small burgh located close to the edge of the sea. There is no carriage other than two small Crigs [?], but it is 8 o'clock and we need three hours to reach Glenarm. We are not expected, as it would be eleven before we arrived, and everyone would be in bed. I suggest that we stop. The house is clean. It is a spa. There is only one bath. Some people are there, bearing the name of MacDonald, even the waitress of the inn.

The priest arrives, who bears the same name. He is 90 years old, solid on his legs, with good eyesight. He was born here, and has been to the seminar in Paris. He stayed six years in that town, where he met Mme Ste Perinne [?], and has forgotten most of his French.

189

7ᵗʰ of July.

At 6 o'clock, we are on our way to Glenarm. We follow the coastline, and come round the tips of headlands. The country is hilly, the land at the foot of the mountains well-cultivated. As we come round the last headland, we see Glenarm, and the Cutter in the bay, taking tacks four miles away. We meet the rowing-boat which has been ordered to be at the bottom of the bay, at the corner of the park at 7 o'clock.

We learn that Milady has been in Antrim for nine or ten days. So, here are forty miles spent in vain and a waste of time. We enter the park and send the carriages back to the Inn to order our lunch.

The castle is half modern, half gothic. It is under repair, being rebuilt in the gothic style. Three facades. The main entrance is by the billiard-room, whose position is being changed; two fine sitting-rooms and a pretty dining-room. These three rooms open on to the park, which is narrow and little wooded. Perhaps it is deep, and better stocked at the back.

The porter expresses his regrets about Milady's absence. Her full-length portrait, painted 25 years ago, is in the billiard-room. Upstairs, we are shown the room which Milady normally occupies. It opens on to the sea, and is lined with flowers, geraniums and hydrangeas. In this room is the painted bust of the unfortunate Queen Mary Stuart and, in a little stained-glass casement which holds various curiosities, is the miniature portrait of the Marchioness of Londonderry, daughter of Milady, who is 22 or 23 years old. In this portrait, she seems a charming and beautiful woman.

After having lunch at the inn, we have nothing better to do than leave. The castle's porter brings an enormous bunch of roses and a little melon. I want to give him a tip, but he refuses politely. Back to the rowing-boat, we find the gardener who has brought cherries, vegetables and salads. He is not as hard to persuade as the porter.

We board the rowing-boat and return to the Cutter. The sea is like a mirror, no wind at all; it can take us to Cambletown. The period of calm lasts long enough, but the wind rises, then becomes strong, and very favourable for our route. We decide to bypass Cambletown and to make use of the wind to go to Inverary. The captain, who is from Cambletown, would have liked to introduce me to his family; but the wind may change. He does not insist, and here we are sailing to the end of our maritime journey.

We reach the junction of the Clyde. The famous rock of Eilsa, which is mentioned in Sir Walter Scott's poem about the words of King Robert the Bruce which make my motto, lies in front of us, and we leave it behind on our right hand side. We enter the Sound of Kilbrannan, leaving on our left the small island of Sandra and the Peninsula of Cantyre, and on our right that of Arran and of Bute.

8th of July.

Inverary

We have come a long way during the night, and it is 9 o'clock when we enter Loch Fine. At 11.30, we discover Inverary, nearly at the head of the Loch. It is resting against a slightly wooded hill with a conical shape. Behind us is a chain of mountains. On the right of Inverary, one may see a gorge; on the left another one, well wooded. The more salient feature which may be seen is a church steeple and the town's jail.

Yesterday, we were discovering castles which had been ruined by the wars between the MacDonalds and the MacLeans; now, since we are in Loch Fine, we can see here and there country houses belonging to the Campbells of the Duke of Argyle's family, who has his castle in Inverary.

The mountains bordering the lake are less bold than those in the islands we have visited, and are wooded enough in the Sound, that is at the mouth of the Clyde. At ten in the evening, we saw the herring fleet; that is the fishing boats, with their sails cast, their nets at sea, tossing on the brisk waves, and letting themselves be carried away by the rising tide. The wind was then blowing very strongly, and I saw what a hard job it was to be a herring fisherman.

Here we are in Inverary. The scene changes. The Duke of Argyle's castle lies in front of us, standing out well against the background of the park. The town is small, but well built and whitewashed, providing a nice contrast with the castle which is made of grey building stones. On top of the hill which I spoke about, lies a kind of tower, sharp like an obelix, separating two valleys [?] which make the park; a third one [?] following the lake, and on the right hand side, a kind of gorge.[84]

At 1.30, we drop the anchor. I take leave of the crew, granting twenty guineas (500 francs) to the forty men, plus some smoking tobacco and ten bottles of whisky. To the rower of our rowing-boat, I give 6 guineas, to the steward and the kitchen boys 5. To the captain, a vermilion snuff-box engraved with my name and "Souvenir to Captain Beatson", 12 bottles of sherry, 12 of Madeira wine, 12 of Port and three dozens of Porter. To the two officers, a dozen bottles of sherry each, and six of Madeira; plus a souvenir that I promise to send them from Glascow. I drink to the health of the crew which answers with three "hoorays" and drinks in its turn. We get into the rowing-boat and after we have parted with the ship, we receive a salute of fifteen gun shots. The echoes from the valleys repeat and prolong the sound, followed by hoorays. We answer, and the crew climbs to the ladders. We reach the pier where the inhabitants have gathered.

I find a Campbell, Major in the Militia, agent to the Duke of Argyll, who is away. He has been ordered to provide us with accommodation at the castle. I thank him, but decline, for I prefer the inn.

We visit the castle: it is of a regular square shape, sided with six big round towers which are crenulated. In their midst is a square tower and another similar one dominating the others. They are shaped like a sort of dome and bring light to the dining room. The kitchen and offices of the ground floor are nearly hidden by a ditch without water. Beautifully furnished sitting-rooms, with hangings made of tapestries from Flanders. The bedrooms and apartments are fine and very practical. The

---

84   *The transcription is very uncertain about these lines.*

castle has two floors built above the offices and a mansard roof. The roof is shaped in the Italian way, the towers [...?] provide flats; all the casement-windows are high, broad and end up in ribbed vaults. The park is beautiful; with magnificent chestnut trees, lime-trees, beech-trees and sycamores. At the end of the valley is a fine meadow; below, a dairy; coming back on our left, we see a poultry-yard which was burnt, and has been rebuilt a short distance away from the castle. Besides this destruction, there are fine lands and some beautiful grazing which I have not surveyed, being very tired.

We return to the Inn. The Duke's agent sends us cherries and strawberries. I give most of them to the captain who stays with us, to take back to his wife in Cambletown, as well as the big bunch of flowers and the small melon I got in Glenarm.

9th of July.

At 9 o'clock in the morning we say goodbye to the captain, whose ship is already under sails. We climb into our gigs and set-off to Chardow,[85] a relay and an inn where we have lunch. The track is good, at the foot of the mountains and alongside the lake which we pass by. The valley then gets narrower. From Chardow's Inn, we only have (after our gigs) some sort of tip-carts, but properly painted and with seats suspended by straps. We have to make do with that.

We climb a rather sharp slope, from where we can see Inverary in the distance, providing us with a pretty picture. We tramp through a narrow gorge, the mountain tops being very precipitous. We keep rising. At the top is a small lake. We san see a deep valley into which we must descend, then the lake we shall have to pass by to get to the inn of [...]. On our left hand side, we leave the Mountain of the Couronnier [?].[86] We still have a mile to do to reach the inn at Tarbat, on the shores of Loch Lomond. There we are, and the Ben [...][87] presents itself to our eyes; with a rocky outcrop on its top which takes

---

85   Read Cairndow.
86   Probably Ben Chorranach.
87   Very likely, Ben Lomond.

the shape of a bonnet, or rather of an helmet.

The steamboat has not arrived yet. It will take us around this beautiful lake. We can see it, and are brought to it. It is laden with people, brought there by curiosity, as well as by the pleasure of seeing the lake, the mountain, and by the sights they have to offer.

I am already known, and the topic of curiosity changes. I become the focus of the general attention, especially from a Lady or elderly spinster,[88] who speaks French and comes to sit beside me. We engage in conversation about the things that surround us. We notice a small cascade on three different levels. We then stop below a rock to see the cave where Rob Roy (Walter Scott's novel) was hidden. I am warned that it is not worth seeing, and that the path to it is difficult. I remain on my seat. Dinner is announced, but I am expected at Ross. It is two o'clock, and I'll get there by 6.

Some small cottages may be found, scattered here and there, which provide charming changes of scenes. The lake opens up and get broader. A large boat is being towed. It is for me, to take me to Ross.

There we are,[89] in the largest boat on the lake, which is itself 8 miles long. The islands, the rocks and the mountains become less elevated. We part from the steamboat, and it is then I notice a white flag[90] which has been hoisted, made with the table-cloth which was used for the dinner. Our own boat carries a similar one. Our boat's purpose is to prevent whisky smuggling. It belongs to the customs, and carries a gun which I notice when it is being fired. It fires fifteen shots. The steamboat travellers salute us with hoorays, which we return.

A mile from the shore is another boat with a double flag, France and England, like the others. On it are two Scotswomen, dressed in the MacDonald colours, and two Scotsmen. They

---

88   *Footnote from the Marshal* : She comes from Geneva, which she often inhabits, and has wit and instruction.

89   The Marshal, Mr de Couëssin and Mr MacDonald Staffa.

90   This is in the Marshal's honour, the white flag being then that of the French army's.*(France is then under the reign of King Charles X, and the white is traditionally the King's colours).*

board, and I recognise the Misses MacDonald Buchanan, daughters of the landowner of Ross, with whom I had dinner at their father's in Edinburgh. This pleasant encounter is very agreeable to me. They can understand a little French, but do not speak it. One of their companions, bearing a Scottish jacket, is Mr Colomne,[91] about 60 years old, a retired marine officer and a Customs Receiver in America; the other one is Mr Baynie, 30 years old [50?] who spends his time travelling; both of them speaking French.

The older one of the Misses MacDonald is called Margaret and the second one Jane. We come ashore, and find Madam their mother and their third sister on the bank. Charming welcome. The husband is still in Edinburgh. He had been home, but our trip to Ireland having delayed our arrival, he has been forced to return, and is expected this evening or tomorrow morning.

We arrive at the castle which, till then, had been hidden by the trees of the park. It is an old abbey which has been rejuvenated in the style cherished by the English, and which especially befits this building, adorned with windows ending up in ribbed-vaults and pyramidal tops. It is arranged in a practical way and the rooms are well distributed.

10th of July.

Visit to Buchanan. The castle is four miles from the Abbey, and belongs to the Duke of Montrose. It is an old house, simple and low-lying. Nothing remarkable. Anyhow it is Sunday, the people are at the service, and the keys cannot be found. I leave some cards.

We visit the spinning-room[92] and the hen-house, which is remarkable because all the poultry are as white as snow. The kitchen-gardens are superb, the greenhouses magnificent. They are the largest ones I have yet had the opportunity to see. They

---

91   Perhaps Colquhoun?
92   *The Marshal uses the word* "filanderie", *which, we assume, comes from the obsolete French word* "filandière", *which describes a woman involved in spinning.*

are filled with all sorts of fruits, and especially grapes which have been available for eating for a month; peaches, nectarines, etc.

Beautiful park, well spread, but with a lot of wetland, as the rushes indicate. The castle, located on a low-lying point, has a limited view over the surrounding countryside, and none over Loch Lomond.

We have a rendez-vous on the shores with the inhabitants of Ross. We join them, the ladies having arrived off the customs boat we used the previous day, with the same flags. They are dressed in the Scottish way. Moreover, the boat is festooned, and the sailors decorated with heather flowers, which are the distinctive sign of the MacDonald Clan. Two or three boats filled with onlookers have come to join us. Gun salute of 15 shots. We leave for the other end of the Loch and, at its head, are met by other boats. I call our captain "Commodore".

We sail to get to Mr Buchanan, MP, at his castle of Balhachim [?].[93] His son-in-law had dined with us the previous evening, and we have promised to have a second lunch at his own place. He greets us as we come ashore, and introduces us to his daughter.

The rain prevents us from walking around, and compels us to come down from the crenulated tower which we had climbed to see the surrounding countryside. The castle has towers and is in the gothic style. His son-in-law, Mr Finchy, from Glasgow, is still young and already has ten children.

We take our leave and come back to Ross. In the carriage, we learn that the owner will be there tomorrow only, but I have already fixed my departure.

11th of July.

In spite of my insistent request, the whole family is up to wish us farewell once again. We were due to leave at 5, but we have mistaken the hour and it is only 4 o'clock, The ladies got up at 3. At long last, we take our leave. Nothing remarkable till Dumbarton, 8 miles away.

---

93   *Balloch Castle, built in 1808.*

Dumbarton – Glasgow.

Castle, steam-boat on the Clyde. Star Inn at Ingram Street. Promenade in town; monuments, buildings, streets, Catholic Church, Museum. We meet the two daughters of Sir Walter Scott, one of whom is married; teachers. I leave [to the Museum?] a grand medal of the Coronation of Charles X. I am presented in return with some peculiar stones which come from the area around Glasgow.

Visit to a jeweller's shop of good repute. I purchase two seals made of gold with double stones for the officers of the Cutter, and at last a gold cross fitted with amethysts for Lady Lucy Stuart's chambermaid. Then we go to M. Mirolt [?] mechanised manufacture of embroidery.

We return to the inn. Considerable crowd. We go out again to visit Glasgow's docks. Two stone bridges, one of which is superb, broadened thanks to iron footpaths; a third bridge made in iron, for pedestrians.

We return at last, and meet Mr Ross, the landowner, who has returned from Edinburgh. We have hardly finished dinner when Mr MacEachan,[94] from Greenock, whom I had invited to come, arrives to see me at the head of his family of ten. They have dinner and tea, and I invite the lot for lunch the next day.

12th of July.

I manage to get Mr and Mrs MacEachan to accept 50 Guineas to get presents [or: as a present?]. It is true they are my relatives. I promise to try my best to arrange to have their son[95] returned from the colonies, and to have him employed with the Customs in England. I also promise 20 Guineas to a young MacDonald from South Uist, who is also my relative, but in a more distant way, so that he may start some sort of business [?] in that island.

We bid each other farewell, and this large family is apparently [?] satisfied with me.

---

94 The Marshal writes MacAichen.
95 Very likely, the older one of the children.

Mr MacDonald Buchanan leaves for Ross. His brother Staffa, accompanies us till Ellenton, to his father in law, where his wife and children are.

Visit to the factory of painted handkerchiefs belonging to Mr Montis, which is some miles from Glasgow. We are given a number of them as a present, especially those which made his fortune. Then we see the process of shearing muslin with fire.

Bothwell.

Old and new castles of the Marquess of Douglas. Abbey with a ruined facade. Run of the Clyde.

Hamilton

This is where the Duke stays: portraits, paintings. Castle of Lord Benclenen [?] named Mi…. [illegible]. It too is being made more gothic. The master of the house is away. We do not see the interior.

Elleston.

We are awaited, to have dinner and to sleep there. We meet Sir James Stuart. He advises us against going to Port Patrick. I quickly abandon the idea of going in that direction.

13th of July.

It is 9 o'clock in the morning. The carriage has been harnessed. The day before, we took our leave of Mrs MacDonald of Staffa. Her father had left to avoid meeting his son-in-law, with whom he is on bad terms. We part with her husband, who has been with us since the 23rd of June. The weather is bad. We had conceived the idea of visiting the Clyde's waterfalls, three miles from Lanark, itself eight to ten miles distant from us. As we arrive there, the weather worsens. We would need to walk a long way, and my feet won't allow it.[96] We give up seeing this curiosity. The information we have received on Port Patrick changes my plans, and I make up my mind to take the road to Manchester, and thereafter Liverpool, which is the harbour where we can board for Dublin.

The horses are ready. One of them is very bad, and we point this out in order to have him changed, but in vain, and, a mile from there, he breaks the [...] in the front of our carriage as well as the harnessing pole. The horse is returned to Lanark and at last another one is brought back.

The ground looks different. We enter the hills and the heather. Poor road and poor weather till Gretna Green, last village in Scotland. Place of clandestine weddings for the English. A river, or rather a stream, separates the two kingdoms. Fine iron bridge over the Eden.

❋ ❋ ❋ ❋ ❋

After leaving Scotland, the Marshal will head towards Carlisle, and then Manchester where he remarks: " We walk upon the heads of thousands of workers employed in the coal mines". *Then onwards to Liverpool, where the party take the ferry to Dublin, which they visit on the 16th of July. Back to Wales (Holyhead on the 18th), then Bangor, Shrewsbury, Birmingham and Banbury. The Marshal is back in London on the 22nd, and heads towards Brighton, where he will sail back to France on the 27th of July, nearly two months after his departure. Leaving England's shores, he writes, in the conclusion of his diary:*

"Farewell, beautiful England,[97] charming country whose inhabitants have welcomed me with so much care and

---

96   The Marshal suffers from gout.
97   *The use of « England » to describe the British Isles is, regrettably, a commonplace error in French. Well acquainted as he was with the existence of "three kingdoms", and with Scotland in particular, the Marshal does not seem to have been immune from it.*

politeness. Farewell for two or three years. I'll come back to see you at that time. "

He then comments:

"No inquiry there, nor any form of inquisition. Nowhere the strangers we were have been asked for their passport. I have been through the three kingdoms, through the islands: no constable or public officer to be seen; everywhere is safe. The people of England are proud of its freedom, of its independence. He benefits from it, but he pays. Everywhere wealth and cleanliness. It is an admirable country in every aspect. "

TOUR OF HIS EXCELLENCY FIELD–MARSHAL MACDONALD, DUKE OF TARENTUM, MARSHAL OF FRANCE, HIGH CHANCELLOR OF THE ORDER OF THE LEGION OF HONOUR, ETC, IN JUNE 1825

(PRESUMABLY WRITTEN BY MACDONALD OF STAFFA)

We have been favoured with the following detail of Field–Marshal MacDonald's tour in this country, which we trust will be acceptable to our readers:

After visiting Hopetoun House, the Palace of Linlithgow, the fields of the battle of Falkirk and Bannockburn, Stirling Castle, the Roman Camp at Ardoch, Crieff, Perth, the Palace of Scone, St Martin's, Kinfauns, Dunkeld, the pass of Killicrankie, the scene of the battle of Harlaw, Blair, Field of Culloden, Inverness, Loch Ness, Fort Augustus, Loch Lochy, Fort William, &c., the Field-Marshal proceeded from Fort William on Tuesday morning the 28th of June for Clanranald's House in Arisaig, where he had resolved to be that night, and which was the first private gentleman's house in which the Marshal had slept since he left France, being resolved to dedicate the very short time he had to spare upon the occasion of his present visit to Great Britain, in seeing as much of the country as possible, and especially in the enjoyment of the scenery and romantic beauty of the Highland hills, and interesting Isles which gave birth to his ancestors. These motives induced Marshal MacDonald to decline, with much reluctance, many kind and pressing invitations from some of the first noblemen and gentlemen of the land to partake of their hospitality and a hearty Scottish welcome. Amongst these were his Grace the Duke of Montrose, the Duke of Argyle, the Duke of Hamilton, Lord Belhaven, Lord MacDonald, Lord Gray, Generals Sir David Baird, Sir Jas. Steuart, Sir Hew Hamilton Dalrymple, Sir David Hunter Blair, Sir Wm.Cumming Gordon, &c. The first stage from Fort William to Arisaig, being the inn at Glenfinnan, the Field–Marshal and his suite breakfasted there, and were shewn the spot where Prince Charles Stuart first erected his standard in 1745, attended by young Clanranald and Kinlochmoidart, and about twenty gentlemen of the name of MacDonald, many of them tacksmen upon the estate of, and all of them immediately descended from, and cadets of, the family of Clanranald; these, with about a thousand men from the Clanranald estates, joined by Lochiel, Glengarry, the Gordons, Macphersons, Frasers, &c. formed the first part of the army of the unfortunate Prince Charles in 1745. From Glenfinnan, the party proceeded by the excellent road and romantic scenery which the district and country of Arisaig present, to Borrodale, the residence of John MacDonald, Esq., who, with Mrs MacDonald and his four amiable daughters and three sons, were all at home, to give a kind reception to their distinguished visitor. Here the Field Marshal surveyed, with feelings of much interest, the place where Prince Charles first landed, in 1745, on the mainland, and afterwards embarked in 1746, when he took his last farewell of Scotland, accompanied by the Field Marshal's father, Neil MacDonald, Esq. of the family of Houghbeg, in South Uist, and the near relation of Clanranald whom he was visiting at Nunton House, when Prince Charles came there, and upon which occasion the Field Marshal's father was introduced for the first time; and from that moment, and from his being a man of very superior education and literary acquirements, the Prince took a great liking to, and never afterwards parted with him. From Borrodale the party proceeded to Clanranald's house in Arisaig, where they dined and slept; and early on the following morning, the 29th, the Field Marshal was waited upon by Captain Henry Dundas Beaton, of his Majesty's cutter Swift, who, by the kind attention of my Lord Melville, and of Sir William Boothby and Captain

Knight, had been ordered to that part of the coast, to receive his Excellency. The party breakfasted at five o'clock in the morning, and immediately thereafter embarked on board the cutter. It had been the intention of the Field Marshal to call upon Mr and Mrs MacDonald of Rhu, but the wind being fair, and it being of much importance to overtake the tide, to work out of the bay of Arisaig, that gentleman and Mrs MacDonald, with their five amiable daughters and three sons, and Colonel MacDonald of Scotos, their son-in-law, very kindly came on board the cutter, to pay their respects to their distinguished clansman, who was not less pleased by their considerate attention, and very judicious arrangement of time, for his convenience, than he was gratified by affability and kindness of the whole family, who had hardly left the cutter, when the Marshal discovered that they had stored the vessel with all sorts of fresh provisions, such as vegetables, fruit, cream, butter, newly caught salmon: which, with two fat six year-old wedders, from Clandranald's parks, and a supply of wines, and some casks of mountain dew, enabled his Excellency and his friends to put to sea, with the comfortable sensation of having abundance of fresh stores on board. The wind having been fair, his Excellency reached the destined port, (Loch Skipport) in South Uist, that same night, about 11 o'clock: and, after sleeping a few hours, he left the cutter at four in the morning, in the barge, and landed at the inn of Craig Goray, upon the ford which separates the island of Benbecula from that of South Uist. Here the Marshal was met by Mr Shaw, Clanranald's factor, who had kindly provided his gig and saddle horses for the whole party, on which they proceeded through the farms in the north end of South Uist to Houghbeg, where Field Marshal had the satisfaction of meeting some near relations of his late respected father and his own, whom his Excellency seemed very happy to see, and to whom he requested Mr MacDonald to say, that he had come all the way from France chiefly to see them.

The overwhelming joy and gratitude of his relations at this mark of kindness may be more easily conceived than described.

In taking leave, his Excellency announced to Mr Shaw his intention of giving a liberal annuity to several of these relations, which should henceforth be paid to them thro' him on the 30th of June in each year; and, in the meanwhile, his Excellency distributed nearly about two hundred sovereigns in various donations. The Field Marshal proceeded from Houghbeg to Nunton House, the seat of the Clanranald family in the Isles and which is at present occupied by his factor, Mr Shaw. On the arrival of his Excellency and suite at Nunton, Mrs Shaw accompanied by her amiable and beautiful sister, Miss Flora McLeod, and Mr Shaw's son, received them with that cordial kindness and hearty welcome for which the inhabitants of the Highlands and Islands of Scotland are so justly celebrated. It may not be uninteresting to mention here, that upon the inhabitants of South Uist being apprised of the arrival of their distinguished visitor, upwards of six hundred of them had assembled near Houghbeg to greet him on his arrival in the isle, which gave birth to his father and a long line of ancestry. Upon this occasion, the Field Marshal ordered a cask of whisky to be given to his kind visitors, and after drinking all their healths, and that of their Chief, Clanranald, and wishing them and their handsome families, of whom he had seen so good a specimen that day, all health, happiness, and prosperity, he left them to enjoy themselves, and proceed with his suite to Nunton. His Excellency and friends having dined and slept at Nunton, (his Excellency in the very room in which the celebrated and lovely Flora MacDonald slept) they started early on the following morning for the cutter, which they reached about seven o'clock, and where they found a fine deer which Clanranald had ordered to be killed, and immediately thereafter set sail from Loch Skipport, and glided along the South Uist coast until they reached the bay of Corrodale, where they landed, and visited the two remarkable caves on that bay, into which the unfortunate Prince Charles Stuart had taken shelter, and where , and in an eagle's cliff at Loch Boisdale, he lay concealed for several weeks, and was attended during that time principally by Neil MacDonald Esq. the father of Marshal MacDonald, and by Alexander MacDonald, Esq. of Boisdale, the grandfather of Mr MacDonald of Staffa. From Corrodale Bay, the cutter proceeded for several hours to follow the *very course* which Prince Charles Stuart, attended by the celebrated Miss Flora MacDonald, who so much contributed to aid the escape of her Prince, took in sailing from Uist to Kingsburgh in Skye, for Armidale castle in Sleate, the property of Lord MacDonald, where the party arrived soon after four o'clock, the cutter having performed the voyage, from Corrodale to the Point of Sleate, in the wonderfully short space of four hours. On landing under Armidale castle, his Excellency and suite were met by Mr McPherson, the factor for Lord MacDonald, Mr McKinnon of Corry, and several of the gentlemen of Skye, who were joined by a large party of the Field Marshal's clansmen, from Borrodale, Rhue, Arisaig, and Morar, who had crossed for the purpose. On leaving the ship, Captain Beatson fired a salute of 15 guns, which was returned from the castle: on approaching which his Excellency was received by three hearty cheers, from several hundreds of Lord MacDonald's tenantry, who had come there for the purpose, and were headed by several of the gentlemen of Skye, which compliment the Field Marshal felt very strongly, and requested of Mr MacDonald of Staffa to state so to the people, in Gaelic, and to express the deep regret his Excellency felt, in not having the good fortune to find the noble proprietor at home. On the following morning, Saturday the 2^d of July, his Excellency went on board the cutter at an early hour, accompanied by all the Arisaig and Morar gentlemen, and proceeded to Castle Tyrrim, at the mouth of Loch Moidart, being the ancient stronghold of the Clan Reginald of the Isles, on the mainland of Scotland, and which forms the crest to this day of all the Clanranald family and its descendants, together with the motto of "My hope is constant in thee", which were the words addressed by King Robert the Bruce to the Lord of the Isles, on the day of the battle of Bannockburn, 1314, and which is of course the Motto of Field Marshal MacDonald. At Castle Tyrrim, about 400 of the Moidart and Arisaig tenantry were assembled to receive their distinguished clansman and visitor, whom they cheered as he ascended the rock and approached the revered walls of the ancient edifice, in a style which few could sufficiently appreciate, who were not accustomed to the ancient usages of these attached, honourable and faithful people; but to the Field Marshal's magnanimous feelings the scene was full of interest, and it was not one of the least striking circumstances, that among those of the tenantry who assembled there that day was a hale old man of the name of Alexander MacDonald, and nearly about 100 years, who detailed the whole circumstances of Prince Charles Stuart's embarking at Borrodale for France, with his suite, which circumstances this veteran had a most perfect recollection of, having been within a few yards of the Prince that day before he embarked. Upon the Field Marshal being informed of this, he immediately approached the old man, and, through the medium of Mr MacDonald of Staffa, put several questions to him relative to the appearance, stature, dress, complexion, &c. &c. of the Prince, and those who accompanied him, to all of which the old man answered readily, and with perfect precision and confidence, which astonished as much as it gratified the Field Marshal, who declared that this man's account entirely corresponded with that which his Excellency's father had often told him, of the departure of Prince Charles and his suite, amongst whom the Field Marshal's father was one. From Castle Tyrrim the party proceeded to Ellan Teona, the residence of Mrs MacDonald of Glenaladale, to whom his Excellency paid his respects, and sincerely consoled with her on the irretrievable loss which she had sustained by the death at so early an age of her only and much esteemed son. From this the party proceeded to Kinlochmoidart, the property of Miss MacDonald, now the representative of that family, and married to Colonel Robertson. The Colonel and Mrs Robertson MacDonald and family being at home, and having kindly pressed the Marshal to remain to dinner, the party spent some pleasant hours at Kinlochmoidart, and afterwards went on board the cutter; and, on the following morning, set sail for the Island of Staffa, where the cutter arrived in the evening, in sufficient time to enable the Marshal not only to view its curiosities from the cutter's boat, which rowed round the island, but also to land, and take a still more

208

complete view of the wonderful construction and arrangement of the stupendous basaltic columns, with which the Field Marshal was much struck and astonished; and in particular with the formation of these columns into large caverns, of which Fingal's Cave is the most remarkable. On the 4th, passed through the Sound of Mull, and after visiting the ancient MacDonald Castles of Mingarry, Aross, Ardtornish, &c. &c. landed in the evening at Lismore, and paid a visit to the Right Reverend Bishop MacDonald, and his amiable niece, Miss MacDonald, with whom his Excellency and suite drank tea. Went on board at seven P.M. and set sail immediately for the Giant's Causeway; reached the Irish shore on the evening of the 5th; landed early on the 6th; visited the Giant's Causeway and Glenluce Castle; slept that night at Cushindall, and proceeded next morning, the 7th, to Glenarm Castle, where his Excellency meant to have passed that day, but unfortunately the Countess of Antrim was from home. Embarked that same day on board the cutter, and reached Inverary on the following morning, the 8th, where immediately on his Excellency's landing, he was waited upon by the Duke of Argyle's Secretary, who kindly invited his Excellency and suite to go to the Castle and remain there during their stay; which kind invitation, from the absence of the noble proprietor, his Excellency politely declined, but availed himself of the opportunity of seeing the Castle, and of viewing the beautiful grounds of that superb and magnificent place. On the 9th, left Inverary at four o'clock A. M.; reached Lochlomond in time for that morning's steam boat, and, after making the complete tour of that beautiful lake, reached the hospitable mansion of Mr MacDonald Buchannan [sic], at Ross Abbey, to dinner; remained there that night, and the whole of next day. During the second day the Marshal took an opportunity of visiting the grounds of Buchanan, and the Duke of Montrose's most superb gardens, which he pronounced to be the finest he had seen in Great Britain. His Grace of Montrose having been detained by official duties in London, had not arrived on the 10th. Visited also on that day Mr Buchanan of Ardoch, at Balloch Castle, which, as well as Tullochewen Castle, on the opposite side of the Leven, are very fine specimens of modern architecture. On Monday the 11th, proceeded from Ross Abbey to Glasgow by Dumbarton. On that same day visited the college of Glasgow, and the Museum there, one of the finest in Europe; also saw Mr Mitchell's tambouring by machinery impelled by steam, likewise the singeing of the cotton and other objects, very much worthy the notice of the stranger in Glasgow. On Tuesday morning the 12th, visited Mr Monteath's extensive dye and bandana works, &c. with which his Excellency was much gratified; and after that the Marshal and suite proceeded by Bothwell Castle, Hamilton Palace, Wishaw Castle, and Coltness, to Sir Henry Stewart's, at Allanton House, on a visit to Mrs MacDonald of Staffa, and her family, where the Field Marshal and his suite met a large party at dinner, and remained that night; and on the following day set out for Dublin, by Lanark, Carlisle, Liverpool, Manchester, and Holyhead, and where his Excellency arrived on Saturday last the 16th.

In the whole course of the above tour, the weather proved most favourable; and when to that is added the unwearied exertion and kind attention of Captain Beatson, of H. M. cutter the Swift, by means of which every thing was rendered comfortable and pleasant while at sea, and wherever his Excellency landed; the warm reception he met with in every place he shewed himself, was calculated to make a powerful impression upon feeling less ardent and susceptible than his; in whom they have excited sentiments of gratification and admiration of every thing he has met and seen in Scotland, which border on enthusiasm, in the admiration of the people and of the country in general, and in particular of the characteristic warmth of feeling and generous hospitality which the Field Marshal experienced throughout the Highlands and Islands. He was particularly struck with the air and gait of the Highlanders, accompanied uniformly as he observed by a courtesy and address, and polished manner, which attracted his admiration not less than his surprise, and he frequently remarked to his fellow travellers, that, from the time he entered the Highlands at Dunkeld, until his return to Glasgow, he never by any accident met with an individual who did *not* put his hand to his hat or bonnet, and accompanied his salute with a very becoming and graceful attitude.

We understand that the Field Marshal felt so strongly the kind attention of Captain Beatson, that at parting he made him a present of a valuable of gold snuff box, and gave 50 guineas to the cutter's crew. His Excellency's stay in Dublin will be limited to a very few days, and it is his intention to proceed from that to London on his way to Paris, with the determination, however, of embracing, at no distant period, an opportunity of coming to Great Britain for a longer stay; in this good feeling his brave and gallant Aid-de-Camp, Count de Couessin, most warmly participates.

We are told that the Field Marshal, and Mr MacDonald, have kept a very full journal of their tour, and in particular about the island of South Uist, Prince Charles Stuart, and the 1745; blended with some very interesting anecdotes of that period and country, never communicated to the public.

Count de Couessin is descended from one of the most ancient families in Brittany, and is married to the niece of Marshal MacDonald.

(Re-typed from original document in The National Library of Scotland, whose co-operation is gratefully acknowledged)

CHRONOLOGY

(This abstract is in no way a comprehensive record of the events of the time. Only some key dates, as well as the main dates in relation to the story are provided).

Entries pertaining directly to the MacEachen or MacDonald History are in italics.

1714
Death of Queen Anne.
Reign of King George the 1st.

1715
Reign of Louis XV King of France.
Regency.
Failure of 1715 Jacobite Rising in Scotland.

1719
Birth of Neil MacEachen in Howbeg, South Uist (26/12/19).

Spanish landing in the Highlands.
Jacobite defeat at Glenshiel.

1727
Reign of King George the 2nd.

1736
At Scots College, Paris (perhaps in Douai too). Possible enlistment in the French service. Becomes known under the name "Neil MacDonald".

1738
Back in Scotland. Does not become priest and refuses to direct seminar of Morar. Probably schoolteacher, or tutor to the Laird of Clanranald's children in Uist.

1740

Austrian Succession War (1740-1748) involving all major European powers.

1744

Storm scatters French fleet and scuppers attempt to restore Stuart monarchy.

1745

French victory at Fontenoy.
Jacobite Rising in Scotland.
Jacobite victory at Prestonpans.

1746

(May-June): Neil is instrumental in ensuring the Prince's escape in the Uists.
(September): Leaves Scotland for France with the Prince aboard l'Heureux *and the* Prince de Conti.

Jacobite victory at Falkirk.
Jacobite Rising crushed at Battle of Culloden.
Prince Charles Edward Stuart a fugitive in the Highlands and Islands, then escapes to France.

1747

Neil probably back in Scotland on a secret mission.
Enlists officially in the French Army (Albany's Regiment).

1748

Prince Charles Edward Stuart asked to leave France. Arrested in Paris, incarcerated at Vincennes Castle, and expelled.

Treaty of Aix-la-Chapelle ending Austrian Succession War.
France to cease assistance to Jacobites.

1749
Neil a Lieutenant in Ogilvy's Regiment.

1756
Military campaign.

Seven Years War (1756-1763) between France and Austria, and Britain and Prussia.

1759
British Naval victory at Quiberon Bay ends hope of French assistance to Jacobite Risings.

1760
Reign of King George III.

1763
Neil marries Alexandrine Gonant (?)

Treaty of Paris. End of Seven Years War.

1764
Scottish Regiments disbanded. Neil pensioned off.
Birth of Neil's daughter, Eulalie Sophie, at Saint Omer (08/11/64).

1765
Family moves to Sedan. Birth of his son, Jacques Etienne Joseph Alexandre MacDonald (17/11/65).

1766
Death in Rome of James VIII of Scotland and III of England, the "Old Pretender".

1767 (?)
Neil settles in Sancerre, amongst community of Scottish Jacobite exiles.
Alexandre's youth in Sancerre. Later education in Paris, at Chevalier Pawlet's School.

1774
Reign of Louis XVI, King of France.

1784
Alexandre a Lieutenant in Holland, in Maillebois's Legion.

1785
Cadet, then Lieutenant in Dillon's Regiment.

1788
Death of Neil at Sancerre (09/06/88).

Death of Charles Edward Stuart, the "Young Pretender".

1789
French Revolution.
Meeting of "Estates General" in France.
Storming of the Bastille.
National Assembly, then National Constituent Assembly.

1791
Alexandre ADC to General Beurnonville in the Army of the North.
First marriage to Marie Constance Jacob (†1797).

Legislative Assembly.

1792
Captain, then Lieutenant-Colonel.
At Valmy and Jemmapes.

Execution of Louis XVI.
First French Republic (1792-1804).
National Convention.
Start of "Great French War" (1792-1815) Period of continuous conflicts between Britain and France, spanning the French Revolution and the Napoléonic Empire.

Only brief spells of peace, such as the Amiens Treaty (1802).
French victories at Valmy and Jemmapes.

1793
Colonel, then General commanding a Brigade.

Regime of "Terror" in France.

1794
General Commanding a Division.

"Thermidorian Reaction". Fall and execution of Robespierre
and end of Terror.
French Victory at Fleurus.

1795
"Directory" governs France.
French campaign in Holland and in Italy.

1796
Bonaparte's Victories at Arcole and Lodi.

1797
In Holland.

"Fructidor" Coup d'Etat. Purge of Royalists in Parliament.

1798
*With Army of Italy. Governor of Rome. Quells insurrection.
General in Chief of the Army of Naples. Defeats army of
King of Naples. Defeated at Trebbia by Suvorow. Wounded
at Modena.*

French expedition in Ireland.
Bonaparte in Egypt.
French Naval defeat at Abukir.
War in Italy.

1799
Back in France.
Approached to lead the "Coup d'Etat" due to topple the Directoire.
Refuses to lead, but backs-up Bonaparte.
In command of the Versailles military area during the Coup.

Bonaparte returns from Egypt.
Coup d'Etat of 18 Brumaire (9/11/99). Bonaparte seizes power.
« Consulate » regime.

1800
Leads the Army of the Grisons. Successful campaign in Switzerland, where he leads his troops over the Alps in mid-winter.

Napoléon Bonaparte First Consul.
Gal. Moreau's victory at Hohenlinden.
Bonaparte's victory at Marengo.

1801
Extraordinary Envoy and Plenipotentiary Minister to the Court of Denmark.

Treaty of Lunéville. Temporary peace with Austria.

1802
Returns to France.
MacDonald suspected by Bonaparte because of his relationship with Gal Moreau.
Not given any command for 5 years.
Landowner at his property of Courcelles-le-Roy.
Second mariage to Félicité Françoise de Montholon († 1804).

Bonaparte "First Consul for Life".
Royalists plots against Bonaparte.
Treaty of Amiens and temporary peace with Britain.

1804
Napoléon Bonaparte Emperor of the French (1804-1814).

1805
French naval defeat at Trafalgar.
French military victories at Ulm and Austerlitz.

1806
French victories at Iena and Auerstädt.

1807
Authorised back to active duty in the army of Naples under Prince Eugène de Beauharnais.

French victories at Eylau and Friedland.

1808
Beginning of Peninsular Wars in Portugal and Spain.

1809
Successful campaign in Italy, then in Austria.
Plays a decisive role in Napoléon's victory at the Battle of Wagram.
Made a Marshal on the battlefield, and Duke of Tarentum.

French victory at Wagram.
Defeat of British Expedition in Holland.
British withdrawal at La Corunna.

1810
Commander in Chief of the Army of Catalunia, and governor of that region.

1812
Commander-in-Chief of the 10th Corps of the Great Army during the Campaign of Russia.
Brings back his troops in good order.

Campaign of Russia 1812-13.
Burning of Moscow.
French retreat and disastrous crossing of the Berezina.

1813
With the Army of Elbe. Narrowly escapes drowning at Leipzig.
Defeated at Katzbach.

Campaign in Prussia.
French defeat at Leipzig.
French retreat from Spain.

1814
Distinguishes himself in the Defensive Campaign of France.
Plays a key role in negotiating.
Napoléon's abdication.
Pledges loyalty to the restored monarchy.

Allies enter France and occupy Paris.
Napoléon's abdication at Fontainebleau and departure to the
Island of Elba.
Restoration of the Monarchy in France. King Louis XVIII.

1815
Sent to oppose Napoléon after his escape from Elba, but his
troops follow the Emperor.
Refuses Napoléon's invitation to join him, and stays faithful
to King Louis XVIII.

At the Restoration of the Monarchy, Commander-in-Chief
of the Army of the Loire, where he disbands the remains of
Napoléon's army.
Made Peer of the Realm, Minister of State, Member of the
King's Privy Council, Arch-Chancellor of the Légion d'Honneur,
Second in Command of the King's Bodyguards, etc.

Napoléon lands from Elba and returns to power.
Battle of Waterloo.

King Louis XVIII returns to power.

1820
Reign of King George IV.

1821
Third marriage with Thérèse Gasparine de Bourgoing
 († 1825).

1824
Reign of Charles X, King of France.

1825
Visits the British Isles, and especially Scotland and the Hebrides
(June-July.)

1830
Begins to cease his various official activities.

"July Revolution" in France.
Charles X abdicates.
Louis-Philippe "King of the French".
Reign of King William IV.

1837
Reign of Queen Victoria.

1840
Dies at Courcelles-le-Roy (25/11/40).
Buried at the Père-Lachaise graveyard in Paris.